D0097882

LIBRARY OF
CCC
GONVILLE CA...

'A STATUE OF FATHER THAMES used to guard the source ... 'unnaturally quiet hidden deep in its COTSWOLD hill'.

A View of the Thames

THE RIVER THAMES.

A View of the Thames

NORMAN SHRAPNEL

with line drawings by George Murray

A DESOLATE ESTUARY SCENE.
near Canvey Island.

COLLINS

by the same author

BLUFFERS GUIDE TO POLITICS

THE PERFORMERS:
THE THEATRICAL ELEMENT IN POLITICIANS
(in preparation)

William Collins Sons & Co. Ltd
London · Glasgow · Sydney · Auckland
Toronto · Johannesburg

First published 1977
© Norman Shrapnel
ISBN 0 00 216551 1
Set in Perpetua
Made and Printed in Great Britain by
William Collins Sons & Co. Ltd, Glasgow

FOR JO

Contents

Introduction   11

1. Palace and Doghouse – *a study in contrasts*   16
2. Downhill from Hampton – *patterns of riverside suburbia*   25
3. Where are the Watermen?
   – *decline of the working river*   39
4. Oil and Orchids – *Brentford v Kew*   52
5. To the Embankments
   – *Putney, Wandsworth, Battersea, Chelsea*   62
6. Castle Perilous – *a parliamentary horror story*   75
7. The Central Scene – *Westminster to the Temple*   84
8. Where it All Began – *Temple to Tower*   98
9. Dead Docks – *Tower to Wapping and Limehouse*   116
10. The Long Street
    – *Bermondsey, Rotherhithe, Deptford*   126
11. The Heart of the Enigma – *Greenwich*   139
12. Woolwich and Thamesmead
    – *shades of past and future*   152
13. Turning Tide? – *the watermen fight back*   166
14. Fighting Country – *Thames barrier to Tilbury Fort*   178
15. Skylarks over the Sewers – *river wild life*   190
16. To the End of the World – *East of Tilbury*   204
17. Riverside Haunts – *Allhallows, Canvey, Southend*   216
18. Pipe-dreams to the Future   228
    Index   243

Introduction

The river is within us,
the sea is all about us
T. S. ELIOT, *The Dry Salvages*

I began this book as an observer and ended it as an addict.
I hope there is no irreconcilable conflict between the two;
though even if there were it could perhaps be forgiven as
one man's subjective backwash from those cold waves of
expert disagreement which have been rocking the argument
about the future of London's riverside.

What I set out to do at the start was provide an impres-
sionistic view of the river scene in the Seventies – a record
of life, so to say, before the flood. There was the London
Thames, on a high tide of change. My impulse was to take a
layman's last look at this ill-used river of ours – so messy
and moody, and with so much to be moody about, yet once
as vital a part of a Londoner's being as the flow through his
veins – before too much that was familiar got swept away.
It would be no formal guide, but rather an individual and no
doubt quirky view. It could be a modest personal memorial,
I thought; or at least a way of waving goodbye. For just as
Architectural Heritage Year and whatever it engendered
would hardly condescend to concern itself with the unspec-
tacular bits of heritage I personally would miss most, so it
seemed to me that the redevelopment planners would be
likely to plan little for my joy.

But there was another reason why such a survey needed
to be done, and done now. It also seemed to me that no
stretch of territory more vividly dramatized our condition.
What has been happening to the metropolitan Thames and
its communities from the western suburbs to the sea, the
river itself and the people who live and work and play on it,
looked like the national predicament concentrated on a
burning focus-point. Here were industrial and social con-

vulsion, squalor and charm, obstinate continuity in some
sectors and violent change in others, inertia and hope and
something near despair, all to be met with round successive
bends. The riverscape was acting out our life.

I found nothing to contradict these impressions, unless
it was that the tide was even higher and swifter, the contrasts more bewildering, than I thought. Here – so it now
looked – was our current state pushed into the front line,
the stretch of the tidal Thames from Teddington to the sea.
But then came the realization that my feeling for the river
ran far deeper than I could have possibly foreseen, and this
has coloured, I don't doubt, all I have written.

It may seem absurd, for someone who has lived by the river
for nearly twenty years, to take so long to realize his true
attachment. I suspect, though, that there are thousands like
me. All that time I have nominally qualified as a proper
Thamessider by living within range of those dejected hoots
– diminishing year by year and sounding all the sadder as they
fade – given out by the rivercraft on misty evenings. To me
they always sounded organic, more like the cries of living
or dying creatures than any mechanical device. They were
mournful and romantic, a sort of swan song. Yet somehow
I heard them with only half an ear.

Half an ear – and half an eye, just now and then, for the
river itself and the life (meaning more than just the traffic)
going on along its banks. In short I had been an average Londoner, vaguely conscious of my Thames in a preoccupied sort
of way but not much involved. (Was it mine, or was it somebody else's?) Suddenly turning into an addict, a looking and
feeling instead of just a theoretical Thamessider, was an
eye-opening and somewhat accusing experience. But I am
glad it happened.

I will not attempt to identify the moment when I ceased to
be a mere observer and became so much more deeply involved. Perhaps it was at one of those exhilarating crests
when the high tide flows and flashes in the sunshine, all but
shouting out its own watermusic. But I doubt it. For usually

I have found its melancholy more moving, when it sulks past its exposed mudbanks around Battersea or out in the estuary. Or I suspect mine may have been one of those clock-stopping moments when the river's desolation is charged with a sudden deep mysteriousness. You overhear odd things in pubs with odd names, like the 'Artichoke' or the 'Magnet and Dewdrop'. The light plays queer tricks. You round the bend at Deptford, past that abandoned entrance through which whalers once sailed into the Greenland Dock; a cloud shifts, Limehouse steeple glows like a candle, and you have a sense of being suspended in time.

The Thames abounds in such effects, and being captivated by them is nothing remarkable. But I soon found that my devotion had a more disquieting ingredient. Quite involuntarily, I began to regard the river as somehow alive – not in the rational sense of life coming back into it as the water grows cleaner, but alive in its own right. It is safe to say that such an aberration never afflicted planners, developers or modern watermen whose engines make them independent of tides, sudden winds and other tantrums. They are not likely to take kindly to an animist's view. Common sense is on their side.

Yet the intimate terms on which Londoners once lived with their river, however far apart they have drifted now, I find hard to see in a purely utilitarian and mechanistic light. Father Thames may be alienated from his family, but the ties of this water seem to me as thick as blood. The river has done so much for – and to – Londoners. It has located and shaped their lives, transported them, from time to time drowned them. It has enriched and beguiled them in peace, been both their defender and their betrayer in war. It has played its part not merely as founding father but as public highway, playground, workshop, common sewer.

Family ties could hardly have been more strongly forged. So how does it happen that we now turn our backs on the water like cats as far as our daily life is concerned? A modern Londoner could easily commute his way home in the evening, skirting miles of metropolitan Thames without ever catching a glimpse of it, and find himself riveted to some television documentary about that very river. It might be a thousand miles away instead of as many yards, and it would never occur to him to go and take a look at the real thing. How far he has abandoned his river, how far he has been deprived of it, would be a circular and profitless argument. Yet the central questions need to be faced. What do we now want from the London Thames? What may we still hope to get from it? What – though it is a thought many would only mock – do we consider it deserves from us?

Even the poets have dried up. Go on a bus-top across Westminster Bridge at night, go on any train leaving Charing Cross Station, and you are confronted with a spectacle that surely calls for a sonnet-substitute. A spasm of hard-rock ecstasy, perhaps? Ships, tower blocks, domes, discos make a familiar daytime scene that each evening is recreated into something astonishing and mysterious. The embankments are looped with strings of light. All dolled up, and nobody looking. Earth – and a new Wordsworth would have to admit it – has not anything to show more unfair.

For Londoners hardly spare a passing glance. You may see a slightly entranced expression on an American or even a Japanese face, but the native on the Number Twelve bus to Peckham? Only tourists and provincials ever seem to walk along the embankments from choice. The river is taken depressingly for granted, left to glide at its own sweet will. 'Sweet' sounds sour now, as if Wordsworth were a satirist. Even poets are careless with words, though Spenser had more excuse with his invocation from an earlier century: 'Sweete Themmes run softly', that other line the whole world knows and quotes. But we have done precious little to keep it sweet. There is one sense, of course, in which the metropolitan river runs more softly than it did in Spenser's day, perhaps than at any time since it became a highway and London became a port. Quite suddenly it has grown quiet, unnaturally quiet.

We should not be deceived by this. The industrial tide may be receding, moving from heart to mouth, but the river is still very much alive. It is in the hope and belief that it will remain so, and that Londoners will increasingly come to share its life again, that I have written this late convert's testament.

It is an account of a brooding voyage downstream, made mostly on foot. Though any kind of conventional guide is the last thing I have aimed at, I should be happy if I felt I had steered a few people to worthwhile parts of the riverside that have been ignored, undervalued or even maligned. Eel Pie Island at one end of my course, the eerie estuary walks at the other, are experiences that nobody ought to miss; and there are many more in between. It is more a meander than a steady course, a landsman's cruise with stops to look at the view and contemplate the prospects.

I have briefly left the river here and there; indeed, anyone who sets out to walk the London Thames will soon find that he has no alternative. Also I have felt free to cast backward and forward a little in time, trying to imagine what the Thames must have been like once, and what may happen to it in the future. Others may well have better and more useful thoughts. If this book started people thinking about the river at all, I should be satisfied.

1. Palace and Doghouse

A STUDY IN CONTRASTS

O, sir, he hath been brought up in the Isle of Dogs,
and can both fawn like a spaniel and bite like a mastiff,
as he finds occasion.

MIDDLETON AND DECKER, *The Roaring Girl*

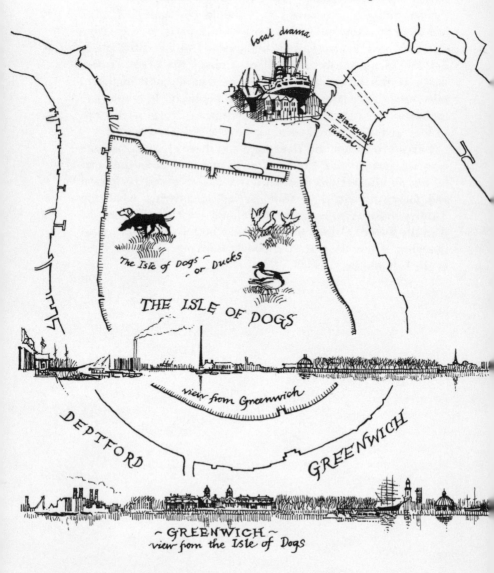

local drama

Blackwall Tunnel

The Isle of Dogs or Ducks

THE ISLE OF DOGS

view from Greenwich

DEPTFORD

GREENWICH

~ GREENWICH ~
view from the Isle of Dogs

My journey was to start above Teddington, moving down – though such distinctions have never been anything like absolute on this mixed-up river – from the domestic and recreational to the working reaches. But before setting out I went for another look at the one stretch of the London Thames I could already claim to know, if 'know' was a possible word. The river itself, these days, scarcely knows what lies round the next bend.

Which is one reason why this view begins, as it will end, at Greenwich. It has been my home longer than anywhere else, yet I still find it a fascinating and enigmatical place. You can't, a philosopher once said, step into the same river twice. I was certainly to find that you can't dip your pen into the same river twice; least of all this river.

Yet if the flow could be anchored anywhere surely it would be here – in a sense time's headquarters, and home of the meridian that measures the earth.

Looking over Greenwich Reach from the bottom of the great horseshoe bend, I have often thought that past and future seem to come together here – or with only the three hundred yards' width of river dividing them, and the sluggish present, seeming to flow in its sleep, lying between.

From Greenwich Pier I looked across, as so many times before, to the Isle of Dogs. The scene on the pier was muted, unmistakeably maritime but giving the impression that it was all part of the location for some early, excessively British film. Windows were plastered with official notices of the Thames River Steamboat Service, complete with bylaws dating from 1905 – the same period, incidentally, that gave birth to the nearby power station which drove all London's long-dead tramcars. A rust-red barge dozed on the quiet water, manned by seagulls in shipshape rows. A few surviving cranes and other impedimenta of dockland had the air of skeletons or the antennae of huge dead insects; and when a blue-and-yellow hovercraft flashed its lights and bumbled off in a cloud of spray, like some clumsy water-beetle far from its home waters, it seemed an exotic intrusion.

Held in this pocket of the past, I found myself peering across the river into the blank future, into the enigma of whatever it was they might be going to do with run-down inner dockland. The great lolling tongue of the Isle of Dogs licked out without affection. The place had a forlorn, abandoned look. The isle is no longer full of noises but it is full of questions about its past, its present, its future – even its name. Why the 'Isle of Dogs'? The most commonly held theory is that the dogs were the hunting dogs belonging to the former royal palace at Greenwich, banished across the river to protect the king's sleep. Or was it named after the dead dogs that got washed against its bending bank by the tide?

Another theory, as likely as any, reads the name as a corruption of 'Isle of Ducks', which certainly must have found the place a popular resort through the ages when it was an undisturbed swamp. 'Isle of Docks' would be the most plausible of all, were it not quite ruled out by the fact that the island had its present name centuries before the Millwall or any other docks were dreamed of. Long before Samuel Pepys wrote about 'the unlucky Isle of Doggs', Elizabethan playwrights were fond of dragging it in as a low comedy line, in the sense of a local Siberia or doghouse.

Dead dogs, ghost dogs, dogs that have had their day? (May be it was the day, back in 1970, they declared their unilateral independence and briefly appointed a president.) As to what their new day may be like when it really comes, not a hint or a scent of that was emerging yet. Great tracts of emptiness met the eye: some flats under construction, a big pink pub, one or two old houses sticking up like live thumbs from a corpse, the leafless trees of a mournful public garden. There was an introverted dome surmounting, apparently, nothing; it looked like a poor man's St Paul's that had sunk into despair. Just a lid: it covered the lift shaft to the turn-of-the-century foot tunnel crossing the river.

I walked across the water to the Isle of Dogs. A strange journey, and even more I had that dislocated sense of being preserved in some deep freeze of time, obeying spooky regulations which went back for their authority to the Thames Tunnel (Greenwich to Millwall) Act of 1897. The panelled lift was the size of a minor Albert Hall, though clearly no concerts took place; no person, it was laid down, was permitted to 'make any loud noise or shrill sound by whistling or otherwise'. You might not take with you any tricycle, loaded firearm or explosive; it was forbidden to be drunk or to spit, or to leave the lift while in motion. Nor, though there was ample room, were you allowed to be accompanied by elephants or wild animals of any kind. (Dogs, presumably, were permitted.) In the white-tiled echoing tunnel I was passed at speed by a gnome-like old man using his bicycle as a scooter. 'Used to do this as a boy,' he confided in a booming, guilty whisper, 'but there was a policeman after me then.' I saw the point of that silence regulation. Every whisper in this extended echo-chamber was a roar. Up the twin shaft, out through the door of another introverted dome exactly like the first one, and – feeling uncannily like Alice – you find yourself in the morose public garden you were looking at from the other side.

Then comes the visual explosion people who see it for the first time, once they have recovered, go home raving about. If you look back at the Greenwich riverfront, the view is sensational. It has been painted and printed and photographed a thousand times – the massive central spread of the Royal Naval College, the white elegance of the Queen's House, the sharp slope of Le Notre's park, crowned by Wren's Royal Observatory.

The college stands on the site of the most famous of the Tudor royal palaces, where Henry VIII held his vigorous court and where Mary and Elizabeth were born. The beautiful Queen's House, built by Inigo Jones as a Palladian villa for Anne of Denmark, survives in its full integrity and now serves as the National Maritime Museum; and the lofty Royal Observatory, though long deserted by the Astronomer Royal for the allegedly clearer skies of Sussex, still drops a

red ball to tell the surviving skippers – such of them as may
be awake and interested – that it is 1300 Greenwich Mean
Time.

All this would be enough to furnish one of the world's
grand panoramas, but there is more. Flanking the college on
one side of the Greenwich riverfront is the elegantly-restored
'Trafalgar Tavern', where ministers used to sail each parliamentary session for a brain-fortifying feast of whitebait.
On the other flank the masts of the Cutty Sark, most famous
of clippers, rise from her dry dock, while Tallis's church –
rebuilt since his day but still resoundingly musical – lifts a
baroque finger as if conducting the incomparable scene.

A great view, in short, for the surviving dockers of the
Isle of Dogs, who are indeed the only people who can see it
in all its glory. From where they stand, this riverside curve
on the south of Greenwich Reach looks like a first and last
word. For them, an unequalled vision of the past. Seen
from the Greenwich side their own curve looks more like a
question-mark which only the unknown and so far unknowable
future can answer.

I was surprised to find somebody else brooding on these
deep matters – or certainly brooding. Surprised, because
although there are 55,000 people still living in the old
docklands it is uncanny how far you can walk without meeting
a soul. And of all the deserted riverside fringes, those hangdog
gardens edging the Isle of Dogs always seem to me the most
conspicuously empty – in spite of (or is it because of?)
being the one place, apart from the river itself, to provide
that superb full frontal of the Greenwich waterside.

But now an oldish man shuffled up, threw me a gloomy if
not positively antagonistic look, sat on the extreme end of
my seat and began muttering to himself. Clearly he was a
creature of habit; this was his regular stroll, when he got
around to strolling at all, and I was trespassing on his bench.
Perhaps he sensed my sympathy, and we talked. At least, he
let me put in a word or two, punctuating his soliloquy; but
I got the impression that he would have been muttering away

just the same whether anybody else happened to be there or not.

LOCK UP LONDON – YOUR CAR, YOUR HOUSE, YOUR BUSINESS – AND BEAT THE BURGLARS, advised a notice not far from where my islander was sitting. It meant nothing to him: that sort of insecurity related more to the southerners across the river, where the mediamen and copywriters and antique-shop proprietors live. Lock up London? You didn't lock your own front door in his street, when it was a street. What happened to Greenwich, across the water, was nothing to do with him. He was an East Ender still; he belonged to the era when east was east and south was south, and three hundred yards of dividing river might have been as many miles.

'It's all changed,' he was saying. 'It's all gone downhill. Look at that dead river.' Well, not quite. At least the hovercraft were having a reasonably busy day: another one flashed and fussed around the Greenwich Pier, and he spat with deliberative scorn. 'Fireworks,' he said. 'Toys. I ask you.'

He wasn't asking me anything. He was telling me. And listening to this lost islander – lost though still at home where he had lived all his life, and his parents and grandparents before him – I learned much about the social crisis of dockland, about the extraordinary tenacity of its roots after the above-ground crop has withered or been abandoned or even destroyed. It seemed that the Isle of Dogs could speak for the changing riverside, just as I had thought of the riverside as epitomizing our national condition.

Yet the island remains its weird self. I always found it so, and everything the old man told me confirmed it. Though it is really a tongue of east London looped by the Thames, the operating of a road bridge can turn it into an actual island; and one which, within walking distance of the City, is in a sense more remote than any tourist-thronged Tresco or Sark. I have met others who spoke, as this man did, of distant Greenwich (five minutes' walk away, under the river) as foreign territory – not inimical exactly, but with nothing in it for him. Yes, he went there some years ago, to the market; but Deptford – though also on the south bank, and as such remote country – used to be more his mark. He had to admit he didn't like the look of the high-rise flats. Also he talked with some air of cautious kinship about Rotherhithe, another traditional river settlement which is all of two miles away on the map and quite out of sight. He spoke of it as an ancient Greek might have spoken of a neighbouring, tolerably friendly island.

But the Isle of Dogs was his country, and I could understand, far more clearly than before, how that serio-comic happening of March 1970 became possible – comic to outsiders, serious enough for him and his friends – when it briefly caught the tele-eye and micro-ear of the world. The island moved its bridge, cut itself off from Britain and unilaterally declared its independence, becoming an internal island republic of twelve thousand people (six times as many, after all, as the Scillies) with its own ruler for a day, one President Ted Johns.

Buffoonery? Not quite, I always suspected. Hardly at all, I thought now. For here was the acting out of a pattern of resentments, some of them self-contradictory in an all-too-human way but none the less real for that. Crucial reactions, as it seemed to me, for our displaced and detribalized era. These islanders resented their spooky physical remoteness right in the heart of London – much was made of the lack of adequate transport and school facilities – but they also resented their invasion by television crews, journalists and other foreign hordes during their brief hour of fame, and many will undoubtedly resent the new underground River Line when it tunnels through their belly to make them just another stretch of inner metropolis. They resent their social isolation – yet some of them also resent the middle-class immigrants from Purley, St John's Wood and such remote parts who are helping to cure it.

And just as they no doubt hated it when the windmills went and the farmlands were superseded by docks and riverside industry, so they deplored it even more when the docks declined and the industry ran down and the jobs were not replaced. If this not-quite-old islander still had any future, where was he to look for it? Hardly back to the land, even though the Isle of Dogs once had the reputation of producing the biggest cattle in England. So which way should he turn his eyes? Across the river and into the ceremonious past? It meant nothing to him.

Downstream, then, to the great deep-water port many were still banking on seeing in the wide estuary of the future, where they hope to rival or beat Rotterdam and worship the oil god in vessels the size of floating cathedrals? A bit late in the day for him. Or should he look away to the right, where the narrowing river loops through London's dead inner dockland, into upper suburban reaches where amateurs mess about in tiny boats? It was there I was going now, to start my journey.

To my friend on the Isle of Dogs, the two ends of London's river might be the ends of the earth. It looked as though his journey was over.

RICHMOND BRIDGE

HAM HOUSE

Spartina Nymphs

"A gloomy Mansion
jealously guarded by trees"

EEL PIE ISLAND

A Boatyard Flourishes.

TEDDINGTON LOCK

where the tidal
river starts

'Never left port in
ten years'

Broomwater

KINGSTON
Royal Borough.

The Palace of

KINGSTON BRIDGE

HAMPTON BRIDGE

Hampton Court

Seven Saxon Kings
Crowned.

Thames Ditton Island.

Three Men in a Boat

2. Downhill from Hampton

PATTERNS OF RIVERSIDE SUBURBIA

> The river bears no empty bottles, sandwich papers,
> Silk handkerchiefs, cardboard boxes, cigarette ends,
> Or other testimony of summer nights. The nymphs
> are departed.
>
> T. S. ELIOT, *The Waste Land*

Touristic Thamesside gets all the available attention, while other strongly characterful parts of the river are neglected. Except from the people who live there, London's riverside suburbia rarely gets the credit it deserves. Many frankly sneer. To some extent it shares the general odium of the suburbs, suggesting a boringly placid and self-immersed community hiding away from life behind its privet hedges and net curtains.

This is a largely unjust reputation, spread abroad by the masochistic and predominantly suburban British themselves; and if it is true of some parts of London the riverside communities – even the middle-class upstream ones – are certainly not among them. River suburbia is the opposite of boring, almost to a fault. To my mind it has an appeal and a vitality all its own. It is fussy and frivolous, with an air of over-acting – often pseudo-timbered, stilted against floods, summer-bungaloid with an affectation of being on permanent holiday. It goes in for absurd little water-ornaments in its front gardens, aquatic gnomes or mock-herons.

Good luck to it, I say. The river, however grand, would be tedious if it were all Hampton Court and no Hampton Wick. Yet there is a link. Riverside suburbia can conveniently be said to begin – the choice is arbitrary – at Hampton Court. Though it is a notably unsuburban-looking property that Henry VIII compulsorily acquired from Wolsey, occupied in a style surpassing even the lavish cardinal's, and reputedly tenanted with the spectres of several queens, the place can be seen as a kind of early super-suburbia, a mammoth exercise in top executive-style river-living.

Here is another great royal boot that treads on London's snaking river, without any apparent backlash. If the river takes kindlier to kings than common people the reason may not be so much snobbish as a liking for being courted. Certainly our kings and queens spent a good deal of history swanning up and down between their riverside homes, adorning and even glorifying the Thames with their frequent barge appearances, their ceremonial rowabouts, their elaborate watermusic – though it has been argued that the main purpose of this was to protect delicate court ears from such uncouthly natural sounds as the language of the watermen. Handel, by this theory, was a mere counterblast to Billingsgate. Incidentally, river language improved after 1761, when offenders started being fined half a crown for each wicked word; and reform went to such lengths a quarter of a century later that a Society for Promoting Religion and Morality amongst Watermen, Bargemen and Rivermen was formed in London. They even launched a floating chapel.

Despite this steady and debilitating increase in seemliness among the professionals – doomed, though the word gives all true rivermen a shudder, to be generally known as 'bargees' – the quality gradually drifted away from the river and gave up most of the old aquatic pomp and ceremony. Royalty, like the rest of us, took to the roads. It increasingly abandoned the state barge for the state coach, and eventually for the all-conquering car. But the ancient tradition of royal river-travel was never quite abandoned. Its infrequent Thames trips today are made in a brisk little craft far removed, both in style and speed, from the traditional state barge; less like a burnished throne than a floating taxicab. The last time I watched the Queen and the Duke of Edinburgh going by water to Greenwich – it was to celebrate Architectural Heritage Year and the tercentenary of the Royal Observatory – they were on the pier and on their way almost before the wash from their boat had subsided. They were in the plainest of plain clothes and their scarlet bargemaster, adorned for an age of greater leisure and pomp, looked like someone the busy royal couple had obligingly given a lift on his way to a fancy dress ball, while they were themselves engaged on more serious affairs. The change is sad, but hardly to be wondered at. Windsor is the nearest approach to a riverside home they have, with Greenwich long since abandoned to pensioners and sea-patients and now to naval students, Westminster to the politicians, Whitehall to the bureaucrats, Sheen and Richmond to the archaeologists and the ghosts.

And Hampton Court to the tourists. For all its splendour, to my mind they are welcome to it: the mental feet ache at the very thought of the place. But I can't resist a passing bow of respect to the riverside town on the massive royal doorstep, if only because it usually gets such churlishly short shrift. The royal borough of Kingston is seldom given much visual credit these days for anything other than its one famous, tourist-grabbing feature.

True, that demands attention. Visiting Kingston without at least a dutiful glance at the place where seven Saxon kings were crowned would be as perversely anti-touristic as going to Canterbury without calling at the cathedral, or omitting the leaning tower from a look round Pisa. Kingston's open-air shrine is a ponderous affair yet it looks vulnerable: the rail guarding it hardly seems a more adequate protection than a thousand years of civilization from the destructive urges of the last quarter of the twentieth century. The coronation stone itself is so massive, of course, that it would undoubtedly be harder to make off with – should, say, any Saxon independence movement break out – than was the stone of Scone.

But Kingston has something rarer than historical shrines. It offers the visitor, once he has accomplished the unnatural act of successfully and legally parking his car and launching himself on his legs, a highly satisfying town centre to explore. That, anyway, is how it looks to me though I know there are purists who disagree. To my eye the architectural ages mix both harmoniously and imaginatively in a way most uncommon

with the British, and the spirits find themselves moving in an
unfamiliar direction – they actually lift. Inhibition is usually
the best virtue we can hope for with our urban renewers
and rebuilders, but I'd say that here the opposite has for
once paid off. Boldness, even brashness, wins. Ages compete,
periods conspire, yet harmony is achieved. Imitation black-
and-white, modern Jacobean, shamelessly echo the real thing;
a circular guildhall, brick dressed with stone, does credit to
the so often discreditable Thirties; there is some sequestered
romanticism from the Victorian era, and a timeless stream
called the Hogsmill meanders thoughtfully into the Thames.
What is old, what new, scarcely matters. Everything – it is
the rarest of urban qualities – seems the right shape and in the
right place. There is even a touch of exoticism in the presence
of an onion dome, and nobody would want to extradite it.

One event that makes it appropriate to launch this journey
from Kingston is that Jerome K. Jerome started there. I
regard Jerome as a kind of prose laureate of the suburban
Thames, expressing its eternal late Victorianism. True, he was
going upstream instead of down, and spent a disproportionate
amount of time at Hampton Court, where he dutifully
got lost in the famous maze: he and his friends were much
prone to confusion and mild misadventure in the interests
of copy, a standby of the humorist's trade in all ages. But
among celebrants of the sporty upper reaches Jerome ranks
high, and it would be a sad or a sinister year in which somebody, somewhere, was not reading *Three Men in a Boat*. Like
so many other boating enthusiasts the author and his friends
arrived by train – on the old London and South Western
Railway it must have been, two Victorian shillings, twenty-
five Victorian minutes from Waterloo – and what they found
is there in essence still:

> The quaint back-streets of Kingston, where they came down
> to the water's edge, looked quite picturesque in the
> flashing sunlight, the glinting river with its drifting barges,
> the wooded towpath, the trim-kept villas on either side,

Harris, in a red and orange blazer, grunting away at the sculls, the distant glimpses of the old grey palace of the Tudors . . .

Something of this has survived – an air, a sense of Victorian ghosts preserved in amber, like flies. Which reminds me of my favourite guidebook, one that Jerome himself might have consulted as he planned the first part of his voyage by steam. 'Flies meet the train,' it says. They were propelled by hooves, not wings. But down on the river the scene I found was much as he must have found it. Inexpert rowers were heaving away with substantial female passengers inexpertly steering, chaperoned by flotillas of surly swans. A pair of mouldering wooden pavilions looked as though they had been made for daring assignations at dusk: still haunted, it could be, by ghosts of girls in leghorn hats and young men in boaters.

Jerome country still, through dark glasses. Not quite, nowadays, as vivid a scene as the one he describes near Hampton, with the sunny river 'a brilliant tangle of bright blazers, and gay caps, and saucy hats, and many-coloured parasols'. Something happened to dim the brightness: something like the First World War, which extinguished so many blazers and so much else. And yet, identifiable still through its shadowed filter, it seemed to me that the jaunty innocence was still there. Near Thames Ditton Island, still pretty in a bungaloid way, an eight was poised for the off. A blue sail, a white sail leaned on the water, but most of the little boats were dozing on the bank, high and dry. I saw no barges, but a black-visaged dredger reminded us that workaday life goes on, even in these sporty waters.

I made my way down to Teddington, where the tidal river starts. (Some people, even locals who ought to know better, are still convinced that the name signifies 'Tide-end-town', and won't be persuaded otherwise.) Here the watery world woke up; I was aware for the first time that there was a lot of water in the river. Sweet Thames was running far from softly in this stretch; the yellow thunder of the weir made people talk to each other through cupped hands. River discipline looks tolerably strict hereabouts. Though warning notices abound for the benefit of the less-well-trained river-dogs, you are expected to know what you are about, or be prepared to learn pretty smartly from those who do.

But some lessons are never learned, warnings or no warnings. DISCARDED FISHING TACKLE IS DANGEROUS — a sign of the times, that one. Whether or not the poet was right in saying that the nymphs are departed, all the rivermen are agreed in boasting that the fish are returning. But modern tackle imperils more than fish, and now the cleaner river carries deadlier flotsam: to the bottles and paper and card-board boxes, the waste land's old contribution to the waste waters, have to be added plastic containers, nylon fishing-lines and other synthetics that water can never destroy.

'This stuff is sheer murder,' a salvage man told me as he indicated a binfull of castaway rope and twine, silver-white and gleaming in the sun. The horror was its immortality: if the river-cleaners missed it there seemed nothing to stop these man-made snakes from swimming up and down with the tides for ever — fouling motors, threatening bird-life, perhaps even endangering bathers if they should be lured back to the river. At the weir canoeists were shooting the rapids, which looked daring: surely that risked a swim? Some things it was forbidden to shoot, like the swans. A notice actually prohibited it. Nothing is taken for granted these days.

Another notice laid down the minimum size of the fish people were allowed to catch — a twenty-four-inch pike, a sixteen-inch barbel, a four-inch bleak, and so on. Even assuming that an angler would recognize a bleak when he saw one, I couldn't help wondering how many carried measuring tapes. I watched a man fishing for roach, for which he had evidently developed a considerable respect. 'They're artful little buggers,' he said, 'but stick around and maybe I'll catch you one for your tea.'

He had no luck while I was there; but more and more fish

are being caught in the de-polluting Thames and the resident species-count is moving steadily up towards a hundred varieties. Some day, who knows, they may really be brave enough to eat what they catch. They still talk about a six-pound eel taken at Kingston not so long ago, but I was assured that this was nothing to the monsters of the old days. It seems the eels have fought a losing battle against natural and unnatural hazards on their way to the spawning-grounds, of which getting past Eel Pie Island must have been about the least.

Unexpected craft are swimming back too. Connoisseurs were clustered round a sloop moored near the lock. She seemed to have sailed out of another age. They were admiring her lines even more than such rare adornments as the blue-and-white mouldings on her patrician prow. A beautiful craft, and beauty still gets its tribute – though at a tacit remove from the admirer, as though implying it may be for others but not for him. Even the fibreglass men know style when they see it. They were talking nostalgically about the virtues of traditional timber.

'They don't build them like that any more,' I heard one man saying. 'You mean,' his companion retorted, 'they don't buy them like that any more.' Such style is admired but not coveted; it is something for other people. Also, it is extremely expensive. The primitive has quite suddenly become the sophisticated luxury. Wood will soon be the rich man's rarity, and such a boat his barely affordable mistress.

Not far from here I discovered what seemed to me one of the most fascinating backwaters of outer London. Leaving the liquid main road, there is a side-turning into an artificial arm of the river, spookily beckoning. It is called 'Broom-water', and its withdrawn, discreetly distinguished houses are a cut above the common flow of riverside villadom. The period air is strong enough to be physical, rotten with drowned leaves, mouldering with memories. Real willows grow, and if real Ophelias are to be met it must surely be here. But there are jollier aspects, or were once. These places were advertised

originally as 'Houses for Boating Gentlemen'. Ideal, any one
of them would have been, for Jerome; ample room to accommodate George and Harris with Montmorency the dog thrown
in. It still looked the sort of haven where it would be correct
to drop in by boat for tea – or something stronger, if the sun
was below the yardarm of *Cleopatra*, or *Blue Bird*, or whatever
the domestic craft may be called.

All the gardens ran down to this authentic leafy lane; all
with their steps and gateposts, some with old-world street
lamps and ornamental urns. It could have been any well-off
outer suburb, lavish with trees and lawns; the only difference
being that the lane was made of water, the parked vehicles
were afloat, the garages were mouldering boathouses. Seductive, intimately strange; a shadowy house-agent's delight. All
the same, I couldn't help wondering if any of those early
boating gentlemen, newly established here from some more
landbound suburb, ever forgot they were boating gentlemen
as they set off through the morning river mist for the Edwardian City – striding healthily down the garden, taking the
steps two at a time, through the gate at the bottom and (surely
it must have happened at least once?) slap into the river.

As for their craft, the pervasive sense of traditionalism
makes it seem unlikely that they ever had names much different
from the current run of River Nymphs, Welsh Dragons and
the like, though a certain relaxation of standards has begun and
I even heard it rumoured that a boat had been sighted in these
reaches called *Dunsailin*. Rivermen like to tell dry yarns
about other rivermen, and there is no malice in it. Well,
not much, though I gathered that they should be taken with
a pinch of salt, which is the nearest to the sea some of these
mariners apparently get. 'See that one?' a Teddington man
said, indicating a neighbour who was working devotedly
on his hull. 'Never left port in ten years, to my certain
knowledge. Only place he gets wet is the Commodore's
Lounge at the local. Drinks there in his yachting cap.'
Another spent so much time servicing his boat that by

the time he had worked through to the end of it the other end had rotted.

They feel they can afford that amount of self-mockery. Visitors are presumed to be aware – and if they aren't, occasion is taken to let them know – that it was from a local boatyard that the little ships mustered for Dunkirk, getting on for forty years back. That was no joke.

There are other and more permanent perils. You may not be able to force a riverman to the water but sometimes the water insists on coming to him. People in these parts are used to being woken by ducks tapping at the window and are seldom surprised to find a swan sailing through their patio. And when the river runs high, every Teddingtonian with half a grain of tidal salt in his veins feels the call. It was running high now. There was a flood alert, which are far from rare. It brought a rising tide of unruffled excitement, a kind of routine tension. I heard terse riverfaring remarks being exchanged. 'Better you than me,' a cabin cruiser said as another lit his pipe and intrepidly took off downstream; he might have been setting out for the Antarctic instead of Isleworth. 'Took fifty minutes from Richmond Lock to the "Three Pigeons",' another reported. 'At eight knots on the engine I wasn't moving.'

The river was restless, flexing its muscles, in a mood for mischief. Not far downstream were swamped boats, submerged garages, parked cars with water over the doorhandles. Several were standing right under a notice near Eel Pie Island saying WARNING – THIS AREA IS LIABLE TO FLOODING. One Twickenham man, with an unquenchable sense of wonder, always goes to view anew the unfailing evidence of human folly revealed by this deep inability or refusal to learn from experience. 'Look at the silly sods,' he was saying softly, with a kind of ever-astonished satisfaction. 'They do it every time. Time after bloody time. Water on the brain, if you ask me.'

The island itself – regretfully, some purists think, as they point to the hash the developers are making out of Eel Pie –

was still safely above water. I went to take a good look at it, the first for several years. Everything looked different – as I had expected. The life of this seven-acre social adventure playground has been full of vicissitudes. In Victorian days, and sometimes no doubt even nights, it was a target for the more enterprising picnickers, rather a dashing place to reach at all; then came successive eras of tea dances, jazz and pop festivals and offbeat community living. These days the modern watermusic of the transistors has the roar of aircraft with which to compete, and the time when there was peace on Eel Pie seems unimaginably remote. Perhaps there never was any. There is always something new cooking in this restless dish, and now they were building impulsively again without any evident concern for an overall plan. A symbol within a symbol: the neurotic urgency of its change – every week a new flavour – looked like a valid if hectic dramatization of the times.

Should the island be tidied up, promoted into gracious living territory, made a fit dish for the residential upper crust? There is a good working boatyard there, which sets a better example. The place is a flavoursome, unashamed hash, and I hope it stays that way. As one who has always prided himself on the right attitudes to visual amenity, who in principle has ardently gone along with furthering what the planners call 'Elements of Positive Environmental Significance', I can only frankly report – with due shame if called for – that the dignifying of Eel Pie Island would get no vote from me. The droll, the offbeat, even the downright messy have their claims, if they can generate as much atmosphere and vitality as this.

I doubt if tourists are often taken to Eel Pie Island. They find their own way across a little concrete footbridge. I hope the adventurous ones go on to nose out my favourite piece of tourist-fodder in these parts, and one that is harder to find. Some may mock it, others may hunt it for quite the wrong reasons, but for sheer barmy charm I still recommend the group of sportive girls in the grounds of York House. I lost my way trying to track them down, and their somewhat obscure site at least suggests a certain modesty. Little else about them does.

TO THE STATUARY: the notice points in a nervously noncommital way, reminding the visitor that this highly historical mansion now serves as council offices, which are not in the habit of encouraging nude swimming parties on their premises even in the lunch hour. One guidebook calls the group 'extraordinary', another 'rather astonishing', both of which comments are true as far as they go. A bevy of symbolic and unselfconscious young ladies are disporting themselves round a fountain, apparently busily engaged in pushing each other into the water or else pulling each other out. Needless to say, they were installed when the place was still privately owned. One of the later and more exotic residents, a rich Indian merchant named Sir Ratan Tata, was eager to brighten the often dispiriting view that even a stately riverside window provides. The girls were good for his melancholia, and fortunately these nymphs, at least, have not departed. This bit of aquatic nonsense is not to be confused, of course, with that older and more authentic cheesecake, the celebrated Maids of Honour whose home is across the river at Richmond. Whether or not these York House young ladies look good enough to eat they put me more in mind of an improbable sister a little way upstream. Outside the Market House at Kingston stands a handsome gilded statue of Queen Anne, and the last time I saw it a stallholder had put a notice at the royal feet saying: CRISP JUICY CRUNCHY GOLDEN DELICIOUS.

The river was rising fast now. Football posts reared like masts out of drowned sports fields, though cattle splashed about the meadows placidly enough, and the 17th Chiswick Sea Scouts looked equally calm as they launched a canoe on a convenient stretch of floodwater. The 'Three Pigeons', so arduously reached by the man at the lock, offered its damply welcome garden for a drink. Precisely the right number of pigeons kept watch on the roof, waiting presumably for the waters to subside, but they were too early. Water, in unexpected as well as obvious ways, had become inimical. At the port of Isleworth – it really is a port in its own right, with a customs house looking more like a church than the rebuilt church does – the vicar was hunting for his prayer-books. Somebody had thrown them into the ornamental pool.

On the other side of the river I discovered the sleepy village of Petersham. I have seldom leapt for my life so often in the space of half an hour. 'Wake up, Petersham,' I wanted to shout. Presumably the warning was unnecessary. For here was a kind of parody of the past, a mock-up of a dozy old riverside village where a moment of actual doziness would be fatal. Surviving pedestrians walked the narrow kerb like a tightrope, the traffic brushing their elbows as it swept round the bend. They must die like flies in this charming and restful-looking spot – or would, if they ever dared to rest.

And there was Ham House: unforgettable Ham House, secret and subtle and dangerous-looking, but conveying an air that would scarcely tolerate any fate so banal as death by road or river. Poison or the jewelled stiletto looked more its mark. The house is curiously underwritten in the guide-books, though that favourite Victorian one of mine describes it as 'a rather gloomy mansion jealously surrounded by trees'. Nice, that 'jealously', and the description still holds. Personally, let me confess it, I am a foot slogger of limited zeal on the stately home front; my heart is inclined to sink into my boots and make them still harder to drag along when confronted with all those acres of routine splendour, those interminable corridors of indifferent family portraits, so lofty and overbearing and exhausting.

But Ham House is different. I would happily exchange a dozen Hampton Courts or Syons, assuming there were as many and I happened to possess them, for this richly sombre Jacobean retreat. Everybody, at a time when the stately home sector has become so important a part of the tourist industry, must by now have spent hours fantasizing about the

sort of grand house they themselves would choose to live in,
if the football pools or some quirk of inheritance gave them
the chance. Does it relate to the house in which they actually
live, or would if they could raise the necessary loan?

Is there, in short, a relationship between the fantasy and
the facts of our life? I think there is. I know exactly the sort
of house I want. I like the Gothic, the sequestered, the offbeat place sulking in trees. There are still hundreds of them
scattered about London, many in quite unmodish parts, and
I doubt if Architectural Heritage Year bothered its elevated
head about them for a moment. Yet a part of the heritage they
undoubtedly are, and perhaps the truest part. The paradox is
that it should have been the Victorians, who brutalized so
much of London for the starkest of material ends, who also
bequeathed it these monuments of introspection, these
moody mountains of brick.

So give me, while there is still time, some bat-haunted
mid-Victorian villa standing in its own weeping shrubberies,
a sad stately home of the London suburbs; and give me, since
I shall undoubtedly need it, a local authority grant to stem the
damp and rescue the creaking floors and roof-timbers.
Certainly such survivals need rescuing, before they are left
to rot and their gardens turned into used car lots and rubbish-
dumps. People seem afraid of such houses, suspecting perhaps
that distinguished Victorian murders were committed in
them, or long poems or oratorios in the manner of Tennyson
or Mendelssohn. Either, even both, may be true. I am
undeterred.

It seems to me that such fitfully romantic gestures are nearer
to the wayward London tradition than are the cool façades
of the eighteenth century or the featureless shapes of the
twentieth. Nearer, surely, to Ham House, which may be
why it strikes me as so much more exciting than many a
blander, grander mansion. True, there is an Italianate whiff
in the air, which is natural enough for English Jacobean.
It could be agitated by the alarming figure that Leigh Hunt
(exaggerating a shade) called 'that infernal old Duke of

Lauderdale, who put people to the rack'. Without my going into the record of its past residents, undoubtedly there is a hint of secret evil lurking about the place. And as I wandered among its ornate shadows the thought struck me what an ideal setting it would provide, some sultry evening, for a domestic production of *The Duchess of Malfi*.

Some evening like that one, heavy and abnormally still; yet seeming to carry a germ of the violence which, Richmond people say, has come back to the river on summer nights – violence both human and natural. I went down to the towing path. The river was rising fast now. The flood warning was red. Great pieces of timber surged down the current like battering rams. Strange sacrifices were deposited on the banks – a dead sheep, a dead swan. Suburban these upper reaches may be, but tame they emphatically are not. They live with a force of nature which often makes its presence felt, as it was doing now.

3. Where are the Watermen?

DECLINE OF THE WORKING RIVER

And did you ne'er hear of a
  jolly young waterman,
Who at Blackfriars Bridge
  used for to ply?
He feather'd his oars with such
  skill and dexterity,
Winning each heart and
  delighting each eye.

CHARLES DIBDIN

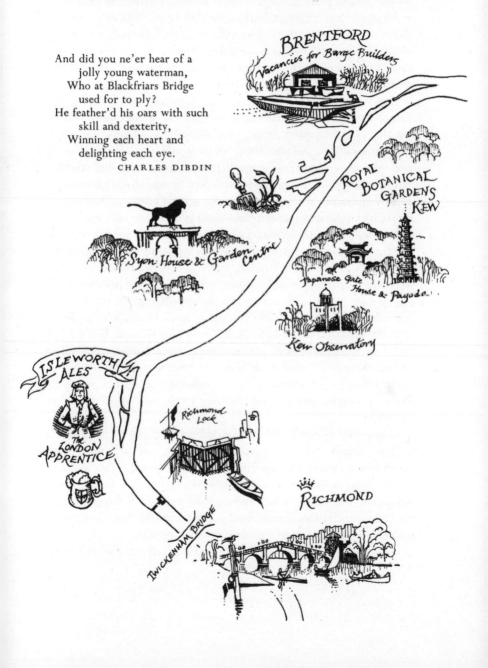

The recreational river manages to keep afloat. The professional river, which knew how to use the tides and cope with floods, is sinking fast. Broadly you could say that the non-tidal river above Teddington belongs to the amateurs while in the tidal reaches the professionals rule – or did once. But as I came to the port of Isleworth on the left bank and Richmond on the right, where the serious working river used to start, one fact became obvious. It was the watermen, not the water-nymphs, who had departed.

For a time they co-existed. In Jerome's day the upper London stretches of the river were shared, none too amicably, by the two interests. Strings of barges and steam-tugs were busy among the pleasure craft, rocking them with their wash and throwing many a straw-hatted punter off his stroke. And the language the professionals let fly was often considered quite unsuitable for the ears of the young ladies of Richmond and Chiswick, and quite unanswerable by their escorts.

No doubt the watermen were aware that already they were on the retreat. The present century saw the serious working river moving fast downstream, and soon the suburban stretches were left virtually to the suburbanites. But the privateers of the upper reaches, the messers-about-with-boats licensed to keep *Sweet Sue* or *Blue Belle* tied up at the end of their gardens, are not so much successors to the river workers as diminished heirs to those powerful citizens who once lorded it in their private barges. With this difference: they now use their mini-barges purely for pleasure, for emulation, to cut a riverside dash, to unwind after a long hot day in the city. Seldom to get anywhere.

The grandees are still with us, minimized but multiplied. It is the bargees who are gone – not that any self-respecting riverman would ever use the forbidden word. The lighter-men, the watermen: the professionals who loaded and unloaded the ships, who moved the people of London in a taxi-service that can hardly have worked worse than the private and public transport of the modern metropolis.

Yet the congestion as well as the vitality of the riverside

scene must have been enormous. How many of them were there plying for hire, rowing and sailing up and down the metropolitan Thames – and drifting too, using the tides like deep breaths to conserve their effort and energy? Not much reliance can be placed on early figures, since it is hard to believe that anybody was actually counting with much accuracy or definition. A contemporary reckoning was that there were forty thousand of them working between Windsor and Gravesend. The crowding if not the sheer chaos represented by such figures must have been unimaginable. More reliably, an official report at the end of the eighteenth century showed over twelve thousand watermen in the central dock area, two thousand of them apprentices.

The passenger-carrying watermen fell away; the lightermen with their barges steadily increased through the nineteenth century. Other river users judged them a turbulent body of men. The years have tamed their survivors. Now, in six hours on an average tide, some thirty rivercraft and strings of barges – occasionally a few more, frequently less – may pass through the busier stretches.

It may look like the end of the river for the traditional waterman's trade, but a way of life already ancient a thousand years ago does not drown easily. Nor will it let itself be run down by the roads – the fear of wheeled competition was already causing dismay to John Taylor and his fellow workers three centuries ago – without a final struggle. Even now the survivors have not abandoned hope of a river revival. They are proud, tenacious, somewhat flamboyant people, and they still know how to put on a show.

Like the Doggett's Coat and Badge Race in which young watermen compete – as they still ceremoniously announce from Fishmonger's Hall – 'for the Livery and Badge provided yearly under the Will of the late Mr Thomas Doggett, a famous Comedian, in commemoration of the happy Accession of His Majesty, George the First, to the Throne of Great Britain in 1714.' This has been described as the oldest surviving annual race we have – always a dangerous sort of claim but never challenged, perhaps because so few know about it. Ask a hundred random Londoners who the famous Doggett was, and you would get some quaint answers. Yet the race he decreed should continue annually 'for ever', from the 'Swan' public house near London Bridge to the 'Swan' public house at Chelsea, still takes place though scarcely anyone notices and both swans are long dead. It is one of those rites that occur like dreams in the heart of waking London, ancient, unbreakable habits that sometimes persist long after anybody can remember when or why they began.

But the beginnings of this one they do remember, and they still row for the original orange-coloured coat, with huge silver badge on the left arm emblazoned with the Horse of Hanover, which surviving Doggett victors – there are some fifty of them still around, with an age range of well over half a century – are entitled to wear. And frequently do wear: as often, I guess, as occasion offers. I saw quite a flock of them, haunting the Tower Pier in their gaudy feathers on a wet and gusty July day, one of the few unfine days of the astonishing summer of 1975. It was the height of the tourist season and a working morning as well, but nobody seemed to look twice at these sturdy men of all ages with their white stockings, brilliant frock coats and glittering arm-badges the size of greedy dinner-plates. (It has always struck me as odd that the British should be regarded as so conventional, when they can appear in public wearing the most extraordinary things without attracting more than a passing glance.)

A few invited guests who knew what it was all about, and uncounted thousands of city workers and overseas visitors who hadn't a clue but looked mildly interested, were watching the start of an archaic event that certainly showed no sign of going under for the last time. On the contrary, there were signs of revival. Again there were six starters, as Doggett laid down; in recent years the numbers had slumped as low as two. There had even been preliminary heats again, as in the good old days when watermen were watermen. Actually it turned out that a touch of artificial respiration had been applied; the ancient rules had been bent a bit; it seemed reasonable, if they insisted on keeping an athlete 260 years old in the field. They now use racing sculls instead of the heavier craft of former days. They still pull upstream, but no longer against the tide.

Yet it is still a long race and a gruelling one, and even the oldest Doggett heart must have lifted to see the full coloured complement stretching like a rainbow from the Middlesex to the Surrey bank, men from traditional waterman localities like Gravesend, Battersea, Blackwall, Rotherhithe, Greenwich, Northfleet. The going was particularly tough this windy day; the man from Greenwich capsized, but climbed back into his boat to finish the course. The end was as exciting as the oldest riverdogs could remember, with less than a boat's length in it after close on five back-breaking miles; but the real significance may well have been that for the first time since Doggett and the first George, the rules now allowing it, the watermen were challenged – and beaten – by a man not employed on the river. The winner was a barrister's clerk, the son of a lighterman.

The beginning of the end? Perhaps, but the end is not yet. The surviving threads of continuity are uncannily strong. Family memory in this trade, laid end to end, as it were, seems to flow back under all the bridges to before the time when most of them were built. There are still watermen who count their own and their immediate relatives' water-service in hundreds of years, and ferrymen who have sailed round the world without ever moving more than a few hundred yards from a single Thames pier.

Recently there was a remarkable if modest display put on at the little Bear Gardens museum on Bankside, one of various imaginative attempts to bring home to the people of Southwark something of their incomparable history; to show that this has been written not only in playwright's ink and in bear's blood but in Thames water as well. There were photographs and other documents portraying the life of a sixth-generation licensed waterman named Harry Harris. At least, six was as

far as they could trace. Harris was born in 1880 and died
in 1962; he lived and died — doubtless like all the other
Harrises — in Southwark, where they were still baiting bears
when the Harrises were already old in their less brutal but
not less dangerous trade.

Harris — and the point about him seemed to have been that
he was typical, not exceptional — was apprenticed to a tug-
master and eventually became a dock lighterage manager.
He swam in the river as a boy, dodged the Thames police,
remembered his grandfather telling of nervous passengers
who would ask to be landed rather than 'shoot' the old
London Bridge on a spring tide. That inhibition, a strictly
practical one when the flow was often fierce between the
massive obstructions, takes us right back to Samuel Pepys
whose diary makes it clear that it was a nervousness he
shared. He too got out of his transport on one side of the
bridge and in again on the other. Possibly one of the long
line of Harrises rowed Pepys in his day and refrained from
mocking him for his timidity. Indeed, following this kind of
thread soon ferries us back to a past far closer than we think:
beyond the shops and houses and heads on old London Bridge,
past the wharves and steps that served the Elizabethan play-
goers and thieves and prostitutes off to Southwark for a
night of business or pleasure or both combined — back even,
shooting not so many bridges as the generations go, to the
foggy centuries that followed the Romans. There could have
been Harrises all the way.

Sometimes crossing a bridge could be more hazardous
than shooting it. Harry Harris tried to walk the parapet of
Southwark Bridge on Mafeking Night and presumably made
it. There were other perils. A frozen Thames is virtually
unheard-of in our day, but Harris recalled a freeze-up in the
nineties when ice smashed barges, tore them from their
moorings and carried them off to sea. He remembered
blanketing fogs, which also seem to have become as scarce
as the watermen themselves. Nowadays it is reckoned that
fog holds up what is left of the river traffic no more than ten

days in a normal year. Fogs were a normal part of the scene in his day, and at such times, as he put it, 'the ears became the eyes'.

With his watery evolution and habitat, his oars for arms and his radar eyes, his acute subsidiary ears and a built-in capacity to smell his way along the river if all else failed, Harris looks like a purely aquatic creature who steered a successful life-cycle. He sailed right round his natural world, from its beginning to its fundamentally unchanged end. He died in time. There was still, as you might say, a wharf with a bollard to tie his last rope to.

The most memorable river character of our day, perhaps of any day, was less lucky. This was no waterman but a water-woman, and she lived too long. Can there ever have been a more remarkable bargee than Dorathea Woodward Fisher, who graduated downstream from the bosky reaches of a Cheltenham College young-ladyhood to marry a rough Thames waterman? The story has all the appeal and vitality of an eighteenth-century ballad, and someone should at least make a modern river-shanty out of it. The lady's wedding present may sound drab, but it was in fact as romantic and auspicious as any in the history of such gifts. It consisted of forty feet of leaky second-hand barge costing twenty pounds, and Dorathea herself helped to pay for it by getting a temporary landlubber's job.

From this improbable beginning she and her husband launched one of the resounding success stories of the commercial river. It lasted until well after the Second World War. They caught the high tide of the post-war trade revival, in which the River Thames and its lightermen had their full share, and by the year 1950 they owned one hundred and twenty-five barges and eleven tugs. Quite a fleet, to build up from nothing.

But she saw it all sink under her, killed by the container revolution. By the time she died in 1974, over eighty years old and all too well aware of what was going on around her (and in particular of what was *not* going on along her beloved home stretches of the river), it was finished. Her sort of barge trade had collapsed, her private fleet was beached, even her devoted bargemen were grumbling because they thought she was rich and could give them at least a silver handshake. So she made a turbulent exit: far from plaintive but in no way reconciled, more the lamentation of a kind of watery Lear, complete with faithful parrot and devoted attendance of cats. She was in mourning, but not for Dorathea Fisher. She was still mourning her husband, an old Doggett's

MOTHER THAMES
DORATHEA WOODWARD-FISHER.

Coat and Badge winner who had died some years before. She was mourning the river itself which seemed, by the measure of anything worthwhile in the eyes of Mrs Fisher, to have predeceased her too.

It was her fierce love of the river, her ardent championing of the men who worked on it, that made her famous and surely unique. Where else would you find so commanding a feminist campaign on behalf of an essentially masculine world? As a dedicated Thames trumpeter she had no equal since John

Taylor stood up for the rights of his fellow workers, and of the river that provided them with their livelihood, three hundred and fifty years earlier. The waterman poet campaigned in a not dissimilar way. He too saw new social and technical developments threatening their survival, as the best-known of his many lines show:

> 'Against the ground we stand and knock our heels,
> Whilst all our profit runs away on wheels . . .'

The difference was that in Taylor's case the alarm was false, or at least premature. Poor Dorathea Fisher's profit, as well as the wages of so many of her workers and hundreds of others like them, really did run away on wheels – those of the container trucks. She was also, by a bitter irony, pushed under by the wage demands of men she had spent her life championing, men she was devoted to and who, in all other respects, returned her devotion. It is always melancholy, and often a bit muddy, when the tide goes out.

'It's becoming an empty river,' Dorathea Fisher told an interviewer near the end of her life. 'I'm glad Billy isn't alive to see it.' Billy was her husband, whose ashes were scattered somewhere in the Limehouse Reach. She was one of those intensely practical romantics English life usually launches from the middle-class female reaches of our society, and it was inevitable that the journalists and mediafolk who gathered round her, unloading her memories like a fleet of her own barges, should christen her 'Mother Thames'. Inevitable, too, that her coffin – that last container which could have been called her first – should be escorted by colourfully costumed representatives of those equally practical and romantic bodies, the Fishmongers' Company and the Company of Watermen and Lightermen. Also, needless to say, that old Doggett's Coat and Badge winners should be her pallbearers.

Whether the occasion is sad or just gaudy, these ancient city companies still know how to put on an impressive show.

Many adore the pomp and circumstance of those highly ceremonious occasions where a fruity voice invites you to 'be pleased to receive the Master of the Worshipful Company of Watermen and Lightermen of the River Thames', followed – whether you are pleased or not – by a procession resplendent in blue gowns and gold chains, frogged and braided coats and cocked hats, the beadle with his mace, the Master with his small posy of flowers to keep the Billingsgate smells at bay.

That, at any rate, is his story. All the best city stories have been told many times, and that one must have been going the rounds for centuries. And Billingsgate, it is true, still reeks of fish, though none of it comes to the market by water any more; nowadays it all swims in on wheels. Perhaps, with the new and much-vaunted respectability of Billingsgate, the porters would be willing to repay the Master's ceremonious compliment by wearing earplugs in symbolic protest against the language they hear about current prices. The watermen once had an even worse reputation for profanity than the porters, and it seems astonishing that they don't let fly occasionally at the sight of all that fish travelling by land. The worshipful company still examines apprentices before passing them out as fully-fledged rivermen, as it has been doing for four centuries; and no bold lad, so far as is known, has threatened a domestic cod war.

I heard the ancient routines explained at the Little Ship Club, which has a splendid plate-glass outlook on to the river against Southwark Bridge. As well as its fetching costume the company was displaying its regalia, including the Great Tankard which dates from 1717 and holds three quarts. This kind of excess is plainly out of date among modern river-dogs, and nobody seemed surprised at a notice at the end of the hall saying that 'smoking is discouraged'. Mrs Fisher and her parrot would have looked out of place sitting under that. She smoked like a paddle-steamer.

And what would Mother Thames have thought of the Thames Barge Sailing Club, which was doing the honours that evening? No doubt her attitude would have been mixed. Some of these barges still sail – marvellous. But they don't work – deplorable. Once they did most of the water-work around London, and the old cargo books show a remarkable range: bricks, hay, coke, oysters, manure to the farms. Now there are perhaps thirty of them surviving – solid, serious-minded craft, looking far too heavy for their crew of two to handle, but still beautifully responsive to those who love them.

'I got mine cheap – nine thousand,' one of the hobby-sailors was saying; the more normal price seemed to be around fifteen thousand. On the club notice board various ketches and other unfrivolous craft were being offered at about the price of country cottages. You could pick up a Bermuda sloop for three thousand (at January 1975 prices), while the vessel billed as having 'led the twenty-fifth anniversary convoy of little ships from Dover to Dunkirk' was going for twelve hundred. But price-cutting seemed to have set in: one sailing yacht was marked down from £450 to £350 in what could, I suppose, have been billed as the 'winter sales'. You could get a sextant for £110, a hand-bearing compass for a mere £12, a barometer also going down; probably it has risen a good deal since then.

A notice warned river-hogs that they could be fined up to £100 for speeding. The limit above Wandsworth Bridge was eight knots – or ten miles an hour, the warning felt it had better add. To all proper sailing men that extra bit of information must have been like telling a hunting novice that he was expected to chase the fox on a horse and not in his Jaguar. Obviously they never quite knew who they were getting on the river nowadays.

One thing would certainly have impressed Mother Thames. Anybody who can manage a Thames sailing barge is a sailor, no doubt whatever about that. So the watermen, a few of them, are still around. They have suffered a sea, or river change. And although Dorathea Fisher liked her fun and her glass of grog, and was the enthusiastic patron of an East End rowing club as well as of that Doggett's Coat and Badge race, her attitude to these skilful hobby-sailors would be conditioned by her deep-seated belief that the river was not really alive unless it was hard at work. And this made her essentially a Victorian at heart, as well as by qualification of birth.

4. Oil and Orchids

BRENTFORD VERSUS KEW

The river sweats
Oil and tar
The barges drift
With the turning tide
T. S. ELIOT, *The Waste Land*

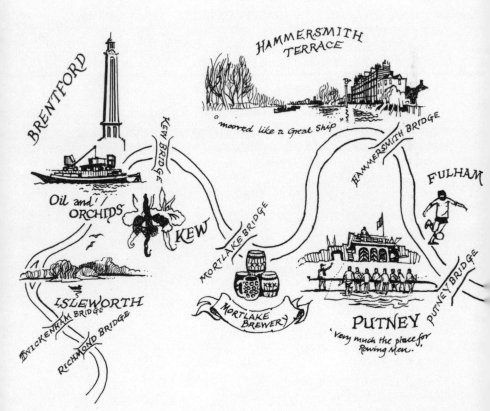

Mother Thames was at home on a river of mixed activity, where the barges barged and the rowers rowed – indeed, in her long day she had a great deal to do with both. She believed in the combative spirit. Yet she would not, I believe, have seen Brentford v. Kew as any kind of contest, even though the two seem to belong to different worlds as they confront each other eyeball to eyeball across the river.

Brentford is unarguably an upper-stream survival of the working river. (Indeed, I discovered that I had the choice there of turning left – a true navigator would say 'to port' – along the Grand Union Canal for Birmingham.) Yet it seemed natural enough that scowling Brentford, so frankly industrial and proud of it, should have lordly Syon as its neighbour and look directly across at the ever-smiling fantasy of the Royal Botanical Gardens. I say 'natural' because the Thames from Isleworth to inner London must be as astonishingly varied a stretch as any metropolitan river in the world can show. Each bend reveals a total change of scene; the starkest contrast is the normal thing; surprise becomes expected. This worries many people who would like more scenic consistency: I think they are wrong. Just as its twists and turns reach their climax here, so the river seems in these stretches to achieve its height of visual tension and vitality.

I could only hope the social mix was as successful.

Londoners pay lip service to mixed communities, even feel the need to plan for them, but are not very good at ensuring that they actually happen. Here – so it seemed to me – they had established themselves over the years by the older processes of haphazard social development, and ought to be none the less cherished. These communities looked excitingly mixed, though the tidy-minded tend to get worried by indeterminate sectors where work and pleasure still jostle each other, where boatyards live next door to bungalows, and surviving barges rub shoulders with lit-up launches hired for floating dances, wedding parties and the more romantic firms' annual outings.

I called at the 'London Apprentice' at Isleworth, a river

pub which boasts so much past – five centuries of it – that much of it must be true. If so it has certainly done its bit in serving the mixed society. That it was used by watermen its name and position make certain. That it was patronized by kings (Charles II, a great river enthusiast, is said to have called with his lady friends from time to time) and by smugglers is plausible. That painters used it in the last century, and rowing men use it in this, is beyond argument.

Equally it appeared to me that Syon House lived up to the mixed spirit of the area. Convent turned palace turned gardening centre, with Capability Brown's famous landscaping now at the service of the gardening capabilities of any number of suburban Mr Browns, nobody could accuse it of living in the past or of being superior about the present. And there, directly opposite, was that Oriental extravaganza of Kew, a vegetable fantasy seeded from across the world, set off against a wealth of chinoiserie scarcely to be met with outside China – or, I should imagine, inside either.

And it was hereabouts that I found myself revising some of my longest-cherished ideas. Every journey, to be of any value, is a process of self-discovery; and if the quest is an honest one the experience can disturb or even shock. Other people's attitudes cry out for revision; seldom one's own. Other people's sacred cows are absurd or unpleasant creatures, but one's own tend to be pampered and are naturally resentful of any ill-treatment. Yet I ended with a number of firmly established attitudes – or so I had always thought of them – severely shaken if not demolished: not least towards one of the oldest, most sacred and most emaciated cows of all.

With the metropolitan Thames facing change more abrupt and fundamental than at any time these last three centuries, nobody could take a sustained look at the riverscape without being forced to have a view on planning. Previously I would never have doubted what this must be. Civilized people – and one hopes one is always that – are invariably on the side of sensible planning because the alternative is a free-for-all, a triumph for the wolves and sharks, a land-grabbers' bonanza, and all the other familiar horrors. And, with so much covetable territory ripe for redevelopment or up for grabs in the disused inner dockland, only the most careful and tenacious of co-ordinated schemes looks capable of saving large areas of Thamesside from a morose decay or, at best, a lucrative sterility. That is the civilized assumption, and before I set out I would have thought it unanswerable. Soon I was not so sure.

Watching the early efforts towards co-ordination I was made even less sure. 'The biggest opportunity since the Great Fire,' they were crying in that fine dawn that always heralds a new planning day. But they were not crying very loud, and soon all too familiar damps and fogs were bringing an ache to the bones of aspiration. And as the pamphlets and surveys began to roll off the presses and the drawing-boards worked overtime, the uneasy feeling grew that we had been there before – and since the Fire, too. I remembered all those post-war plans, pioneered by Hitler's bombs, leading to an enlightened frenzy of paper work – most of which came to nothing. I suspect that the British are not good planners because their hearts are not in it. Having spent four years fighting the planes they were prepared to spend at least as long subconsciously fighting the plans, making sure that nothing measurable would come of them just as they had done three centuries earlier.

Moving on downstream, experiencing the visual impact of the communities it has shaped and destroyed, the life and death it has brought to London, I was beginning to suspect that the river makes its own laws, such as they are – that it rules its fifty-odd miles of metropolitan territory with a kind of inspired chaos, using people to exert its will or its passing whim. The result is not always pretty but it is alive. And the heretical thought occurred to me that I preferred this chaos to a planner's paradise even if we could get it, just as a man with all his warts is preferable to a statue, or an ugly child to a beautiful doll.

But 'ugly' is only half of it. It would be perverse, though

as I now realize not impossible, to prefer gloomy Fulham to Twickenham, or Brentford to Kew, or rows of decayed warehouses to the South Bank central development. Yet I also now know I would not want a river that was all elegance and sweetness and light. The dark is needed too.

Round every curve a different prospect strikes the eye, and 'strikes' is often the word. Certainly it struck me how right it was that it should have been a famous riverman who invented the word 'serendipity'. Horace Walpole had his extravagances and this was one of the more agreeable. The dictionary defines the word as 'the faculty of making happy and unexpected discoveries by accident'.

I found the Thames living up to his word. Some of the discoveries were happier than others, but the surprise was constant. Indeed, it soon seemed an inadequate word. Variety gave way to something not far from scenic violence, and then to surrealism. I met a flotilla of swans, followed by a flock of elderly men with schoolboy caps and megaphones. I came upon the mountainous Mortlake Brewery and then the Harrods Furniture Depository. Such sights take strong nerves. The Depository, especially, looks like something straight out of an alarming dream, a Hammer Films château in terracotta. I have often wondered what they deposited there. Massive mahogany tables, perhaps, too huge for any normal storeroom; or chandeliers in delayed transit between stately homes; or field trunks left by Boer War colonels, still waiting to be reclaimed; or disused cupboards for skeletons. The eye – my eye, anyway – never grows accustomed to this extraordinary building. Yet who, except the more correct planner, would want it away? I have actually seen the Depository classified in an official survey as an 'Element of Negative Environmental Significance', which must be among the most surprising uses of the word 'negative' on record.

It would not be surprising, however negatively the experts regard its environmental significance, if the apparition put visiting oarsmen off their stroke. Oxford and Cambridge men presumably know what to expect. I was now in Boat Race waters, and some big river event was clearly expected; but could even surrealism go to such lengths as to row the Boat Race backwards?

But there is another annual race, more spectacular if less famous, which covers the same course though in the opposite direction from the university event, downstream from Mortlake to Putney. Less famous, I mean, among Londoners; for all rowing men the Head of the River race is prestigious enough, bringing hundreds of competing crews from all over Britain and Europe. That landbound metropolitans seem scarcely to have heard of it, hardly bothering to ask what all the fuss is about if they happen to find themselves in the neighbourhood of Putney Bridge on the March morning when it takes place, is yet another emphatic sign of their divorce from the river. (I searched the Sunday papers next day and managed to find half a dozen lines about it.)

Yet for sheer spectacle alone this event deserves to be one of the top events of the London spring. Ancient rowing men in their juvenile caps (the men in the boats tended to wear woolly hats or, still more strangely, Börg-style bandeaux) got extremely animated as they awaited the off, and no wonder. It put me in mind of a very wet Grand National. Gaudy confusion reigned, with a disorderly armada of crews facing all ways, looking from above like a scatter of coloured matchsticks on the ebb tide. The river's ancient chaos and congestion were back again, it seemed. But control was miraculously established: they started at ten-second intervals, and a computer timed them. To see them swinging home past the Putney boathouses, famous crews and obscure ones, from clubs and colleges, schools and business houses across the land and far beyond, deserved to exhilarate even those of us who can scarcely fit a hired oar into a rowlock. For addicts the excitement was intense. There was little actual cheering, since it was not that kind of race, and even the computer needs a short interval to produce its individual timings. But the hoots of the coxes came off the water like the cries of strange birds, and the colours clashed brilliantly as the spaced crews surged

Competitors assemble at the Start !

HEAD OF THE RIVER RACE.

LIKE A SCATTER OF COLOURED MATCHSTICKS ON THE EBB-TIDE.

into the final stretch, a dozen boats crossing the line within seconds. Only experts could judge the form, but it looked a wonderful way to get from Mortlake to Putney.

And Putney looked very much the place for rowing men to live. If they are not river-conscious here, they can't be anywhere. More than Kingston, which turns its pleasant face mostly away from the water, more even than Richmond, which had the style once but has largely lost it, Putney possesses the definitive riverside air. Agreeing to pose as a London suburb it is fully aware of being its own town at heart; and unmistakably a river town, with something jaunty about it, something casual, lacking a lick of paint and not bothering, cheerfully fond of itself without being too town-proud. Putney looked an attractive example of the lazy old let-it-grow technique, encouraging eccentricity and the offbeat gesture.

This can take strange forms. A middle-aged man was jogging along the towpath, fully and indeed rather formally clothed. He was pressing a little, as though with a train to catch. But it was evidently no question of *catching* a train. 'He's running a bit late today,' somebody remarked. I thought it best to leave it at that. Less innocent sports go on than rowing, or running your own personal railway. There is an old church at each end of the bridge; at least, I found there was one church and the other would be back shortly: the parish church announced its rebuilding after being destroyed by vandals. All Saints, at the other end, prudently maintained a guard during opening hours. An armed guard? Not that, yet, a woman tourist was assured.

'But it's so beautiful – surely they wouldn't wreck a place like this?' The duty guard smiled sadly. They kept watch on a rota system, was all he said. Wrecked churches, locked churches, guarded churches – the new pattern seems universal. Do they ever get caught? What can be done if they are? Even punishment implies a kind of consent; total alienation poses different problems. Even if they could be rounded up, squads of over-energetic young culprits could hardly be set to work making good the damage, since they are unlikely to be well versed in the field of stained glass or the English Perpendicular. The English Horizontal is more their mark. They do not, presumably, row. I couldn't help asking myself, all the same, if vandalizing for mischief is all that much worse than vandalizing for money.

Leaving aside such extreme anti-environmentalists, I feel places like Putney preserve a nice balance between caring and not caring, set a good example of doing what you will within decent limits, healthily advance the unpretentious banners of the Ad-Lib movement. Short of any necessary or possible defence works against juggernauts, wreckers, aircraft noise and grandiose development schemes, they should be left alone – encouraged, indeed, to carry on the commendable way they are.

In daring to think that the British are on my side in their deep suspicion of the big-time planners, whether public or private, I am also aware of the strong psychological pressures working the other way. They are induced to feel guilty about not thinking big, failing to take the forward-looking view, and the rest of it. Yet I trust their deep disruptive urges. Once a long-term plan is actually adopted, or shows dangerous signs of being so, then the British carry on the fight obliquely. They set about frustrating or 'denaturing' it. Their hope, deep down, is that such projects will be quietly shelved, or sink from inertia, or be scuttled by a change of government, or prove too expensive in the light or the shadow of one of our recurrent financial crises, or die the death of a thousand cuts which modern joint planning techniques make easy. At least one of these chances will almost certainly come off. The wastage of effort, of mental and moral energy, is enormous: but all is considered worthwhile if nothing much happens at the end.

So in confronting their capital city's greatest planning opportunity since the Great Fire my guess is that the British will loyally do, or rather fail to do, what they failed to do three centuries earlier. And can anybody – hand on heart, knowing the sort of people we are – truly wish that Wren's or Evelyn's rebuilding plans after the Great Fire had been realized? Ways would have been found of dealing with that constructional logic, that Frenchified radial grandeur. It would not have been London's style at all.

London's way, conditioned by the snaky river and by the temperament of Londoners it has so largely but subtly formed, is more capricious, more impulsive, more human than even great planners can understand. And I doubt if the ones we have available today could be called that. But we can rest fairly secure, I think. So far we have always been saved from paying more than lip service to global schemes and final solutions. If the national instinct for piecemeal progression, for often deplorable but sometimes inspired makeshift, is now shamed out of court we still have a last line of defence – the state of national crisis which, as I write, seems to have become accepted as a permanent condition. Perhaps we shall be saved from final calamity – not for the first time, I suspect – by lack of resources.

5. To the Embankments

PUTNEY, WANDSWORTH, BATTERSEA, CHELSEA

And when the evening mist clothes the riverside with poetry, as with a veil, the poor buildings lose themselves in the dim sky, and the tall chimneys become *campanili*, and the warehouses are palaces in the night

WHISTLER

Filthy river, filthy river,
Foul from London to the Nore . . .

Punch, 1858

The HOUSES of PARLIAMENT

Westminster Bridge

Albert Bridge

LAMBETH BRIDGE

HAMMERSMITH BRIDGE

CHELSEA BRIDGE

VAUXHALL BRIDGE

LAMBETH Palace

University BOAT RACE

Hurlingham Sports Club

BATTERSEA BRIDGE

ALBERT BRIDGE

COVENT GARDEN fruit & vegetable market.

PUTNEY BRIDGE

WANDSWORTH BRIDGE

St Mary's Battersea

WANDSWORTH where gas-holders dominate!

Moving downstream from Putney, I was increasingly aware of the different way two different men can look at the same thing. Or the same man, in different moods. It is the Kew and Brentford dilemma – for those who see it as a dilemma – stretched out through such scenically clashing areas as Wandsworth, Battersea, Chelsea and the new concrete market garden of Nine Elms.

And the way you look at it conditions, inevitably, the way you see the river's future: industrial or scenic, residential or active, black or green or shades of grey. Two men I talked to, one unknown and the other famous, knew exactly the way they wanted to see the river's future and expressed it with an enviable certitude. They took starkly opposite views – the Brentford and Kew of the argument, so to speak – and as one predisposed in favour of both Kew and Brentford, committed to mixed development or maybe just hooked on contrast like some kind of visual drug, it is a debate that will always find me floundering in midstream.

I came upon a man hunched behind a large canvas, gloomily painting away at a gloomy scene. He seemed relieved, though at the same time resentful over the interruption, to pause a minute from his study of a junkyard piled high with the dismembered corpses of machinery. The future? As far as he could see, it would go one of two ways. Either they would just let go, with an occasional spasm of ad-hoc activity and a bit of shoring up here and there, some minimal rehousing and a few sad pleasure boats; or if enough prosperity came back to encourage the speculators it would be all trade marts and pink gins and marinaland, smart flats for trendy media-folk with river views, and to hell with everybody else.

Having made it plain that he much preferred the first prospect he got busy again on his junkyard. This man was more traditional than probably he would like to be accused of. He was a direct descendant of the Miasmal School, which already has the longest and most respectable ancestry. Over more than a century the river has developed a seductive aura of decay, a low-tide distillation from the mud and mist and industrial fumes, a fog-and-Whistler cocktail which is not what the smart yachtsmen drink but is both potent and deep – perhaps hopelessly deep – in the craving of artists and of those who learn to see through their eyes and respond through their nerves. Reacting against an earlier convention, it became a convention itself. Canaletto's offering of a Mediterranean Thames of clear sunshine and sharp outlines was an alien whim; though, perversely, there are vistas that grow nearer to him now, with the relatively smoke-free and fog-free air and those cleaned central buildings and glittering new shapes.

Yet just as my painter was reacting against the routine prettiness of boats and swans and tree-lined riverscapes as churned out by a thousand amateurs, so his weightier predecessors had rebelled against the washed-out formalism of the eighteenth century. Poets and painters alike, they were all ripe for redevelopment. The Thames brought out the worst in the more fashionable poets, from Pope downwards. The roughest ballads, the coarsest watermen's songs, are far superior to all that tired, grandiloquent versifying about the silver Thames (was it so silver, even then?), or Horace Walpole twittering about his beloved 'Twit'nam'. How one prefers his prose joke praising the river because it separated him from the Duchess of Queensberry, or the lordly complaint from the fourth duke that all the damned thing did was flow, flow, flow.

As for the painters, it was as though the theatrical changes in the river scene brought by the industrial revolution compelled them to re-equip their visual apparatus. Turner was the great innovator. Ruskin, in *Modern Painters*, points in admiring contrast to the Venetian masters with their background of marble halls and young Turner lurking among the cabbage leaves of Covent Garden, or haunting his beloved Thames shore where he would satisfy his yearning for black barges, patched sails, rotting wharves, smoke and soot and 'every possible condition of fog'. This equips the gifted boy to celebrate nature and human labour in what Ruskin calls (a phrase impossible to our age) 'blind, tormented, unwearied, marvellous England'.

As the Miasmal School developed fog became a drug, industrial murk a medium of romantic introversion, until the school acquired its own extreme rhetoric of paint and of word. There was even Henry James confessing that he loved the Thames most when it was 'all dyed and disfigured', going enthusiastically on about 'the brown, greasy current, the barges and the penny steamers, the black, sordid, heterogeneous shores'.

They were on the brink of overdoing it, and it was not altogether surprising that a brisk counter-Miasmal movement set in soon after the 1914 war, accompanied by an anti-bardic impatience with derelict warehouses, crumbling wharves and other useless riverside impedimenta. Some thought it high time to clean things up, and one celebrated writer and river champion who decided that a little less mess would not come amiss was the late A. P. Herbert.

It is still impossible, or at least insensitive, to round the Hammersmith bend without thinking of Herbert. If Dorathea Fisher was the Thames leading lady of our time, he was undoubtedly its top male star. What saved him from an over-aesthetical approach to the river and its problems was his skill as a waterman, his authority as an administrator, and his personal experience of what the river can do to you if it happens to be feeling unfriendly. He must have survived some forty thousand tides in his charming but vulnerable riverside house, part of a terrace moored like a great ship except, of course, that it was unable to lift with the rising flood. One of the forty thousand was churlish enough to jump his garden wall and sink his basement kitchen and dining room in six feet of reeking river water.

That was back in 1928. In 1953, another great flood year, it would have been far worse if the river wall had not been raised by eighteen inches. Further inundations were always on the cards, but when I went to see APH on his seventy-fifth birthday I found him preoccupied with other things – some watery, others to do with dry land. He was not the sort of man to be satisfied with one project at a time.

A table as big as a hold carried a huge cargo of work in progress, his walls were covered with river maps and faded photographs of beloved old boats and musical comedy stars. He was busy on at least two books and navigating several campaigns: one of them – for authors' lending rights – had to wait until several years after his death before making it to harbour. Large angle-lamps loomed like cranes over the authentically riverlike chaos of his desk. Yet all that work, all those congratulations jangling the telephone every few minutes, were not permitted to get in the way of the necessities of life.

'Let's go to the pub,' said APH – meaning the 'Black Lion', a stroll away along the riverfront, where he achieved the difficult feat of being a revered and famous figure and an ordinary regular, both at the same time. The customers talked about rivers and boats but not, I felt, in deference to Sir Alan. He would not have thanked them for that. It so happened that many of them were genuinely interested in the river and boats. It would be odd, come to think of it, to live in or around Hammersmith Terrace if you were not.

Back in his garden there was peace of a kind, with even the aircraft tolerably silent as a lucky birthday present and the west-bound traffic no more than an endless rumour. We leaned on the heightened wall, wondering how much higher it would eventually have to be if nothing was done to curb the ever-rising river. A swan peevishly thrust its way through a tangle of driftwood knocking against the handsome blue sterns of some barges. There was far too much of it, APH said. They ought to put nets. 'We used to catch it and burn it for firewood when I was a boy.' It hardly seemed likely at the time that that particular wheel could possibly come full circle and make us mudlarks for driftwood again, but who could be so sure now, with the size of the current fuel bills?

Sadly, nobody will call on APH the right way any more, steering through the driftwood past the blue barges, tying up at the garden wall. Or any way, for that matter. In his last book about the Thames – it was on the stocks in that boatyard of a study when I saw him – Herbert writes about the fine sunset view from his beloved Hammersmith to Chiswick. 'Refuse to look at the factories beyond, and you are deep in the country.'

Yet *should* you refuse to look at the factories? This sort of contrast, however deplorable to the orthodox environmentalists I would hardly have thought APH would seek as shipmates, is of the essence of the urban Thames.

Certainly he had a surfeit of it in his stretch of river. Downstream beyond Putney a leftward swing provides a total change of visual mood, green echoing green from bank to bank, Hurlingham on the north bank and Wandsworth Park on the south. A second left bend and the scene darkens again as though a black backdrop had descended. There is no denying that Wandsworth Bridge is emphatically a working bridge. Mighty gasholders rule the skies here; already they have acquired patina, looking like ancient monuments, liable to be preserved for the nation. But it is a mistake to revere nothing but industrial giants, to worship exclusively at power stations. Houses and streets have their rights, too often neglected and frequently outraged.

I walked down Battersea High Street and Battersea Church Road with a sense of deep desolation. Clearly they had seen better days, and looked as though they might soon see no days at all. Which would be tragic, for they project a riverside atmosphere – or the ghost of one – as strong as any I found along the Thames; a village air, sinuous and organic, seeming to echo the river they skirted. The old brick church – no architectural masterpiece, the purists say, but I was in no mood to care about that – had a rare charm and rightness; rare because, although the Thames is not short of churches helping to form its riverscape, it is hard to find one actually sitting on its bank.

To me St Mary's was not only comely but distinctly maritime. Churchyard mast, sailing barges, the great sluggish riverscape magnified by bends – the whole scene had a Low Countries look but in the English way: single-Dutch, the sort we can understand. Seen in the distance, Cheyne Walk and the Chelsea houseboats were an ocean away. It seems right enough, in Chelsea, that a boat should be transformed into a house. But Chelsea Flour Mill looked comfortingly homely, like a flour mill; and my heart almost warmed to the messiness of Lots Road Power Station because it chose to *look* like a power station instead of a cathedral.

Going to Chelsea by way of Wandsworth Bridge has the advantage of novelty. It is a small circuit but unfashionable. No tourists will jostle you, no addicted river-wanderer even. Crossing the bridge by foot brought glances of surprise from the high cabs of lorries. Yet surprise remained normal, even here. Among the sand, cement and beer-wagons plunging across the bridge I met a very old horse, pulling some scrap metal and a very young man. He (the young man) was modishly dressed, and gave a theatrical wave as he passed.

'Junk Boutique', a shop on the far side of the bridge was called. It said a lot about this area, where Wandsworth emulates Chelsea and any old iron prepares to turn itself into an *objet d'art*. Northward, parallel to the unapproachable river, along mysterious Townmead Road, past the Fulham Power Station with its four phallic chimneys, one of them gently fuming; past stark, run-down but still solid looking rows of terrace houses. Everywhere, in the middle of a desperate housing shortage, were to be seen these heart-breaking acres of basically sound yet abandoned property. Much of it would be tolerable to live in, some positively attractive. Nothing could be more desolating than this vista of ravaged houses, mortally sick with planning blight, delayed rapacity, designated area disease or just plain neglect. It lifted the spirits just to see ordinary people carrying on their ordinary lives. Why should that seem so special? I felt absurdly reassured – and half unbelieving, as though it was all being laid on for a film or television feature – to find a cluster of Victorian back-to-back houses with windows intact and curtained and lines rigged with washing, signalling human survival.

'Rather deathe than False of Faythe,' a grammar school (foundation 1700) announced on its rebuilt front wall; but it was not all that easy to know with any certainty what faith was, or what false was, or what death was, even. There seemed to be a kind of limbo, an ill-defined not-quite-ending and not-yet-becoming, to which whole sections of the riverside had been currently consigned. At the unfashionable end of Chelsea construction workers were drinking in unmodish bars without removing their white helmets. Or were they demolition men? So many areas appear uncertain whether they are on the way up, down or out.

Skirting Chelsea Creek and Lots Road, I soon achieved the reassurance of Cheyne Walk and the village of houseboats at its western end. This stretch of beached suburbia looked delightful but no doubt had its trials. Fraught, fashionably dressed young women were walking up the ramp from their dreamboat home into the sea of real life. Was this where all the barges went? Had all the watermen been transformed into water-birds? It made an agreeable sight from above. On the standard barge foundation endless variations of superstructure had been devised, ringing the changes from frank homeliness to glossy sophistication to high flights of fantasy. There were floating country cottages, Roman villas, show boats; there were coloured pillars and porticos, cats dozing or prowling around the potted palms, yellow and pink and apple-green decors. One of the bonuses of belonging to the houseboat set, presumably, is that if the river floods they ride it.

Not long after admiring this pleasing domestic scene – so gay, in the obsolete sense of the word, and so Chelsea-like – I saw it reported that official attempts were being made to damp down on the visual fantasy in order to make the houseboat scene more shipshape, riverworthy and generally disciplined. I fervently hoped the move would get the response it deserved, as rude a one as Chelsea knew how.

One thing I envied the beach-dwellers for. It was quieter down there. Up on dry – normally dry – land the traffic roared along the embankment, provoking nostalgic thoughts about the days when this was a village where fairly rich citizens came to avoid the noise and the people, at least as much as the smoke. But how long since it was truly peaceful? Thomas Carlyle was so maddened by pianos, dogs, parrots, crowing cocks and other assorted noises of Chelsea that he built himself an early form of sound-proofing under the roof of his tall house. It was successful – too successful, since it also excluded ventilation, and history nearly had a suffocated sage on its hands.

Much has changed in Chelsea since the time when Carlyle improbably swam in its river, contemplated the windmills and watched the watermen drinking with their tarts. ('Improper females', as he recorded it.) The fact is, the place was going to the dogs quite early on, with rough sights and cruelty to horses and noisy hymn-singers, and distinguished letters of protest were soon appearing in *The Times*. Yet there appears to be an impressive continuity of life among the Chelsea rich, who can no doubt afford better sound-proofing than Carlyle and who maintain along the elegant Cheyne Walk a remarkable level of taste and standards, grandly oblivious of the traffic.

The motor traffic, at least. 'THIS ROAD IS RESERVED FOR RESIDENTS AND THEIR HORSES AND VEHICLES,' I was astonished to find a notice in copperplate script proclaiming at the entrance to Cheyne Mews. Another courteously reminded residents of the desirability, in the interests of their friends and neighbours, of *walking* their horses when passing under the archway. The restrained clip-clopping of ghostly hooves after midnight now has the less inhibited snarl of sports cars with which to contend, but if there are ghosts anywhere they ought to abound here. Not just those of Rossetti and Swinburne and George Eliot, of bargemen and improper females and horses. There is the ghost of the old wooden Battersea Bridge, of Whistler and his Nocturnes; and the much younger ghost of the lamented 'Pier', a riverside pub done to death as recently as the late 1960s. It had a turbulent life, and getting barred from the 'Pier' was an almost compulsory feature of the post-war Chelsea set. Vague revenants, strangely dressed in the manner of thirty years ago, still haunt the site, waiting for opening time outside a pub no longer there.

But the Albert Bridge, mercifully, is still with us. Flaunting its ineffectual charm, its largely functionless make-up, it looks entirely out of tune with the age, a ghost before its time. I even found a notice instructing people to break step if they ventured across in groups. I liked the idea that only the out of step were wanted here. If it is inertia or meanness that has saved this bridge from replacement by something more solid, a structure that could take Eurolorries and that troops could march across without bringing the whole thing crashing down, then long may inertia and meanness survive.

This most endearing of all the Thames bridges took me across to Battersea Park where, in the days when it was still called Battersea Fields, the first Duke of Wellington fought the last political duel. It was over the eternal issue of a statesman's right to change his mind and his course without dishonour: 'to do a U-turn', as we have learned to put it. They have different moral problems at Battersea now. When I walked through the park it was plastered with posters about whether or not it should accommodate a Disneyland. Perish the thought, everybody I met seemed to be saying. But perhaps Battersea's serene interlude, however attractive, is unnatural. See it as the ghost of the old Vauxhall Gardens, that earlier and more fashionable South Bank pleasure haunt, and you could call it a case of beaux to gnomes in five generations.

East of the park I found myself in the diocese of Battersea Power Station and the developing spread of the vast new riverside Covent Garden. It is one of the strangest reversions of fate that has brought, in a manner of speaking, the countryside back to Nine Elms, which was a famous market gardening area two centuries ago. Now it plants concrete pillars and aluminium stockades, glowing in fluorescent light, and digs great beds for the lorry parks; all the apples, tomatoes, oranges and pineapples are safely gathered in their containers, the square seeds of the future. There is no denying the rationality of the move from central London, and only those – there are many – who are far gone in nostalgia will lament those bizarre operatic confusions of the old market north of the Strand, where you could really see your fruit. True, you could never be sure whether a barrowload of melons was for saleyard or stage, or whether the colourful characters who never quite bumped into each other were marketmen or chorus singers. Sad, of course, that it should all have to end. It had a Marx Brothers as well as a permanent 'Pygmalion' flavour, and those ghosts will hardly travel to Nine Elms.

Moving eastward, I preferred to keep to the south side of the river, for a number of reasons – one of them being the Wandsworth Road area, an untidy region of recognizable human beings and neighbourhood shops where no tourist is ever likely to set foot unless he gets lost. I got lost myself, and liked it. I liked the comparatively relaxed atmosphere, or so it seemed. I liked the black fun that induced a shop to call itself the 'Friendly Zulu'. Another good reason for choosing this way was that beyond Vauxhall Bridge the approach to central London took me along the Albert Embankment instead of the more familiar Millbank. This has several distinct advantages. There is a full view of the contentious Millbank Tower, all three hundred and eighty-seven feet of it, and a fair opportunity of deciding whether it is really as deplorable as so many commentators maintain.

Those who insist – and it is surely a quaint attitude – that the Almighty decreed the Victoria Tower of Barry's Palace of Westminster to be the scale-setter for the central embankment buildings will naturally deplore the Millbank as an impudent intruder on the sacred skyline. I don't see it that way. I find it rather beautiful, discreet and quite unaggressive. For me, the main benefit of approaching on this side is that one can see this fine high-riser and *avoid* seeing the clumsy crate-like blocks one is walking under. A century ago they demolished the riverside village of Lambeth to make way for this Albert Embankment. According to the records it was a picturesque spot. Nobody could say that of what eventually took its place.

There is always, of course, Lambeth Palace, the traditional residence of archbishops and an ancient among upstarts. It is swooning with age and looks it, yet it is not one of those highly historical buildings I feel any great urge to linger at. Heresy, no doubt, but I would call it uninviting. Could it be that there is too much of the wrong sort of history, and it shows? It was once, they say, a great place for top-level hospitality – some of it enforced, as the Lollards Tower with its iron chain-rings for the convenience of guests still testifies. It doesn't look hospitable now. The aura of the adjoining St Mary's Church I found equally unenticing; there was an empty bottle leaning against the sealed door, though one could get round to look at the tomb of Bligh of the Bounty. He was Vice-Admiral of the Blue, and goes down mildly enough on this record as the man 'who first transplanted the breadfruit tree from Otaheite to the West Indies'. Surely there was something else?

Past the back of St Thomas's Hospital, Westminster's architectural opposition, busy shedding its old skin and boxing itself into the statutory cubes that are now required packaging. And so to the best view there is of the Palace of Westminster. Seen from across the river it drops sheer into the water, as Thames palaces should, its terrace wall white for a few inches above the green tidemark.

Not enough inches, really, even though the walls have recently been raised.

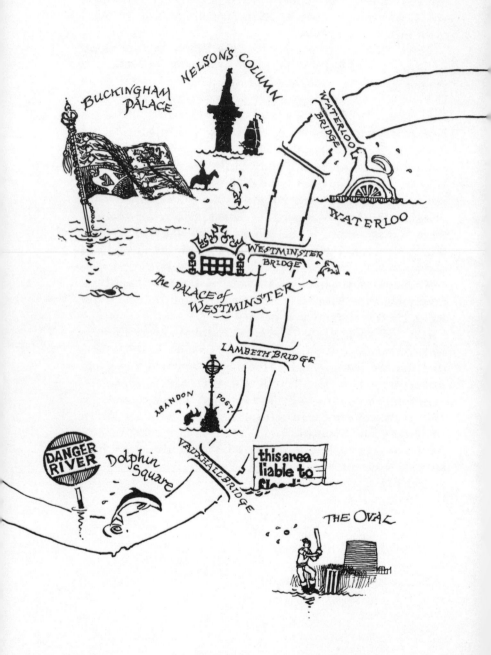

6. Castle Perilous

A PARLIAMENTARY HORROR STORY

And all the proud and dreadful sea
And all his tributary streams
A constant tribute pays to thee
And all the liquid world is one extended Thames
ABRAHAM COWLEY

Natural disaster is something that strikes others, never ourselves, or so we have come to believe. Yet Londoners live dangerously, more dangerously than they appear to have realized; and their chances of death or destruction from flooding have been increasing. Even the House of Commons got to hear of it.

One summer evening in 1972, strawberries-and-cream time on the famous terrace, a debate was going on in the House which was more than just unusual. It was horrifying enough to curdle the cream.

It would have been unusual anyway because it was about the river. Although members of Parliament might be assumed to live with the river in terms of the greatest intimacy they hardly ever talk about it, still less formally debate it, and probably notice it no more than ordinary Londoners do. Their Victorian Gothic palace plummets straight into the Thames with a theatrical effect that can hardly have been matched since the truly Gothic Baynard's Castle did its ancient plunge from the medieval Strand. But it is best to cross the bridge to see it properly; and that is rather far for most MPs, apart from being the unfashionable side of the river.

The Thames, frankly, is seldom in their mind. They seem to have forgotten that five of their number, on a famous occasion three centuries ago, got away by water when a king was after them. Gratitude apart, it is sensible in politics to keep as many escape routes open as possible. The Lords do a little better. A peer – a very tall peer, as indeed he needed to be –

recently tried to walk across the water near Westminster Bridge. His idea was to establish where the ancient crossing-place used to be a thousand years before there was any bridge at all, and to prove that we could still ford the river if ever we needed to: exactly the sort of offbeat foresight, some believe, that justifies the continued existence of the Upper House. What Lord Noel-Buxton did establish was that peers may have got taller – and six-foot-three was a good enough foundation, anyone would think, for an experiment of that kind – but the river has grown disproportionately deeper. He failed, though only by a few inches, to make it without swimming. But the knot of spectators who gathered on the bridge voted it a noble effort, particularly at a time (it was the early 1950s) when the river was still badly polluted, before fish had been seen to be coming back in any measurable numbers and when only eels were reckoned to survive.

Only a member of the Upper House, appropriately a little upstream from the Commons, would have that sort of impulse. At least he provided a reminder of a brutal fact, for those willing to take due warning. London is sinking like a slower-motion Venice, and its river is rising. As for the great majority of Commons members, they seemed content to let others worry. They only give their attention to the river if they must, and now that they no longer have to smell it the occasion need seldom arise. It is simply what lies beyond the wall of the terrace where they like to sit with a drink, or nibble their strawberries and cream with favoured guests.

As some of them were doing, no doubt, that June evening while inside the chamber of the Commons a comparative handful of MPs, mostly London members with what nobody could deny was a strong constituency interest, were discussing the chances of calamitous London floods. They were plotting it in terms of a thriller. One speaker even envisaged it as a horror film, seeing the tidal surge that was to inundate central London sweeping down the North Sea coast with, mercifully, a certain amount of warning one could only hope was accurately estimated.

The surge, this man reckoned, would reach the Wash with six hours to go before hitting the capital. In that time the inhabitants of forty-five square miles of London would have to be warned, the underground train system evacuated, the House of Commons and other riverside institutions abandoned. The film – even now they could hardly contemplate it as a real-life possibility – would have spirited shots of members of Parliament running for their lives. What was more – so a bluff ex-admiral pointed out – they would need to devise a new public warning system because the existing sirens would merely convey to most Londoners the idea that somebody was making another Battle of Britain film and no notice would be taken. Half real fear, half incredulous fantasy-mongering: that was the mood. Well, they would know all right when the Thames came cascading over the embankment and water climbed the walls of Westminster Hall.

They talked themselves out of the fantasy part of their mood. Soon they were laying odds on the chances of such a disaster, and these seemed alarmingly short. It sounded as though a Londoner had a better chance of being sunk in the next Thames flood than of backing the winner of the Grand National. One impeccably sober MP – the member for the cities of London and Westminster, no less – estimated that not only the Commons but Green Park, half of St James's Park and Buckingham Palace faced the prospect of being inundated before the decade was out. Having forced themselves to confront the facts, the most optimistic seemed to agree that there was one chance in ten of the river reaching the highest protection levels in any given year, and one chance in thirty of its overtopping them sufficiently to cause a major disaster.

'We have a one-in-thirty chance of being drowned during one of our debates.' That was the graphic way their peril was put by the member for London and Westminster, a seat that hardly encourages hotheads. Indeed, Mr Christopher Tugendhat was listened to with the attention deserved by so gifted a man of figures, well-known for his measured financial writing.

Suddenly they realized that the horror film could be a documentary – that Commons, Lords, flannelled fools on the terrace, drinkers, debaters and all could indeed be engulfed, if the conditions were right, by a devastating tidal wave.

Earlier debates, on the rare occasions they had been held, sounded less urgent. There was one in 1968, for instance, which called the fears 'overstated' and put the risk, much more mildly and vaguely, at around a hundred to one. The odds could hardly have shortened as much as that in four years. Though it is true, of course, that they are shortening all the time, because of that obstinate habit the land has of sinking in relation to the water level.

The risk was always there. The story of London flooding is older than parliament, older than the sixteenth-century historian John Stow, who writes of calamitous events at Westminster, Woolwich and Lambeth:

> We read also, that in the year 1236, the river of Thames overflowing the banks, caused the marshes about Woolwitch to be all on a sea, wherein boats and other vessels were carried with the stream; so that besides cattle, the greatest number of men, women and children, inhabitants there, were drowned: and in the great palace of Westminster men did row with wherries in the midst of the hall, being forced to ride to their chambers.
>
> Moreover, in the year 1242, the Thames overflowing the banks about Lambhithe, drowned houses and fields by the space of six miles, so that in the Great Hall at Westminster men took their horses, because the water ran over all.

Pepys records the inundation of Whitehall, and many another historical flood has gone into the records. In our own time the worst have been in 1928 and 1953, which between them drowned some three hundred people. It was after the 1953 catastrophe that Lord Waverley produced a report and the various statutory authorities began their agitated ritual dance over some kind of river barrier.

Something, clearly, would have to be done, and preferably before thirty more actuarial years were up. In 1966 a mathematician from the University of London, Professor Bondi, was commissioned to study and report on London flooding risks. His findings could not have been plainer. The risks were unacceptable as they stood, and were increasing year by year. The professor thought it might be a good idea to stage a trial evacuation of the underground railway system, since its flooding could be (as he put it) 'a knockout blow to the nerve centre of the country'.

What could cause such a disaster would be the clicking together, as by some diabolical one-armed bandit, of a high spring tide, heavy rainfall and a North Sea surge. And if the worst happened the government were obviously depending on those predicted hours of warning before catastrophe struck – allowing, in particular, time for the bulkhead gates protecting the underground system to be closed. But innocent, non-technical MPs – not innocent enough, all the same, to be entirely reassured by governmental statements which seemed to be getting less soothing every time the subject came up – at once thought of the tube station at Westminster. Naturally it is the one they know best. They are used to entering the House through the cloisters leading from the station stair head, a pleasant fusing of the secular and spiritual worlds. But suddenly they felt uncomfortably close to the next world. They could not for the life of them see, nor was it at all convincingly explained to them, how that particular station could possibly be protected from any Thames water that had so little regard for parliamentary privilege as to come flooding into New Palace Yard, not to mention its new and vastly expensive car park beneath. Perhaps they would have done better, some of them were beginning to think, to spend their money on diving suits and a mooring basin for boats.

The professor had delivered his report in 1967. Parliament, faced with the inescapable need for action, once again responded: put on its wellingtons, blew up its water-wings, staged debates in three successive years. During the first of

THE THAMES BARRIER

... Could control the flood water
in central reaches.

these, which took place in 1970, the government revealed
that an evacuation exercise as advocated by the professor
had actually been held; apparently this involved various
headquarters moves and strategic telephone calls, if nothing
as untidy as actual people. Still, the government spokesman
was already admitting the danger of tidal flooding to be 'real
and imminent', which was quite a stride forward in urgency.

And so, less than twenty years after the last disaster, and
with ten full actuarial years before the deadline for the next,
we came to that cataclysmic debate of 1972. It was an eerie
affair. Death by water, of cities and of men, was in the air.

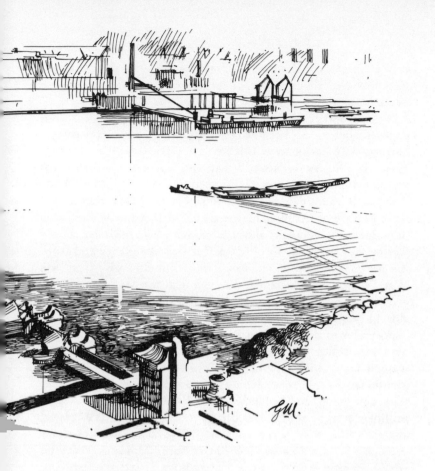

Florence had suffered its ruinous floods. Venice was sinking and so, steadily and relentlessly, were we. London's walls had again been raised, but the idea of progressively adding to their height, in measure with the ever-rising river, had a nightmare touch. Clearly that contest had to stop somewhere.

Another answer had to be found. They settled for a Thames barrier which could control the floodwater in the central reaches, a rising sector-gate system to be placed across the river at Woolwich. It could be ready, they thought at first, a little over-optimistically as things turned out, by 1978 –

just a quarter of a century after the last big floods which launched the shock wave of urgency, though well over a century since the original barrage plan was launched.

As long ago as the 1850s Herbert Spencer, who was a civil engineer before he became a philosopher, was advocating a barrage with locks to eliminate the tides from the London river. In the 1930s such a barrage was championed with ardent campaigns and spirited slogans like DAM THE THAMES! The Lords had a debate in which it was reckoned that a full-scale barrage at Woolwich, complete with roadway and some new docks, would cost about four-and-a-half millions. There was opposition from the Port of London Authority and from the government; also, no doubt more conclusively, from the War Council which ended the technical investigation on the grounds of the security risk. The structure would be vulnerable to bombs.

So that was that. What a British War Council said in those days went. But – under five millions! The money tide has washed away such figures into dreamland. Compare those mentioned in the 1972 debate, for a scheme nothing like as thorough-going and including no locks. A figure of £75 millions 'at 1970 prices' was mentioned first, but this escalated almost while they were speaking. The then parliamentary secretary to the Ministry of Agriculture calculated that the whole scheme would cost £125 millions – and the estimate was 'only very tentative' at that.

His caution was justified. If nothing else, the inflation surge was at our gates, and soon they were looking at such major items of public expenditure through the doom-tinted spectacles of financial crisis. It was revealed in a 1975 debate that the estimate had risen to £168 millions; then it lifted to £250 and (almost before you could say the figures) to £370 millions. The mid-1975 estimate of the probable ultimate cost was £500 millions.

It all had to be reckoned against the £1000 millions (at 1966 prices, and you could certainly multiply that figure now) which Professor Bondi reckoned a major flood disaster might cost. And since hypothetical spending may be the only sort we can afford if the inflation flood engulfs us, we are left with some pensive hindsight views up the might-have-been reach of the river. For an insignificant fraction of what the barrier will cost, we could have had a far more complete defence.

But there would have been another sort of cost. A dam would wall away the tidal movement altogether. Above it, the former estuary would be a fixed-level lake, a narrow lagoon gently wafting seaward. No more floods, but no more tides either. No more breathing, the end of the river's life? There are many who would prefer it that way. They argue that the two-way flow below Teddington causes such complexities, dangers and frustrations that we all ought to be happier to see it eliminated.

They point seductively to the lotus-land this change of the river's life would bring. Clean, placid water at an eternal half-tide. Peace, perfect peace, and navigation made easy for all mini-mariners. The tidal range, which can be twenty feet or more at London Bridge, would be ended. No more boats breaking their spines in the mud, or left hanging from iron hooks because their owners are called away and forget the state of the tide. No more bothersome calculations because the ebb tide lasts longer than the flood.

No more bothering about anything much. But would something fundamental, something we should be reluctant to lose lightly, go with the last tide? There are many practical and knowledgeable Thames-lovers – the late Sir Alan Herbert was among them or, should one say leading them – who are all in favour of a non-tidal Thames. Leaving the navigational side out of it, they say, think of the visual improvement. No more mudbanks and sleazy exposed shores at low tide – what a blessing that would be!

The painters would hardly agree. The seabirds certainly would not. But at least the MPs would be able to attend to their strawberries and cream without any need to worry about the sleeping monster over the terrace wall.

7. The Central Scene

WESTMINSTER TO THE TEMPLE

I have seen the four great empires disappear!
I was when London was not! I am here!
ALFRED LORD TENNYSON

Tennyson, forefinger no doubt erected in powerful poetic climax, was speaking not for himself but for Cleopatra's Needle, that larger and still more ancient finger reared so theatrically from the river wall of the Victoria Embankment, new in the Laureate's day. The sixty-foot immigrant from Heliopolis had in fact nothing to do with Cleopatra, predating even her by fifteen hundred years; but that was what Londoners christened the famous obelisk, and that is what they will go on calling it as long as London exists.

After that, who knows? For me those startling alarm-cries from the Commons gave Tennyson's hectic lines fresh point, and made me look at the old granite erection with a new and nervous eye. If the worst happened, and Parliament, palace, royal parks and central riverside areas were inundated by some deadly confluence of tide, wind and rain, I had nightmare visions of the Needle emerging above a waste of the most expensive floodwater in history.

The Laureate's lines would have been equally applicable if he had appointed himself the mouthpiece of the river itself. If a lump of granite can talk, why not Father Thames? By our own day at least one other 'great empire' would have to be added to Tennyson's list of casualties. And of the two that concern him particularly, the Roman and the British, the river god would have more cause to commend the Romans, if only because any god has a natural prejudice in favour of those who believe in him. That the Romans, though practical people to a fault, held the river in ritual awe is made evident by the vast number of coins found in the vicinity of the wooden bridge they built. These range over centuries of the occupation and could never have got there by accident: no citizens of any age could have been as consistently careless with their loose change as that. They were votive offerings. And if the down-to-earth Romans felt they had to placate the spirit of the river, what might not be due from us?

There was that dreadful period when we treated the Thames like a common prostitute, abusing and polluting it until it imperilled our own health. Then we decided – in the high Victorian period, appropriately – that the time had come for reform and regeneration. So the river was corseted in embankments, cleaned up and made to look respectable, soberly jewelled with lights. In short, they did a Pygmalion on it, gave it the right accent, more Chelsea than Cockney. They made amends, of a sort.

The embankments certainly brought a number of measurable benefits. By curbing the horror of untreated sewage going straight into the river they saved uncountable thousands from death by disease. They eased and sped the land traffic flow, though that may look a dubious advantage today. They reclaimed for public use precious ribbons of central territory. Visually they are far from unimpressive. With all but remnants of Georgian and Regency London now gone, they provide a substantial part of the only formalized sectors of townscape worth looking at. The river's restless curves save them from monotony. And their strips of riverside garden – if only these were not separated from the river by the thunder and fume of the embankment traffic – would be the most precious of their by-products.

By a happy accident, as it seems, one stretch escapes this disadvantage and shows what a riverside garden really ought to be. Since the palace of Westminster (as all the great waterside houses and palaces once did) drops sheer into the Thames, with no public access past the river flank, the wedge-shaped Victoria Tower Gardens, running up to the dead-end of the House of Lords from Lambeth Bridge, are undivided from the river except, of course, by the obligatory flood wall. The gain in intimacy is enormous. Here, for a few hundred precious yards, land and water are truly linked. And all because the great Duke of Wellington was afraid of the mob! For it was no accident after all, nor Gothic traditionalism either, that plunged the palace into the river. The Duke insisted that crowds must not be able to surround it when Barry rebuilt it after the 1834 fire. Another triumph for timidity, and from an unexpected quarter.

We all have our favourites; to me this is one of the most

attractive corners of London, and it even contrives a domestic air. It is quite the most pleasant approach to the Houses of Parliament; and occasionally one or another of our statesmen who still live within the sound of division bells, and are not afraid of the mob, can be seen taking a walk there with their cares of office, dogs, wives or friends, or just themselves. Even when it rains – and although it strains credulity to think it rains more in the Victoria Tower Gardens than in other parts of London, my memory always presents me with a wet scene when I think of it – people still linger. They like to take their time looking at the great Lords façade, at eroded Lambeth Palace, at St Thomas's Hospital shedding its old skin like a chrysalis and revealing its great pale new wings, glistening in an eternal drizzle.

And, of course, the most famous group of statuary in town. Black with despair and wet, huddled as much against the weather as the king they were submitting to, raindrops on each nose-end; the last time I saw Rodin's Burghers of Calais they were put to shame by an undaunted Emmeline Pankhurst who lifted her liberated head near by. The prison badge worn by those who suffered with her for Women's suffrage, a broad arrow on the Westminster arms, was proudly displayed. She gazed without enthusiasm at Henry Moore's beautifully textured construction across the road, marrying the centuries against the ancient stone of the Jewel Tower, a surviving fragment of the original palace. 'But what is it supposed to be?' her lips would be saying, if they could only speak. 'And what is it *for*?'

Inside a little Victorian fountain looking like a miniature Albert Memorial, commemorating Wilberforce and Macaulay and Brougham and other emancipators, I found another emblem at least as eloquent as Mrs Pankhurst's – a broken bottle, with dregs. In fact I found it all over inner London. It was to be seen in every public place: the drop-outs' coat of arms. The derelicts who haunt the embankment gardens of late years are a *memento mori*, a glimpse of the skeleton beneath the ailing social skin. I say 'of late years' because

PARLIAMENTARY APPROACH.

" TO ME, THIS IS ONE OF THE MOST ATTRACTIVE CORNERS OF LONDON."

although they have always been around, on seats and benches and even pavements, and may now be in less danger of starving or freezing to death than they were fifty years ago, there is a sinister difference between the old drop-outs and the new.

They used to be a fringe section of society. Anybody could belong – join and leave and join again, according to fortune or sometimes sheer whim. Now they are detached, a race apart. Bearded old men, looking like displaced eastern sages, and younger ones with shuttered eyes still commandeer park seats and share their bottle; but it is a private rite in a private world, and what the bottle often contains would appal the public one. Their drop-outs' club is exclusive; as far as the rest of society goes they seem to have nothing to communicate, nothing they want to hear.

The plausible old cadgers, however roguish, were more reassuring – the old soldier, the chap fallen on hard times, the casher-in on his Irish charm. These are so rare now that when they do emerge they sound like satirists, or small-part actors from some period film. 'Pardon me, sir,' said a man in Villiers Street, edging up like a character from between the wars, 'I wonder if you could spare a bob or two?'

'Bob or two': how disquieting, and how dating. A chap fastening on another chap to whom 'bob or two' would sound better than 'ten-pee'. It would have been vulgar, rather than incomprehensible, if he had made it 'half a dollar'. Clearly the fellow wrapped himself in the *Daily Telegraph* on his park bench. Or did he join the others, with some natural distaste, under the sheltering railway bridge in Embankment Place, beneath the notice – presumably no satire intended there – saying DEPARTMENT OF SOCIAL ENGINEERING?

But the appearance and the reality of London as viewed from Westminster Bridge have always been stark in their contrast; and the embankments which Tennyson lived to see, though Wordsworth did not, scarcely changed that aspect much. Tourists who flock to the bridge still get a fair return for their effort, and sign their appreciation on the green paint covering the central stretches of the parapet. So hideous a colour that disfigurement can only improve it, this has been turned into one long scrawl of signatures and occasional comments, an extended open-air visitor's book. Every tourist in London, from Abu to Zuckermann, seems to have made it a point of honour to leave his mark on Westminster Bridge. From Corsica, Sweden, Argentina; from Essen, Firenze, Napoli – they have all been here. There are some who leave their message in Cyrillic, some in Arabic script. Mostly very neat, all (so far as the English reader can translate) conspicuously clean. And when the book is full it can be renewed with a long lick of paint.

Clean looks odd. Is it only the British who go in for public lewdness? Certainly none of these visitors show any sign of behaving in the abandoned way James Boswell did on a day in May of 1763, when he picked up a 'strong, jolly young damsel' in the Haymarket, walked her to the bridge, and proceeded to 'engage her upon this noble edifice'. He adds that 'the whim of doing it there with the Thames rolling below us amused me much'. At least he wrote it up in his *London Journal* and not, as far as we know, on the 'noble edifice' itself. That was the original stone bridge, then a mere fourteen years old, and its graffiti would have been harder to remove.

I stopped on the successor to Boswell's and Wordsworth's bridge and took the full impact of the fantasy of lights, with the Italianate curve of County Hall luscious as a slice of melon against the cold white face of the Shell building beyond. Impressive, but a shade overdone? When austerity hit us in the mid-seventies the dimmer lighting was to some tastes an embellishment, subduing the Festival Hall complex into a particularly seductive and mysterious half-glow.

A man leaned on the parapet at my side and I wondered, since he was unlikely to be a Londoner, from what part of the world he came. No doubt he would have inscribed his name and place of origin if there had been any room. It turned out he was from New York. 'Makes you want to get down there and explore,' he remarked; and I told him with a host's due sense of appreciation that a view couldn't do more for a man than make him feel like that.

'And you're lucky,' he then said, 'because in my town you'd think twice before you did that, this time of night.' Here I felt rather less the proud host, thinking it necessary to warn him that even solid, reliable London, once the envy of the world's capitals at least in this respect, was no longer the secure place it was once. People get mugged in that civilized concrete jungle, built in the Festive Fifties between the river and the massive rail terminus of Waterloo. And junkies abound on the station steps, castaways who leave their signatures in vomit or sometimes blood. We are back, in many respects, in Boswell's rough century.

There are daylight fantasies too, daydreams with the occasional snarl of nightmare. The most malign riverside sight I discovered was in the Victoria Embankment Gardens, apparently unnoticed by the passing strollers and lunchtime sandwich-eaters. Or rather they had stopped looking at it, accepting it as part of the regular scene. Two bronze feet, child's feet, still in the stance they would occupy if the legs and body were there, stood on a pedestal. But there was no body. It had been sawn off at the ankles and taken away. The inscription, which had no loot value, remained: it informed the unsurprised world that the figure had been provided by children 'in memory of the work done for the temperance cause by Lady Henry Somerset, June 1896'. She was president of the National British Women's Temperance Association, and the dedication added, 'I was thirsty and ye gave me drink.' Ironical, if that was what it was stolen to buy.

Equally strange, though less afflictingly, is the York Water-gate. Surely the least curious of tourists must wonder what on earth this great squat chunk of classical masonry is doing so far from the water, like a morose hippo tethered a hundred yards from its pool. It once led from the Duke of Buckingham's town house to the river which, in pre-embankment days, flowed past its steps. Now its landbound pillars are all at

sea, its pollution-fed lions reduced to skeletons; its steps lead
not to the arrogant ducal barge but to a jazzy band enclosure
that might have been imported straight from Margate. Behind,
clumsy concrete blocks have not quite been able to lay the
ghost of the murdered Adelphi, that noble eighteenth-century
terrace done to death between the wars. Various flights of
old stone stairs set place-nerves twitching and preserve an
illusion of being on the river's brink. A lot of time can be
spent here arousing suspicion by tracking former riverside
paths, invariably ending in prestigious garages or up against
blank stone walls; or hunting oddities like the caricature of
John Rowlandson's old house; or fruitlessly lamenting the
vulgarization of Villiers Street. That watergate apart, the
mighty Buckinghams have left little behind they would want
to keep. Still, Pepys's house is near, and the headquarters
(as it describes itself in bold lettering) of the 'Royal Society
for the Encouragement of Arts, Manufactures and Commerce'
goes back to Adam.

For me the streets in these parts have lost too much not to
be dispiriting; but I find the main embankment gardens
stronger in atmosphere, with a heavy sleepwalking air which
the statues do much to provide. These are massively and
irredeemably ugly, too high and mighty to loot, Victorian
to a man and a camel – the camel being the memorial to the
Camel Corps, quaintly neighbouring the one to Robert
Burns. Burns and a camel! A mouse, it surely ought to be:
the Mouse Corps Memorial, some insist, would be more in
keeping with our diminished times as well as more in the
poet's line of country. The other statuary is human, in a
manner of speaking. Nobody ever seems to look at them, the
members of this petrified club for the famous and the forgotten, though not all preserve a decent Victorian reticence.
Do Savoy guests ever peer out from their suites at a nervous-
looking Arthur Sullivan being clutched by his tempestuous
and scantily-clad bronze weeper? I doubt it.

How many Londoners recognize Henry Fawcett Raikes,

who founded the Sunday schools, that once-great British institution? There is Outram, but who now remembers the Bayard of India? Or Bartle Frere, eternalized by public subscription? I put it to the test. I asked several passers-by if they knew who Raikes was, or if the name Bartle Frere meant anything to them. Some looked deeply embarrassed, some indignant: you just don't ask questions like that in London parks, least of all from Londoners. But even allowing for a few satirical guesses one fact was obvious. They were not just hazy. Their ignorance of these once-famous men was total.

Whether or not our imperial statesmen deserve to be forgotten – as Frere certainly did, if Gladstone's stern disapproval is anything to go by – they can never have suspected such a fate, and I can't help wondering if their statues ever feel the ache of this monumental ingratitude. Yet they have achieved their immortality. Short of H-bombs or major earthquakes, they are there for ever. Even the most devastating flood would hardly move them; their stern, calm faces would surely rise above it.

They are forbidding but powerful, with a sepulchral grandeur, spectral figures twice the size of life. Like Whitehall Court with its alpine range of turrets, like the palace of Westminster which broodingly rules the entire scene, they express what is now the dominant London note – Victorian Romantic, which will stay in command until the bland packing-case era manages to pack it away. It will be extraordinarily hard to shift. Those who complain that the scale of the Westminster skyline has been outraged by the high-rise interlopers ignore the fact that cold measurements or even hotly angry ones are not everything – not necessarily anything much. What could dwarf that marvellous monster the Victoria Tower, but something of its own kind?

When Barry reared his Neo-Gothic palace against the Abbey, the traditional ruler of the Westminster skies for so many centuries, that was true audacity. Both survive as mighty presences, the real abbey and that newer Nightmare Abbey of genius, ruling the scene unmoved by the lofty impotent giants surrounding it. Nothing recent counts for much, or intrudes much. The Festival Hall complex, so alluring by night, fades by day into a range of concrete barns: almost a modern agricultural aspect, a Harvest Festival Hall. Next to it the vast inert face of the Shell building expresses total absence. But Wren's surviving churches, however small, refuse to be extinguished. They ignore monsters; they spike the scene like exclamation marks, commanding attention. And wherever you happen to be sailing or driving or walking, whether you are as near as Southwark or as far as Greenwich, St Paul's pops up all over the skyline like a floating bubble nobody can burst. If it had been anchored in a vista, as its creator intended, that dome would never have had the same capricious and buoyant appeal.

But it hardly seemed to me, as I plodded on along my concrete water-walk, that the embankments could be claimed, except in strictly limited terms, to have restored the river to the people. Rather the opposite, in one sense. They provide dignity, formality, those sometimes neurotic quirks of fantasy. In some sectors, though by no means all, they improved the view. But as far as the river is concerned they define and emphasize separation rather than remove it. People are walled away, and if the point is missed the walls heavily underline it. Anybody who looks for the human dimension, as much associated at one time with the Thames in London as it still is (though diminishingly) with the Seine in Paris, will have to look again. Bazalgette's great strips of stone are in a sense rivals – anti-rivers which have not only usurped part of its bed but, far from adding to it, have served to drain the Thames still further of the life it once shared with Londoners. The wall is a frontier; the lines of traffic people must cross to reach it are additional defences. Even the few gestures towards a shared life are in land rather than water terms: floating pubs, floating restaurants, a floating police station, floating exhibitions and publicity shows of one kind and another. All this is as null, measured against any true conception of river life, as the floating mortuary which, should you need it, is also to be found in these central reaches.

The embankment turns its back on the river, like Boadicea. She is the most English, the most Victorian, of all London's frozen population. It is not easy to associate her with her true period, so much does she have that air of an important personage in some early carriage section of the Women's Institute: one is confident, somehow, that she always drove on the left, made correct signals, and did her best to remove prejudice against lady charioteers. Knives in her wheels? A touch un-English, to be sure. But how many have read her inscription? 'Regions Caesar never knew Thy posterity shall sway.' Sway, mark you, not slay. But she certainly slays the tourists, who gaze at her with a curiosity more avid than any other national worthy manages to attract.

Is it simply that they find it hard to reconcile this stalwart though ladylike figure with the one they will have read about in their history books, a huge and ferocious woman with a furnace of red hair and a voice that could halt an army in its tracks? She looks more like someone whose daughters were born to be fashionably married – rather than raped, which was what actually happened to them. This bronzed lady belonged essentially to a brief interregnum, a mere ribbon of time, the Victorian Embankment period. The ferocious flesh and blood of Boadicea's real age was perhaps nearer to our own.

Such thoughts – any thoughts – are dangerous. I risked my life cutting across the surging traffic to the river wall. MURDER, cried a notice displayed on their pier by the Thames Division of the Metropolitan Police. HAVE YOU SEEN THIS CHILD? I was in a flood risk area, the warnings added. And Cleopatra's Needle: surely that was timeless and reassuring enough, making even the real Boadicea an arriviste? 'This obelisk, prostrate for centuries on the shores of Alexandria,' the legend boomed – Churchillian language before his time. But even the Needle looked sick. Eternity's eroded phallus has started crumbling from the London disease in the last few minutes, so to speak, of its three thousand years.

I climbed into one of the seats that ostensibly overlook the river and the sense of wrongness, of veiled conflict, subtly grew. It took some little time to see why. The point was what I could *not* see: only a tawny strip on the far side of the river was in view. For anybody unnaturally tall, eight feet or so, the situation would be different. It took quite a time for the truth to dawn. The wall had been heightened since the seats were fixed. YOU ARE IN A FLOOD RISK AREA, the notice said, after all.

But the river, what could be seen of it, looked harmless enough, forgettable and forgotten. One day, perhaps, they will turn the seats round. And why not? The scene remained implacably landbound. I watched urban dogs on short walks risking substantial fines for misbehaviour as they sniffed around the dolphin-decorated lamp standards. Long-distance runners pursued their mysterious cult; impossible to know where they came from or went to, but their flow was as constant as that of the water – at which they never glanced. If anything could stop them, surely they would pause for a look at the Plimsoll memorial? But it turned out to have nothing to do with them after all, being one of the few with maritime links.

Eeriness persisted. Sir Walter Besant, the London historian, gazed on the scene through bronze spectacles. PLEASE EXERCISE GREAT CARE WHEN USING THE GANGPLANK. Sensible advice to customers of the 'Old California', the floating pub. Come to think of it, anyone could slip into the river, here in the heart of London, without causing more than a momentary disturbance to the gulls bobbing among the driftwood, the plastic cartons and the nylon rope that never dies. Really, the landward prospect was more cheerful. Some jolly heraldic dragons, looking ravenous with their forked red tongues and silver fangs, marked the embankment boundary between Westminster and the City.

Here the Temple gardens, where the Wars of the Roses traditionally broke out, overlooked the river with an air of owning it, of never having accepted the vulgar intrusion of the embankment. They excluded the common herd in antique script. Fish-tailed cherubs, looking succulent as whitebait, adorned the flamboyant gateway. I found myself centuries down memory lane in Paper Buildings, and among resonant legal names like Boreham, Goodenday and Griffinhoofe. King's Bench Walk, with its plane trees and suave cobbled contours, still looks like what it has always been, the most desirable town address in the world; but no journalist should find it in his heart to forgive the disappearance of the old 'Feathers' and its replacement by a pub called the 'Witness Box', looking – though I could hardly bring myself to enter it – as coldly welcoming as a lawyer's smile.

But lawyers have a genius for finding themselves the most agreeable places to live and work; who wouldn't want to do either in the Temple, let alone both? Decent of them, I thought, to admit the common herd. Middle Temple is pleasantly accommodating to the stroller, with sequestered little terraces lit by (can it be?) gas lamps of the earliest style. Does the lamplighter still come on his ghostly rounds about muffin-time, when wigs are whipped off and parchment documents tucked away in eighteenth-century drawers? This still looked authentic Dickens country, only a few steps away from Fountain Court with its goldfish and propped-up mulberry; only the fogs seemed to be lacking, anyway out of doors. And here was Middle Temple Hall, where Shakespeare first presented *Twelfth Night*.

PLEASE CLOSE THE GATE QUIETLY, pleaded the Honourable Society of the Middle Temple in its hushed though firm copperplate tones. It was the least anyone could do, despite the quaintness of the request against the roars of the embankment traffic. But the sun was suddenly out, and the empty river shimmering; and in the distance, back the way I had come, the turrets of Westminster lorded it over the restless, demented beauty of London.

8. Where it All Began

TEMPLE TO TOWER

Nay, boy, I will bring thee to the sluts and the roysters
At Billingsgate, feasting with claret-wine and oysters
     BEN JONSON, 'The Devil is an Ass'

Though a mere interlude in the flow of time, the central embankments – Victorian Imperial on the left, Twentieth-Century Cultural on the right – seem fully prepared to go on for ever. Further downstream, where the river divides the City from Southwark, the contrast is stark. Here the tide of renewal has been so swift that the riverside looks all past and future and virtually no present.

I found it a sector of remarkable turmoil, of visual excitement and alarm, as though a medieval and a modern city were locked in combat. Ancient wharves and ranks of surviving warehouses, looking romantically older than their years and not well equipped for modern property warfare, were fighting it out as best they could with the new developments. I earnestly hoped that at the end of it all such veterans as Queenhythe, Dowgate and Billingsgate would be spared, and that Bankside would emerge from the struggle not just without further harm but with due honour. For these made the nucleus of the London we know, and still appeal to the eye as well as to the imagination.

It was Bankside I was making for. South Bank culture ended at Waterloo. From then on the waterside was a cacophony of rumbling lorries, growling cement mixers and guard dogs, strident slogans about the need to preserve the riverside for the people. I found myself in Upper Ground, divided from the river by a forlorn hope of old warehouse buildings still precariously standing if not actually fighting, and then in Barge House Street, a name that rang a cracked yet persistent bell. Barge House Street . . . Barge House Stairs, which centuries of rivermen must have clustered round like water-flies: could it be possible that they survived?

And there, amid the nostril-pricking cement dust, was the unmistakable whiff of history. What does history smell like? In this case, perhaps, nothing more than an exhalation of ancient river mud and rotting wharf timbers, working on a hunch. If the old lightermen could navigate through fog to the cinnamon wharves of Wapping or the malt berths at Deptford, smell their way not only to cloves and soap and whale-oil but to teak and ivory, it may not be too mystical to be led by the nose – without really believing they could possibly be there – to the Barge House Stairs.

There are still, it turned out, hidden doorways that can take you back a thousand years. I found a narrow alley guarded by lurching bollards that might have been made for W. W. Jacobs characters to perch themselves on. At the end of it was a flight of mouldering wooden steps leading down to an old stone causeway, with ravaged timbers held by huge rusted clamps. I sat on the low-tide beach, hundreds of yards and years from the tourists on the Victoria Embankment opposite. The place was insulated from the noises of central London. The stillness, the silence, were intense. I shared a luxurious chill of loneliness with the sleeping hulk of a barge, improbably named William. It was like being thrown overboard by the twentieth century.

Climbing back on board a little hurriedly, and making my way to the lower regions of Blackfriars Bridge, I found myself in an area where history's vibrations were far from soothing but not, in the light of the throbbing turmoil now going on, inappropriate. This was Paris Gardens, scene of some of the nastiest bear and bull baiting. It was also the western end of Bankside, with ancient and modern at each other's throats. Everybody was trying to get a fingerhold, it seemed; lucky the ones who got in early, like Mr Charles Hopton who established those elegant almshouses of his two centuries ago. Not that there looked much room for latecomers, for this is the diocese of the Bankside Power Station – enormous and demure with its clipped lawns, its austere fluted tower, its brickwork decorations of the best Industrial Perpendicular period, its monstrous and inappropriate good taste.

It looked like a vast crematorium and some see it as just that – a crematorium for the ashes of living London. The prayers rose up all around: STOP BANKSIDE BEING RAPED – LET'S PLAN OUR FUTURE NOW – SAVE OUR RIVERSIDE. Next to the power station, a glowing example of the urge for bizarre juxtaposition so dear to the English, I found what looked like the most charming and elegant small house in central London. Cardinal's Wharf is reputedly where Christopher Wren lived, watching the dome of his own cathedral rising across the river. When not busy admiring his own handiwork he no doubt took a stroll in the local lanes, Maid Lane or Love Lane, or (if in that sort of mood) Foul Lane or Melancholy Walk. Southwark brothels were famous once and brought many Londoners over the bridge on a night out. They had names like pubs and a favourite Tudor house was called the 'Cardinal's Hat'. It reformed later and became a fashionable theatrical eating place – a species of early Ivy, so to speak.

Now real ivy festoons the walls of Cardinal's Wharf, and the original Cardinal's Cap Alley still runs by the side of it, dividing it now from the power station. As I turned into this ancient lane the metropolitan racket was silenced as if by a cut-off switch and massed birdsong broke out instead, staying with me until I re-emerged on Bankside when it stopped as suddenly as it had started. The birds were real too, though this of course was famous theatrical territory once, and valiant efforts have been made to bring about a revival. The surviving residents should back them, since from the time its first theatres were built Southwark had a tradition of putting on shows to celebrate public events, or deplore them if need be. If Southwark feels threatened, what more fitting than that it should dramatize its plight? Nobody would be likely to go to gaol for sedition, as Ben Jonson did in his day.

Roving riverside groups, here and elsewhere, have in fact tried their hand and voice in the environmental cause, playing out the over-simplified morality of helpless people against monster developers. We live in a time when the theatre, like the church, feels the need to go to the customers. There are dangers. It could be counter-productive if this kind of social protest became a form of travelling folk art. It could be equally so if campaigners indulged in over-romantic views about social continuity. Southwark may indeed be one of the few parts of London where people had grandparents living in the same area, but they would mostly feel it was pushing things to claim any kinship with their Elizabethan predecessors.

SOUTHWARK HAS A GREAT PAST . . . GIVE THE KIDS A CHANCE TO KNOW WHY SOUTHWARK IS WORLD FAMOUS – I found it hard not to warm to posters like that. The great story is, of course, double-edged and even two-faced. How can we begin to understand people who could see *Hamlet* one night, watch a blind bear being whipped the next, with the following evening occupied with a bloody sabre-match between a waterman and a butcher, cheered by partisans so violent that they would make a modern football crowd seem inhibited? The answer is not that there were civilized audiences and brutalized audiences, since the same spectators often watched the whole range. Pepys certainly did, and his diary reveals the ambivalence. Having recorded how he saw 'some very good sport of the bull's tossing of the dogs, one into the boxes', he makes a point of adding that it was 'a very rude and nasty pleasure'.

If the baitings were watched by the sophisticated as well as the simple, no doubt they sometimes went for the same reasons that prompt reluctant modern Londoners to take their visiting guests or clients to night spots – because it is expected of them. There was a surviving Roman element, mixing cruelty with fashionable spectacle. Both Queen Elizabeth and her successor King James used these shows to entertain ambassadors. At the same time they were so popular with the crowds that some of the tougher and longer-surviving animals were given names like favourite actors or wrestlers – Sackerson or Hairy Harry or Paris Jack – which can in no way have mitigated the hideousness of the proceedings. Once the Spanish Ambassador was accorded the special treat of watching a white bear turned into the Thames and attacked by swimming dogs. The dogs used in the baiting were also kept to guard private houses, and they understandably had a reputation for extreme ferocity. Now that we are back in the guard-dog era, and prowling alsatians can no longer be trusted to recognize their best friends, at least one sinister link with the Tudors seems to be re-established.

Various brands of historical shiver were evidently due as I walked past or over the graves of the Globe Theatre, the Bull Ring, the Bear Garden, the equally famous Clink where the bishops of Winchester kept their prisoners. Remnants of the bishops' palace unearthed from the rubble give more than a hint of its grandeur; but the oddest piece of continuity I found was at St Mary Overie's Dock, an inlet dating from the fifteenth century and originally belonging to the priory that became the parish church of St Saviour at the Dissolution, and eventually Southwark Cathedral. It still carried a notice certifying that THIS DOCK IS A FREE LANDING PLACE AT WHICH THE PARISHIONERS OF ST SAVIOUR'S PARISH ARE ENTITLED TO LAND GOODS FREE OF TOLL. Since the dock was securely barred from human approach the ancient privilege looked academic: or did they keep a heavy old key somewhere?

As for St Saviour's itself – the real cathedral, looking far less portentous than the sacred powerhouse down the road – that was entirely friendly and approachable, spreading its net for the preoccupied city-bound shoals and hoping in its blandly modest way to catch a few of them. No over-insistence, simply a quiet reminder that Christians had worshipped here for thirteen centuries and one might like to look in and join them. It just so happened that a lunchtime programme of recorded music was going on, so why not have a listen too? BRING YOUR SANDWICHES, a notice suggested. TEA PROVIDED.

The interior was as warm and human as the invitation promised. I soon rated this high among my favourite London churches and certainly one of the most cheerful, an accusation that could hardly be levelled against the other cathedrals. It even brings itself, uniquely in my experience of churches great or small, to make monumental jokes. A large memorial to a quack doctor named Lockyer carries a sequence of mock-heroic couplets, unless one ought to call them sick-heroic, about 'his virtues and his Pills'; while John Gower's glamorous tomb has an effigy of the poet with his head resting on his three most famous works, surely the most impressive commercial to be found anywhere on the ecclesiastical rounds.

And out through the west door I was in another world which could have been hundreds of miles instead of yards from London Bridge Station, that least inviting of the great commuter termini. Past a mighty plane tree, past the old borough market with its surviving air of trapped countryside – and there was Winchester Square, and the place where the Clink prison stood until the Gordon rioters burned it down two centuries ago, and looming cliffs of brick with catwalks high overhead, and a ruined fragment of Winchester palace with weeds springing from the rich masonry, and a surreal notice AUX CHAUFFEURS DE CAMIONS CONTINENTAUX.

In the 'Johnsonian Anchor' I stood at the bar with my shoulder against a mark showing where the high tide reached in 1928. If this was ever a simple waterman's inn it had long stopped being that, as any diner choosing the tournedos Rossini would soon discover. How high was the price tide going to reach? But one was also paying (assuming one could get near the window) for that incomparable North Bank vista spread out like a living print across the river, dominated by that other cathedral which was a mere upstart, centuries before Wren hatched its new dome, against the ancient harbours it shadowed: Queenhythe and Dowgate, and Billingsgate a little way downstream, founding fathers of all the docks and harbours of London.

It was these I now set out to reach, crossing the newest London Bridge which, with its three strictly functional though elegant concrete spans, is less of an attraction to loiterers than its predecessors. The London habit of bridge-gazing was highly popular until quite recently. As well as flowing over London Bridge from the morning commuter-trains to please Mr T. S. Eliot ('I had not thought death had undone so many'), many city workers used to come back at lunchtime to look at the ships, a habit he never got round to celebrating. Probably throughout history, and certainly since Stuart days when its shops were the most fashionable in London, the bridge was always a centre of human activity and inactivity.

People used to watch the ships loading and unloading. That rarely happens now, but race-memories die hard and a few river-gazers still lean over the steely new parapet, watching whatever there is to be watched: the cruiser Belfast permanently at home to the tourists, or the romantic seediness of the doomed warehouses looking like the stables of extinct river-monsters which in a sense they are, or the weaving antennae of the giant insects busy devouring them. Finding the bridge no longer sympathetic to lingering I made my way straight – or after only a little hunting – to the church of St Magnus Martyr, still smelling of sanctity and history and fish.

It was not where it ought to be. I found it cleverly hidden against the obliterating flank of one of the riverside's most hideous utility blocks, perpetrated between the wars. But it is not the church that has moved. St Magnus used to mark the northern entrance to the bridge, with Wren's Monument built in line; but the British, with their congenital distaste for even so modest a vista as this, defeated the plan in the most elaborate way they could devise – by moving the bridge. John Rennie's replacement to the famous structure that had stood for over six centuries was sited thirty yards upstream. Rennie's bridge, which took over in 1831, got away not only from the church but, in the end, from the country. When its own turn came to be replaced a few years ago it was bought by an American corporation and reconstructed across a lake in Arizona, making it by far the most notable bridge ever to emigrate.

Perhaps it was just as well that St Magnus was out of sight or they might have had that too. Being pushed off-stage has its consolations. The little church still had its handsome gilded clock – the one appearing on the old prints of the original bridge – but there was nobody to tell the time to now. The road across the bridge used to go through the church-yard; follow that path now, and you run up against the wall of a cold storage depot. This dead-end churchyard repays the trouble of hunting it down, all the same, because of two relics it hides – a piece of the old bridge's first arch, and a vastly older chunk from the original Roman wharf. This, when I managed to find it, had rubbish packed at the back, presumably making it the only authentic Roman litter-bin in London.

Those ancient harbours of Dowgate and Queenhythe are also, in the humiliation of their present limbo, frequently made to act as rubbish receptacles. Once it was silks, casks of wine, all the riches that came to town. London Bridge originally had a drawbridge which let the ships upstream to Queenhythe, just as the bascules of Tower Bridge were raised in later years. It would be eccentric, not to say highly suspicious, to go by water to Queenhythe now. I approached it through a convulsion of new buildings in Upper Thames Street, past premises still labelled with aromatic and far-voyaging names like 'Garfunkel' and 'Wanderer'. I couldn't help marvelling that Queenhythe should still be there; a square-cut harbour that was old when the Normans came, already virtually obsolete by Tudor times because ships had got too big for it, but later flourishing again on a specialist lighter-trade in luxuries like aromatic oils. The ancient barge bed is still bared at low water. But soon I was sleepwalking along an iron ramp, down a flight of old steps, stopping just short of a rusted ladder dropping straight into the tawny river. All too easy, here, to plunge over-deep into reveries of Tudor refugees and oceans of Rhenish and Bordeaux. You could drown in it.

This primal beach, the cradle of mercantile London, is much frequented during breaks from work by young men with trowels and small picks, hunting for treasure. I watched a group of them – 'team' would be too disciplined a word – probing without much obvious expertise but with a large optimism along a foreshore which to eyes like mine offered nothing but derelict accumulators, plastic cups, chunks of wood, detergent bottles, broken crockery and the odd shoe. The hunters were not discouraged by this normal clutter. They were aware that besides vast numbers of coins the London river has yielded prehistoric flints, bronze and iron age swords, Saxon ornaments, pieces of medieval armour, beads, brooches and spurs, witch bottles and manacles, clay pipes belonging to every smoking generation from the earliest, not to mention such strange and triumphant finds as a Roman bikini made of leather, the head of an emperor and a head of Christ. I left them hopefully tapping and pecking away.

I walked back to London Bridge and beyond it to Billingsgate, a general dock centuries before it specialized in fish.
Old John Stow provided some early Port of London statistics:

> Touching the ancient customs of Belinsgate in the reign
> of Edward III, every great ship landing there paid for
> standage two-pence, every little ship with orelocks a
> penny, the lesser boat called a Battle a halfpenny; of
> two quarters of corn measured the king was to have one
> farthing, of a combe of corn a penny, of every weight going
> out of the city a halfpenny, of two quarters of sea coal
> measured a farthing, and of every tun going out of England
> beyond the seas, by merchant strangers, fourpence, of
> every thousand herrings a farthing . . .

Clearly a lot of counting went on, and I began to see why the
Custom House stood at Billingsgate's side for a thousand years.
As it does still, though there is nothing to watch now on the
nearby waterfront. Queenhythe and Billingsgate docks are
long dead. But the death of the founding docks has spread
and is creeping along the water.

I looked downstream a little way and there, as though
guarding or obscuring the future, were three massive shapes
like figures in a Gothic fairy tale: the Tower, Tower Bridge
and the new Tower Hotel, squatting like a great toad by the
waterside. They seemed to be presiding over some great
transformation scene. Below them the riverside was waiting
– to be changed into what?

There had been some truly theatrical transformation
scenes before. The three wildly different yet related structures
– Norman, Victorian and neo-Elizabethan – were power-
symbols, representing three separate ages of brutality. And
perhaps the toughest age, and the most revolutionary when it
came to changing the river scene, was the Victorian. The sheer
toughness of the Victorian age and the Victorian inheritance
is something to marvel at, sometimes shudder at. All this
century's attempts to bury the era, to rise above it or lay
it under concrete, have so far merely served to emphasize its

astonishing survivability. Victorian London itself did a thoroughgoing job of demolishing all but remnants of Georgian London, but put up a sterner resistance when its own time came. Perhaps it was harder to put down. Perhaps the undertakers lacked the same determination.

The Father Thames we were born with and still occasionally visit even though we have grown estranged – certainly the one 'Mother Thames', that remarkable bargemaster Dorathea Fisher, loved and honoured and obeyed – was a late Victorian father, reflecting the current morality of hard work and a growing concern, all the stronger because it was also good business, for the well-being of the hard workers. And although this strongly romantic and slightly ethical attitude to industry has gone so deep in the British spirit, only in the most recent years showing signs of disappearing, it was essentially a development of the closing decades of the last century. Things could still be tough, particularly for those who failed to play along with the age and its ethos, but they were much tougher earlier on. Grandfather Thames must have been in many respects a very nasty old man.

He was certainly a very dirty old man. There was a grandeur, undoubtedly, that got lost in the smoke. The early days of the swiftly growing port of London must have had a cosmopolitan exhilaration and a visual splendour matched in few corners of the world. But life around the docks had special hazards. As well as silks and spices and Far Eastern porcelain, ivory and ostrich feathers, tea and tobacco and more exotic drugs, the regular imports included plague, smallpox, cholera and typhus. Moreover, the violence and uncertainty of modern life would have seemed enviably safe, if more than a little tame, to past generations of rivermen. Over a long period press gangs made frequent raids on the dock areas, finding likely material for a brutalized navy. For life among the Thames workers was not only dangerous but crooked, as bent as the stream itself. Watermen, at any rate until their worshipful company established and managed to enforce its rules, were commonly lawless and frequently vicious. Menaces, looting and customs-dodging were the normal order of the day and still more of the night. Over the years whole oceans of contraband tea and spirits have flowed their way through British gullets.

Of the thieves who abounded on the river the neediest were the most vulnerable. Henry Mayhew, in *London Labour and the London Poor* – that remarkable pioneer study of the way Victorians actually lived, an island of reality in an ocean of sentimental and moralistic fiction – describes how children would wade in the mud between the abounding barges, lifting each other up when they assumed nobody was looking and knocking off lumps of coal or metal. Small wonder they were so often caught. Older mudlarks, frequently women in their sixties which was an advanced age in those days and conditions, would wade up to their knees for scraps of salvage or fuel which would then be sold for coppers in back streets to those who could afford the luxury of fires. Magistrates – perhaps surprisingly, in the light of what we know of that atrocious period – were often sympathetic. The same sad pilfering happened around the mining areas during the depression of the 1930s, and the later magistrates were by no means invariably more lenient than the earlier ones. Clearly, some of them flinched from sending children to prison for stealing lumps of coal, or old women whose knees-up had to be performed through Thames mud.

The real villains, they knew all the time, were never likely to be caught. Mayhew describes the vigorous activities of the river pirates who raided shipping from London Bridge to Greenhithe twenty-odd miles downstream and also, as he puts it in his unemotional way, 'the numerous depredations perpetrated by the lightermen'. The temptation must have been great, since a man could easily find himself in charge of a bargeful of brandy, opium, tea or tobacco worth (at early Victorian prices) twenty thousand pounds or more. Mayhew takes a firm line:

These unprincipled lightermen could get a good livelihood by honest labour, varying from thirty shillings to two pounds a week; but they are dissipated and idle in their habits, and resort to thieving. They often spend their time in dancing and concert-rooms, and are to be seen at the Mahogany Bar at Close Square and Paddy's Goose, Ratcliff Highway.

They often lived with prostitutes, but Mayhew adds the interesting social footnote that the lightermen's women, unlike those of the river pirates, were 'generally smart and well-dressed'.

Standing on this newest version of the oldest bridge of all, looking down the Pool of London which was the heart of where it all happened, I imagined the scene as it lasted for so many centuries: the water almost solid with anchored ships and lighters clearing their cargoes, the streets flanking the river teeming with watermen and sailors, rogues and prostitutes. What a documentary it would make, I thought, if a modern television team, or just a roving reporter with a microphone, could revisit these once notorious haunts. After several changes of name, as though for shame, Ratcliff Highway is now identifiable again as 'The Highway'. But the bar that was in Close Square is long closed; it must be as long since they cooked Paddy's Goose. Looking for the ghosts of thieves and tarts in the ghosts of pubs is a job for more than a camera team. And just as well, no doubt, since these characters would have had less than our tolerance for sociological study. Contemporary writers who were by no means timid men agree about how dangerous it was for affluent intruders to walk those streets alone, particularly if an ill wind had made it a bad day at the docks.

Mayhew's cool observation would be rare at any period. Writers and artists, reporters too, usually see what they want to see, find what they set out to find. The scope in his day was vast. Already the metropolitan scene was a whole world, with fantastic contrasts round successive bends. Here was the best and the worst life had to offer; and the worst of this mid-Victorian London, not least its riverside, was moving into

a kind of hell which a few gifted artists, notably Gustave
Doré, have partially trapped in pictures.

Doré's view is particularly valuable because it is urgently
involved in the visual sense and yet emotionally detached, a
paradox perhaps only possible with a foreign observer. It
enables him to treat the starkest subjects in a fluent and un-
inhibited way, without the shield of satire which is as often
a defensive as an attacking weapon, obstructing the clear
picture. His powerful sense of human drama, driven by a near-
manic vitality, may lead to overstatement here and there
but never, I think, to deceit. It would in any case have been
hard to overstate the misery and horror of life among the poor,
and there are occasions when Doré manages to locate an
unrhetorical expression of evil or sadness that would be
unattainable by a native cartoonist. Those who escape the
distortions of satire often founder on sentimentality; Doré
steers clear of both. His extraordinary theatrical gift is
happiest with crowd scenes, and it is still possible in a short
stroll from the City to visit the now empty stages he populated
so vividly – waterside alleys like Pickle Herring Street and
Shad Thames, lurking virtually unnoticed on each side of
Tower Bridge, that preposterous gesture of Late Victorianism
which in his day was not even a dream of the future. How he
would have loved it.

The street scene, the empty stage, is exactly as he saw it:
steep banks of brick converging above the narrow alley as
you look up at the giddy catwalk bridges, the pulleys and
cranes, the trapdoors and working apparatus of the great
crowds of actors and technicians and public who gave life to
the scene. Deserted now; nothing but a pallid figure, covered
in all-white protective clothing, flickering from some hole in
the wall and disappearing again as quickly, and a spectral smell
of spices like a memory of the past. In Doré's picture the place
is teeming with life and toil and treadmilling humanity.
Another of his drawings shows a city lane looking like a river
of fish – dead fish, fish for sale – through which men in caps and
women with baskets are swimming for their lives.

But the Doré that haunts me most, a nightmare I would never want to be rid of, is the one he called 'Hayboats on the Thames'. Men are sprawled in an exhausted, deathlike sleep on a great floating haystack, making its way at night through a forest of masts. It must have been a common enough sight but his avid eye seems to have been the only one to record it. Like Charles Dickens, he saw the extraordinariness of familiar things. Why did the two never collaborate? They would have made a wonderful working partnership.

For when we consider the river in fiction it is Dickens first, the rest nowhere. What river-haunter can forget Quilp's sinister wharf in *The Old Curiosity Shop*, with a light in the counting-house window blinking redly through the fog like an inflamed eye? And through that superb though painful novel *Our Mutual Friend* the river seems to run like a diseased artery. The meandering violence of the plot adds to the total and deliberate morbidity of effect in what seems to me an entirely original way. This book has never had its due. The most ardent of Dickensians found it disturbing. Of course it is; it was meant to disturb. Critics judged it too wayward and lacking in narrative urgency, surely a total misconception of what Dickens was about.

The story flows, but it is no sparkling stream, any more than was the befouled river which served, in a marvellously sustained way, as the main presence – one could almost say the main character – in one of the few English masterpieces of symbolic fiction. There is a dark jollity about it, appropriate enough to the mid-Victorian scene, but even the cosiness of the riverside pub is from time to time disturbed by the knocking of corpses against the door. The book seems to ride the river and mingle with it, spreading itself over corrupted banks and mud flats in a slack, sinister tide which goes out to reveal bodies and a more deadly sort of treasure than Mayhew's mudlarks were hunting.

That is what this greatest of Thames novels is about, death and decay and the pollutions of a new money-grubbing society. It is a novel of deep protest, though not in pulpiteering terms, since good art never preaches that way. Modern London may seem a dangerous and at times downright nasty place, and documentary reporters have unearthed horrors with which Dickens himself would be at home; but I doubt if it can begin to compare with the sinister nature of Dickens's town. And despite the nightmare character of some of his scenes it should never be assumed that they are fevered, romantic imaginings. Not only was he a trained reporter but he remained an addictive one. He never tired of exploring the darkest streets at night, talking to crooks and drop-outs and policemen, haunting wharves and thieves' warrens. And he had that best of gifts for a novelist, an avid and retentive ear for talk. With the dawn he would take himself home, play back his mental tape, and produce limitless quantities of that never-fading dialogue.

As for the miseries of the Victorian poor, awful enough anywhere, these were accentuated in dockland which was already clogged with verminous slums and appallingly vulnerable to the ebb-tides of trade. London's reputation was dark in the world, behind the glowing front of Victorian morality and a dawning social conscience which was to make new growth industries out of charity and the improvement of the more deserving poor.

As far as the river went, pollution could hardly have been more physical. The Thames was by now in its open sewer phase; even Parliament had to take notice, and some action, when the reek became intolerable. The windows of the Palace of Westminster were draped with disinfectant-soaked curtains, and parliamentary papers referred to 'noisome effluvia', which was strong language for the day.

The year was 1858 which – so close down the river of time to that more salubrious landmark, the Great Exhibition – became known as the year of the Great Stink. The Thames sank unusually low, the weather was more than commonly propitious for the sluggish horror creeping through the metropolis to make itself felt, and some awful epidemic was feared. Our legislators, who may be slow off the mark (particularly in mid-summer) but know how to act when driven to it, decided that the disinfected curtains were not enough. Resolutely holding its nose, the government of the day took steps to end the session somewhat earlier than usual.

They even had debates in both houses. Disgraceful, they called the situation in the Lords, referring perhaps to the unrestrained excretory habits of the lower orders. Mr Disraeli actually went so far as to introduce a bill in that malodorous mid-July, authorizing the river's cleansing; but this soon found itself bogged down in the familiar argument about whether the cost should be met from central or local funds. But they got the measure through in the end, and it even received a prominent though vicarious mention in the Queen's Speech closing the session, when Queen Victoria's subjects were assured that 'the sanitary condition of the metropolis must always be a subject of deep interest to Her Majesty,' and that there was an undoubted need 'for the purification of that noble river, the present state of which is little creditable to a great country.'

Her Majesty could say that again. It is alarming to ponder what Wordsworth, not long dead, might have written if – handkerchief clutched to face, which was the way most people crossed Westminster Bridge – he had revised his most famous sonnet as a last offering. Even *Punch* produced some stern verses:

> All beside thy sludgy waters,
> All beside thy reeking ooze
> Christian folk inhale memphitis
> Which thy bubbly bosom brews . . .

The Thames, incidentally, provided the water most Londoners drank. Might that help to explain the gin addiction of the day? You had to be brave to be a temperance reformer in some parts of the metropolis. Perhaps you had to be even braver to be reformed.

Well, there was Mr Disraeli's Act, and soon there were the embankments with proper sewers under them, and the vested interests of the water companies were finally (though not until the turn of the century) washed away by the Metropolitan Water Board. A wicked blow against private rights *that* was, some maintained. But there is always a price to pay, and not just in cash. The British seem to find it hard to be clean and jolly at the same time. Soon, instead of the brassy old pleasure steamers taking East Enders jaunting out to Margate and Clacton, it was the SSDVs – sewage sludge disposal vessels – chugging out into the estuary to deposit millions of tons of solid waste a year.

Then came the most potent cleansing influence of all. With bird-watchers in the inner docks, herons standing guard where river police were recently on duty, butterflies reconnoitring over Southwark, wild flowers rooting themselves on abandoned wharves, the Port of London Authority itself – surely against its own commercial interests – has been able to claim with pride that so many different kinds of fish are now to be found again in the tideway. So are shelduck, tufted duck, mallard, teal, redshank and thousands of wading birds. It is the people, those who have lived and worked and suffered on the river for generations, who now look in danger of becoming extinct.

9. Dead Docks

TOWER TO WAPPING
AND LIMEHOUSE

She'd shine at the play and jig
   at the ball
All rigged out so gay and so topping,
For she married six husbands and
   buried them all
     (Pull away, pull away, I say!),
What d'ye think of my Meg of Wapping?

CHARLES DIBDIN

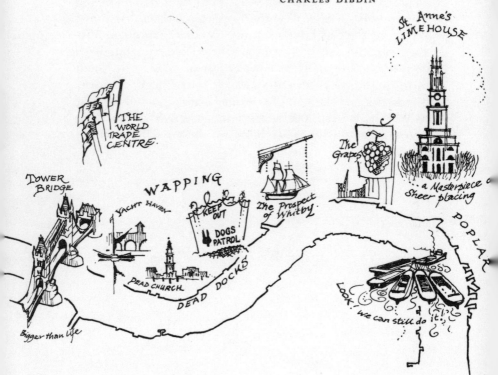

Those three Tower sisters, like something out of Grimm, dominated the next stage of my journey – and in a sense all the remaining stages, since here, in our own day, the heavy work of the river starts. Started, rather. In the shadow of the Tower the uppermost of the modern docks were born ('modern' in the sense of being a thousand years younger than Queenhythe and Billingsgate), and are now dying downstream.

The Tower of London, Tower Bridge, the Tower Hotel. I have little to say about the first and the third. William's famous castle is the most invincible of tourist attractions, despite its recent reversion to a violent past when some visitors were injured and one woman killed in a bomb attack. The new hotel provides magnificent if expensive riverside views including that of the Tower itself; though it may well be thought that one of the Tower's less inspiring assets is the view of the new hotel.

Ruder things than that have been said about Tower Bridge in its day, but never by me. I find that great sham-Gothic gesture of Victorian self-indulgence quite irresistible. I can never look at it too long, cross it or sail under it too often. From time to time it is said to be under threat, but to lose it would be as unthinkable as for Paris to lose its Eiffel. There is a modern legend growing up that some Americans were disappointed when they saw Rennie's London Bridge installed in its new Arizona home, as they had been mentally confusing it with the vastly more flamboyant Tower Bridge. I have heard American tourists repeating the story as they pass under the bridge on river boats, so if it was not true to start with it has in a sense become so now. Not that they complain they have actually been conned over the deal. They just feel they landed up with the wrong bridge, and I see their point.

But let me start on a quieter and, paradoxically, a more modern-seeming note, even though it takes us back a thousand years before the Conqueror. Before braving the Three Sisters there is another member of the Tower family well worth a visit, the mildest and least spectacular as well as the oldest of the four historical generations. Up on Tower Hill there is a surviving slab of Roman wall, and there may be found an inscription in memory of Gaius Julius Alpinus Classicianus, who seems to have been an administrator considerably more civilized than London was used to in that distant day, or for that matter has often been since. To judge from the bronze figure erected to commemorate him, Classicianus was a sensitive bureaucrat much burdened by his responsibilities; he has a worried look, and a hand is raised as though tentatively conducting a small and unpredictable chamber orchestra. History justifies this character reading, as he was sent here to do a reconcilement job after the ruthlessness that came in the wake of the Boadicea rebellion. He performed it faithfully. Evidently he hated excess. If he could have seen two thousand years into the future he might have winced at Tower Bridge.

The bridge is excessive, and nobody could deny it. It is bigger than life, certainly bigger than taste or function – even though, surprisingly enough, it works. The twin Gothic towers house the machinery – as horrific as that in Poe's story about the pit and the pendulum – which operates the bascules. (The original idea was to have chains lifting the drawbridge, but evidently it was thought that would be carrying even the urges of Victorian Gothic too far.) Yet the thing is mostly theatrical gesture. Just as Barry's Palace of Westminster manages to look more antique than the authentically Norman Westminster Hall, so Tower Bridge, born 1894, makes the authentically Norman Tower of London appear no more than middle-aged. Like all great structures of whatever period it looks as though it has been and will be there for ever – a crazed stately home, a titanic folly straddling its own moat with a pair of heavy-footed gatehouses.

All those lancet windows that can never be looked into, all those dungeon doors; who, or what, would answer if anybody knocked? The pedestrian walk high overhead is long since disused; people leaped off it too eagerly. And as I crossed the main bridge I again had the unnerving sense that the mobile part of the massive structure shuddered and creaked a little beneath my feet, making me feel rather the way a fly must when it steps on to a web. Few cross the bridge these days except on wheels, though even that is not always safe. Once the spider-jaw bascules nearly got a double-decker bus. They began to open while it was crossing, and it had to jump.

One way of seeing the bridge – a macabre way, perhaps – is as a mausoleum to dead dockland. The innermost docks it looms over, St Katharine's and London, were born in the expansionist period of the industrial revolution, flourished in the Victorian and Edwardian heyday, and were the first to close as the port's trade moved relentlessly down river. The docks were dying from the head down, and for anybody wanting to view the body this is the place to start. It is essential to go on foot, though one is at some risk from guard dogs and others alerted by the unfamiliar sight of a pedestrian, and not unnaturally concerned about drugs, illegal immigrants or explosives. Still, there was a spice of danger appealing to all good frontiersmen when the West was being born, so a little can be accepted when the East is dying. And East London, we can be sure, will die hard.

But before entering the waste land of Wapping, I experienced another sophisticated interlude. Plodding down the patched stone setts of St Katharine's Way towards St Katharine's Dock, which had been recently transformed into a yacht haven and commercial centre variously described as a social disaster and an environmental triumph, I was not expecting much to lift the heart. If the Tower Hotel and the World Trade Centre were anything to go by, the environmental gain must be limited at best, while the ruthless start to the St Katharine story all those years ago – the displacing of hundreds of poor families, not to mention an ancient hospital and religious house, to make way for the docks – was an unpromising social precedent for the new commercial chapter.

TEA . . . MINT BONDED WAREHOUSES . . . Such obsolete labels on the outer walls of the dock buildings suggested either absent-mindedness or a strong sense of chic on the part of the developers. The dead dock had been tastefully laid out, that had to be admitted at once. The new 'haven' was a considerable pleasure to the eye. One of the rarest of contemporary planning virtues is the ability to recognize something good and leave it alone, or accommodate it imaginatively in a new scheme; on that score the developers had done well. In particular they had made much of the central feature called the Ivory House, a mid-century Italianate building which must be the most graceful in the whole of dockland, dead or alive; it was this that contributed much to the Venetian air of the place. The revealed brick vaulting, the elegance of cast-iron columns, the black-and-white bollards repainted and left unstraightened, the ragwort also left brilliantly growing out of the old dock walls – it looked as though a formidably cultivated eye had been busy here. A red sail hung from a mast in the windless afternoon. I watched a bearded youth painting his Dutch barge. There was peace here, at a price.

Yards away, on the other side of the wall, was Wapping. Or rather, not so much Wapping as the absence of Wapping. There was the shape of a riverside community, the outline of a main street (WAPPING HIGH STREET, E I, it confirmed on a surviving wall), a site on which human life once recognizably went on. But Wapping was now a devastation area apparently ruled by guard dogs. It seemed a strange commentary on the times, that guard dogs should now be kept to deter people in the way that cats used to be kept to deal with mice. But what people? For a full hour, nervously walking about Wapping, I did not see a single human being. Had the alsatians devoured them all? More likely the surviving inhabitants saw nothing to come into the stricken streets for.

Saw plenty, indeed, to keep them away including illustrations, in case plain warning notices were not enough, of pinpoint eyes and lolling tongues and teeth. They say there are seventeen separate firms specializing in crime prevention guards, and most of them seemed to be operating here. Guarding what? London Docks were once a forest of masts, then a sumptuous hell of smoke through which would waft

the smell of spices and coffee, the reek of hides, the fumes of
wine and rum. Now, nothing. High walls, cemetery walls,
screened the dead docks while the streets of Wapping, the
ones that still clearly traced its once-living shape, were a
wilderness of dumps and lorry-parks, blind-eyed derelict
houses and corrugated iron fencing. Even decline must have
its rhythms. These upper dockland areas were dealt a succes-
sion of blows more shattering than humanity can take and live.
Stunned by the bombs, they then had to watch their livelihood
disappear with paralysing speed. Now, they are clearly
beyond recovery in anything like their original shape.

Weeds, less enticing than the pampered ones at St Katharine's, grew from the steps of Wapping Old Stairs, heavily
locked with a notice saying that the river police kept the
keys. So there was no approach to Execution Dock, in case
anyone felt the morbid urge to tread the spot where pirates
and less romantic sea and river criminals hung in chains
while the tides washed over them. But I found a beautiful
brick church, quite dead, with the skeleton of a school next
to it (INFANTS, a ghostly notice said); and the 'Turk's Head',
next door again, was dead too.

Up Wapping Lane were car cemeteries, any number of
guard-dog warnings, a housing estate that looked curiously
devoid of humanity. Or was it so curious? I saw no children,
and no wonder. NO BALL GAMES, NO CYCLING, the rules
laid down. NO LIVING, one almost expected. Yet signs of
life I did manage to find. There was a pub strangely called
'Welcome to the Cuckoo', and in the neighbourhood of
Cinnamon Street a cluster of small shops provided some much-
needed human welcome. No future perhaps, certainly no
present, but a sense of the past managed to emerge. In the
bar at the 'Prospect of Whitby', where the sophisticated
simplicity of bare stone floor suggested that customers came
from afar, I discovered a symphonion, a kind of early juke-
box. (Put in an old penny and it would sing you 'Star of my
soul' from 'The Geisha'.) There was an odder, more modern
exhibit dating from 1953, evidently – what with the floods

and the gangsters – the river's *Annus Horribilis*. This was a press cutting about a raid on the house in which guests were made to lie on the floor while thieves absconded with £3000. Exciting, but it looked a curious advertisement.

Once there were forty pubs along this Wapping riverfront, and though the Saturday night scenes were no doubt lively to a fault, a touch of Meg of Wapping's spirit would be a joy to see today. Even one or two of her buried husbands might add a touch of vitality to the picture as we see it now. They would be unlikely to materialize in tourist haunts like the 'Prospect' or the 'Town of Ramsgate'. But for every famous pub there is an unfamous one where the locals go. It was from one of these that I saw a docker of the old school emerge in expansive mood, arms flung wide.

'Hullo, darling!' he shouted to the lady member of a stiffly dressed group who had obviously strayed from the Tower Hotel or the World Trade Centre, if not both. Undeterred by their nervousness and surprise he insisted on telling them in colourful detail, and at the top of his perfectly amiable voice, precisely what he thought of the great St Katharine's development, which was apparently not much.

But there is little common ground in these parts. WARNING – SHARK INFESTED WATER, shouted a wall-message in Narrow Street, beyond Wapping Wall. The land also began to have its perils again, with a swish of cars and a frequent hurtling lorry. A certain recovery of spirit seemed evident, together with a change of accent. A new type of immigrant was moving in, professional eyes open to possibilities, capable of seeing not simply what was good but what could be made good. Anybody in the market for jetties could find some choice specimens here. One short row of façades looked, with its studious and well-bred shabbiness, about the nearest thing to the Ile Saint-Louis that London had to offer.

Here I found the 'Grapes', claimed as the original of the 'Six Jolly Fellowship-Porters' (my favourite literary pub) in *Our Mutual Friend*. It was here that Miss Abbey ruled her watery customers with such a firm hand. Most of Dickens's affectionate description of this poky, friendly, river-haunted little house could apply perfectly well today, including the 'crazy wooden verandah impending over the water', like a faint-hearted diver unable to make up his mind to go in. I still found it trembling at the brink. Archaic regulations about flood prevention – not quite as old as Dickens, but authorized by the obsolete London County Council – still hung on the walls, managing to convey the impression that they were not trying to be quaint but had quite simply been overlooked. Across the river, looking from the balcony, could be seen the third set of recently disused docks, the Surrey Commercial.

Still very much a riverman's house, it seemed to me, and a Dickensian one too : I half expected to hear Miss Abbey giving her orders to her customers – 'George Jones, your time's up! I told your wife you should be punctual,' and, 'William Williams, Bob Glamour, and Jonathan, you are all due.' There are, of course, rivermen and rivermen, as some of the sophisticated new river-gardens nearby indicated. However, nobody could object to a touch of waterside grace in these stricken reaches. And at Limehouse Basin I actually saw a tug at work pulling a string of six barges, its nose in the air as if to say 'Look – we can still do it.'

So to Limehouse Causeway, Chinatown, where a whole generation of spine-chillers led by Sax Rohmer wove their deliciously horrifying fictional tapestries out of the supposed Yellow Peril. There is little cause to linger now, since the local Chinese are as close to model citizens as we are likely to get these days. It seems a pity that social virtue, when it can be found, should have to operate in such singularly ugly housing estates. But ugly is as ugly does; and near here I found another of my favourite unknown, unpraised, unlovely yet irreplaceable London corners. Limehouse Church is a familiar sight from the river, its odd steeple – not quite sure whether it set out to be a spire or a tower – dominating the great horseshoe bend where Limehouse Reach swings into Wapping. Few go to look at it at close quarters; it is no orthodox architectural beauty, but if it were as ugly as sin it would still be superb, a great hulk of a church made buoyant by the spreading sails of its trees. Another masterpiece of sheer placing; and to say there would *have* to be a pub near by called the 'Five Bells and Bladebone' would be stretching the matter. But there is, and it is right.

Back, then, along the once notorious Highway, running parallel with the even more notorious Cable Street. Both look thoroughly tamed now. No disreputable seamen's haunts on that bad old Ratcliff Highway these days; no wild beast shops such as there were once, when it was possible to buy a lion cub, anteater or baboon, or perhaps a small alligator to rear in the bathtub. No sign either of those old opium dens in Cable Street. If Chinatown was never quite as sinister as the early paperback-writers portrayed it there was always something to justify the sense of daring or even danger with which West-Enders on a night out, or conducted groups of the more adventurous tourists, would take the road eastward towards the docks. Now, where blank yellow faces once flickered at dark windows, there are only the still more expressionless faces of tall rehousing blocks to be seen.

Yet two points between these tamed thoroughfares held me. There was St George's-in-the-East, Hawksmoor's great sister ship, so to speak, to the church at Limehouse. Many a skipper and many a mate must haunt this churchyard, the more so as I found that some of their gravestones were helping to wall up the gently steaming back of a coin-operated automatic laundry. And near here was buried – until, early this century, they removed his body to Sweden – that spooky philosopher Swedenborg, who was as much at ease in London eighteenth-century society as he was in the company of spirits who had passed on.

Before turning his attention to these transcendental concerns Swedenborg made an early study of worldly matters like docks and sluices, the force of tides, and how to determine longitude at sea by observing the moon and stars. Also, more disconcertingly, he applied himself to the invention of devices for transporting boats over land. There was nothing vague about this visionary. Land and water, mind and spirit, he was an amphibian of many parts.

If it were possible to interview Emanuel Swedenborg – and it should be, if his teachings are true – it would be interesting to learn what happened to some of his wide acquaintanceship when they entered the spirit world. King George the Second, as he has told us already, became an angel: a success that may well have lifted some eyebrows in surprise. But did Swedenborg ever hear anything more of Meg of Wapping, or any of her husbands? The great mystic lived with us long enough and a local square is still named after him, so presumably he retains some concern. And for those of us who have to live in this world the future of dead docklands and their people provokes speculation as fascinating as the future of dead kings, and perhaps more urgent.

10. The Long Street

BERMONDSEY, ROTHERHITHE, DEPTFORD

Besides the disagreeable situation in which we then lay,
in the confines of Wapping and Rotherhithe, tasting a
delicious mixture of the air of both these sweet places,
and enjoying the concord of sweet sounds of seamen,
watermen, fish-women, oyster-women, and of all the
vociferous inhabitants of both shores . . .

HENRY FIELDING, *The Journal of a Voyage to Lisbon*

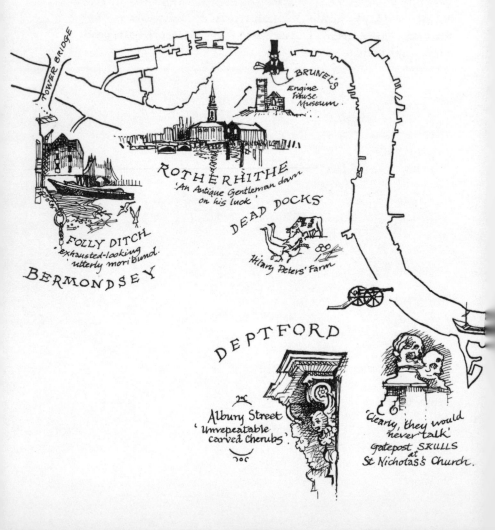

TOWER BRIDGE

BRUNEL'S
Engine
house.
Museum.

ROTHERHITHE
'An Antique Gentleman down
on his luck'

DEAD DOCKS

Hilary Peters' Farm

FOLLY DITCH
'exhausted-looking
utterly moribund'

BERMONDSEY

DEPTFORD

Albury Street
'Unrepeatable
carved Cherubs'.

'Clearly, they would
never talk'
Gatepost SKULLS
at
St Nicholas's Church.

I have often been struck, in the course of this journey and in reading about other people's, by the sometimes quite alarming degree to which the experience itself is conditioned by the traveller's state and mood. When poor Henry Fielding set out on his last voyage in 1754, desperately ill with dropsy and jeered at by watermen as they hoisted him on board at Rotherhithe, he was in no mood to respond to the vitality of the scene. Conditions would have been better for him today.

I was in Rotherhithe one bitter evening when powdery snow was flecking the spire of the handsome eighteenth-century church, peering through the cloud of my own breath at the wooden effigies of children – they must have come from about Fielding's time – on watch outside the dead schoolhouse. The silence was intense. Then I heard music, and was astonished by it. The music was older than the church from which it came, and so were the instruments on which it was being played; the strings had a husky antique sound and the jangle of a harpsichord broke in.

Not that the mixing of the centuries seemed at all un-natural in Rotherhithe. Of all the inner riverside settlements this was the most variously haunted, with ghosts of market gardens and vineyards, of medieval war fleets fitted out against the French, of master mariners and merchants without number, of condemned tobacco they used to burn here in sacrificial clouds; also, most famously, of the Pilgrim Fathers who sailed from here, not to mention some of their crew who lie buried in the graveyard of that same church from which the music was emerging.

The journey from Tower Bridge had been strange and ambiguous from the start. Walking eastward along the south bank, I felt 'prospecting' seemed more the word, as I skirted sick warehouses and tracked and countertracked a tangle of alleys to round that befouled inlet of the river made eternally infamous by Dickens. Only a pedant would lay down the law as to where you leave the ghost of Bermondsey and enter the ghost of Rotherhithe. Behind the wharves and warehouses, when they lived, rose the sustaining ranks of slums; and they, in their day and after their fashion, had life too. They were a close community, hugging the river but not part of it, walled away from the dominant Thames. It would come to them only in apparitions: the glimmering space at the end of an alley would suddenly be filled, as on some early television screen, by the enormous shape of a passing ship. Many a child who had never seen the river must have been terrified at the sight of a grotesque figurehead, king or goddess or staring hero, swimming through his back yard.

It still begins at Dockhead, where the lanes bottled away on the waterfront join the road running east. Bermondsey – or is it Rotherhithe? – has scarcely recovered from the searing Dickens descriptions in *Oliver Twist* of the life, if such it could be called, bordering on St Saviour's Dock, which he calls Folly Ditch. He writes with sustained invective about the 'dirt-besmeared walls and decaying foundations; every repulsive lineament of poverty, every loathsome indication of filth, rot and garbage'. Empty warehouses, crumbling walls, shattered windows, crazy galleries crossing overhead – the scene is not so different now, though largely depopulated.

And in our own day the neighbourhood has turned the other (and cleaner) cheek by giving its rehousing blocks Dickensian names like Copperfield House, Trotwood House, Weller House; though not, understandably enough, Fagin or Sikes or even Oliver House. The Dickensian horror was a shade over-written but no doubt fully justified as a piece of social campaigning, since the area had an appalling reputation throughout the eighteenth century and would not have been likely to improve when the dock era set in. Not until near the outbreak of the Second World War had it hauled itself into a state of tolerable respectability and sanitation – and then the bombs came, and hit it harder than they hit anywhere else in London. Some places, like some people, seem to be singled out for all the knocks.

I took a close look – not so easy to come by these days – at Folly Ditch, alias St Saviour's Dock, approaching it along the cavernous Shad Thames which remains theatrically Dickensian in appearance. But it was as though – and again I was reminded of a Doré scene – the actors had all walked out or been eliminated. There were the ghosts of smells, a whiff of curry and a hint of spice, but little that looked alive. Now and again the metallic booming of brewery tubs (a new sound since Dickens's day) would echo between the high close walls; the thunder of a lorry heralded a rare monster and the more dangerous for its rarity, since a casual pedestrian in those narrow lanes was the last thing a driver would expect.

The creek itself, its morbidity apart, offered a marked contrast to that nightmare chase when Sikes tried to escape from the mob. It must be many a long year since a mob was last seen here. The desolation was such that no novelist or stage designer could hope to emulate. I had never seen any-thing so exhausted-looking, so utterly moribund. The tide was out, leaving a lane of littered mud between the sick walls, their brooding monotony broken only by the blind eyes of old warehouse doors. A pair of barges lay in the mud like stranded whales.

It was on the eastward side of the creek that Dickens placed his action. Mill Street, his Mill Lane, looks much as it must have done then, though mercifully without women lowering their pails and buckets to scoop up their water. Jacob Street has moved on a little since he featured it. One firm more lately established there, evidently reacting to that influential outburst about filth and desolation and decay, rather pointedly calls itself Clean Walls Limited.

Now, they claim in these parts, nobody lives in slums any more, though this is a somewhat negative achievement since the Bermondsey population must have dropped fourfold compared with its one-time peak of 126,000; also a circular one, since a main reason for the fall in population is the lack of adequate places in which to live. Again, all is past and future – dead past, largely left unburied, and future not yet born. And since it is young people, particularly young married people, that the area chiefly lacks, where is the future to come from?

Recolonization, perhaps; even some sort of interplanetary

movement. Certainly there were parts of Bermondsey Wall that looked, when I saw them, weirder than any moon landscape; so pulverized that it was impossible to say which hand, past or future, had dealt the heavier blows. Farther east, the corpses of warehouses were laid out in seemlier rows. Screening the abundant gaps, makeshift metal walls and multistrand barbed wire kept people away from – what? Surviving waterfront-dwellers obediently shunned the waterfront, as though it were infected, or mined.

They kept away from the warehouses, no doubt, in sensible response to notices warning them that some of these were unsafe. They kept away from the river itself through sheer force of social habit, allied to what looked like a new kind of quiet, routine intimidation. Cherry Garden Pier, a key point where ships traditionally hoot their approach to Tower Bridge, had no welcome for foot-voyagers. No loitering, no trespassing, it warned. Former rights of way to the river had been closed and padlocked. By way of official compensation a short stretch of authorized river terrace had been opened up not far away. But, whether through personal cussedness or normal human nature, it was along the locked lanes I found myself wanting to go, not that bland bit of approved public walk. An illogical attitude? No doubt, but it could be an attitude to this forbidding and mostly forbidden waterfront that many shared. The question it raised could be a key to those padlocks. Surely there was something between a hazardous free-for-all and this stark exclusion, some acceptable way of bringing the river into river-dwellers' lives?

I turned down empty Elephant Lane, past a deserted children's playground walled with old gravestones, past the comely 'Mayflower Inn', which must be the only pub in England offering postage stamps for sale. I roamed among wharves and some fine warehouse buildings until dark fell and the snow started. Then, confronted by those eerie Georgian children on eternal sentry duty outside their long-closed school, I heard that music coming from the church. It turned out they were holding a concert to celebrate the anniversary of the Thames Tunnel which Marc Isambard Brunel began cutting from here a century and a half ago.

Why they should be saluting this ever-astonishing engineering feat with music of an earlier century, played on baroque strings, was not at once apparent. A counter-tenor sang Purcell, the viola da gamba and harpsichord added works by Restoration composers like Matthew Locke and Pelham Humfrey. Restoration: a clue there, perhaps. They were not just remembering Brunel but trying to do something about him, and about Rotherhithe in the process. Their immediate aim was to turn Brunel's old engine house into a permanent museum, and to rescue derelict warehouses and set them up as craft centres – including workshops for making old musical instruments. So there was an admirable logic about it all.

Was this, then, the new horizon – men-o'-war turned into spinets and Thames barges into baroque fiddles? It sounded magnificent, if hardly industrial redeployment. On and on went Rotherhithe Street, out into the wilderness again, circling the abandoned Surrey Commercial Docks. And here was one of time's strangest revenges. These dead dock basins, where some of the shyest wild birds were now breeding and such interesting plant species were rooting themselves that entranced botanists were writing about it to *The Times*, have in their day been cemeteries for half the forests, jungles and oceans of the world. Mountains of timber, lakes of whale oil have been deposited there. All over now; but the birds and flowers would have to make the most of their brief revival, for the next stage – another possible trade mart and hotel complex – was already being hatched.

Riverside redevelopment, or so it began to seem, was already establishing its own evolutionary life-cycle. First came the co-ordinated plan, or at least the acceptance of the need for one; but this, being visionary, was doomed from the start though it might influence people's thinking a little. Next, various projects for piecemeal development, basically commercial with a social seasoning; and these – offering some prospect of immediate jobs, accommodation and benefit to the rates – were plainly more the stuff of real life. Then came the reactions, the many manifestations of the ever-fascinating, ever-baffling Voice of the People.

More a chorus than a voice; more a cacophony, some would say, than a chorus. Yet wise or wrong-headed, prejudiced or disinterested, spontaneous or rehearsed or even prerecorded, it could no longer be ignored. Nor did the authorities, their confidence and sense of purpose at a low ebb, want to ignore it. On the contrary, they were uncommonly anxious to listen. They were eager to saddle public opinion with the responsi-bility for their actions – provided, of course, that they could satisfactorily identify it.

Small wonder, though, that the voice was confused and confusing. It depended largely on the starting point. Starting with a wilderness, a total future, the problem was in a way the most straightforward. Starting with little or nothing but a past, some distinguished wharves and broken-down Georgian houses, the challenge was more complex. But beginning with a going concern, a community enfeebled and run-down but still identifiably alive, posed the biggest difficulties of all when its traditional livelihood had gone. Here, as in some other sectors of the riverside, they seemed to be having to cope with all three conditions at once.

The voice – the voices, rather – of the people were extremely active though they can have given little reliable guidance to the town halls. A few wrote letters or gave reasoned views to professional interviewers. Some left their fierce libretto on the public walls. Some played viols and sang. Small theatrical groups presented satirical entertain-ments with titles like 'Sold Down the River'. Others of a more practical turn of mind converted derelict land into adventure playgrounds for children, or launched farming projects. There were also those who, aware that all the schemes, slogans and satire in the world would not of themselves save a single good old building from fire-raisers, lead-stealers or vandals private or public, busied themselves with rescue projects and imaginative pioneer work of the Brunel Museum kind.

Voices from outside were important, but what needed to be heard most of all was the voice of the dockland community. But where was it to be located? Who spoke for Thameside? People like Bob Mellish, pre-eminently. They listened to Mellish with the closest attention when he gave evidence before a parliamentary committee on these matters – and rightly, for nobody has been fiercer in his devotion to the riverside and its people than the member for Bermondsey over so many years. However, long before he had finished it was obvious that even Bob Mellish had had second thoughts. Nobody – and he made this very clear – loved the traditional life of the East End more than he. At the same time he was not going to sentimentalize about the days when dockland slums abounded, when a child could live yards from the river without ever setting eyes on it, until the time came for him to start his hard and precarious life's work on it.

So what I supposed they might say they wanted, those unidentified dockland voices, was nothing more demanding than jobs and decent houses and a sight of the river. But that was not all, and the rest was harder to get into words. They needed familiarity, a touch of recognizable character about the place they lived in; this was something they invariably had in the past even if the character was not always good. One of the many self-contradictions, however understandable, over the long agonizing about what to do with these run-down areas was the claim in one breath that they had built up precious local communities to be preserved at all costs, and the demand in the next breath that better transport was needed to get out of them. Their curious isolation near the heart of London has indeed been a potent character-builder, and it would be an illusion to think that easy escape on wheels would not change things radically. Perhaps it is inevitable that the individual Cockney should be ironed out into the general-ized Londoner, but it hasn't happened yet and it will be sad when it does.

That these regional characters exist, distinguishing places half a mile apart as sharply as the personalities of people standing side by side, could not be denied by anyone using his eyes and ears around London. I doubt whether even Shaw's Professor Higgins could now pretend to distinguish a Bermondsey man from a Rotherhithe man by the cut of his vowels, yet even these – no more, in truth, than two stretches of the same derelict street – seem to me to possess quite different images. Or different ghosts: is that it?

Rotherhithe – and what was left of it appeared to support the notion – had connotations of grandeur and high endeavour. I thought of Turner, seated on Cherry Garden Pier (it would have been a valiant official who tried to keep *him* out), painting the *Fighting Téméraire*. And those extraordinary Brunels, father and son: Marc Isambard, who finally got his tunnel built after an eighteen-year struggle with the Thames; and Isambard Kingdom, scarcely taller than his own stovepipe hat, who -built the biggest ship in the world. This was the *Great Eastern*, which stuck on its sideways launching – they still mark the site on the river at Millwall – and lived up to this inauspicious start by proving one of the most colossal failures of maritime history. But the conception was vast, and half a century before its time. They say the monster could have sailed round the world without refuelling. It was never asked to do that.

Bermondsey also had its grand period, with one of the greatest abbeys in Christendom; and even (more surprisingly) its chic period, when they tried to turn it into a fashionable spa. But the operative image is much nearer in time and very different in style, an almost too human mixture. On the one hand, poverty, drunkenness, violence; on the other, an air of jollity and jellied eels, baked potatoes and barrel organs, street celebrations (both public and private) on the least provocation, and down-river jaunts to Southend and Margate in high-spirited steamers far too gay to survive into our own day.

So although Daniel Defoe was and remains right in his description of the way from London Bridge to Greenwich as one long street, 'winding and turning as the river winds and turns', its character changes dramatically as it meanders along.

Bermondsey I would personify as a retired publican, friendly but touchy and dangerous in his cups; Rotherhithe as an antique gentleman down on his luck; Deptford – quite different again – as a Cockney pearly queen as old as any of them but determined to keep it dark. Deptford has more history and fewer signs of it than any other part of London. It could hardly wait to get rid of its treasures, and must have been embarrassed to discover that by some oversight it had retained just one street full of precious and highly individual old houses. Still, every time I revisit Albury Street there seems to be less of it. Some of the houses have been drawn from their terraces like decayed teeth, others – complete with carved wooden cherubs on the doorposts – carefully restored. The last time I was there it looked as though many of those unrepeatable cherubs had been knocked off – in both senses of the phrase; and a jazzy youth centre had been established at the end to ensure that Albury Street did not feel its age.

The fact is that Deptford is not really interested in any past that stretches further than the memories of its oldest inhabitants, and this makes it truly East End. Perhaps it lost its historical pride the day in 1869 when Princess Louise launched the last warship from its naval dockyard, an occasion mourned by *Punch* with some verses starting "'Tis the last launch from Deptford', presumably to be sung to the tune of 'The last rose of summer'. Yet there were signs of local casualness, a distinct lack of ceremonial awe, long before that. After the first Queen Elizabeth had knighted Sir Francis Drake on board the *Golden Hind* – not a mile away from where the second Queen Elizabeth was to knight another Sir Francis for another circumnavigation of the world – the famous ship was left aimlessly drifting around the dockyard for years until somebody had the idea of turning it into an early kind of floating snack bar, a fate Greenwich would never allow to befall Sir Francis Chichester's *Gipsy Moth*.

Now this most prestigious of the royal dockyards, to which Samuel Pepys commuted so regularly by river in the course of his Admiralty duties, has been usurped and obliterated by the

Pepys Estate, a massive exercise in modern rehousing which the local children, loyal to Deptford's anti-historical instincts, tend to call the Pepsie Estate. There are in fact two totally contrasting halves to Deptford, adding a schizoid touch to its understandably baffled nature. A frontier pub called the 'Harp of Erin' divides this new high-rise Deptford from its Edwardian-style, typically East End High Street. It is hard to imagine these two worlds ever meeting – or if they do meet, as I suppose they must, can they ever understand one another? Around the High Street there are still people who like to talk about the half-crown joints they bought on old Saturday nights, the days of the muffin man and the shrimp and winkle man, and of Flo the Fishgirl who also had ninepenny rabbits (skinning included in the price) dangling from her cart. There are also uglier corners to this Memory Lane, such as those in which harmless German porkbutchers had their shops and their houses smashed to pieces when the 1914 war broke out. Could the equivalent happen again? I hope we never have to find out.

Now it looks like an age barrier. It might be thought that these old inhabitants would never venture from choice into territory where entire streets were up-ended into tower blocks. But the housing estate covers the waterfront, and I saw several obvious rivermen, lonely as stowaways, lurking in new pubs with no hint of water about them except their nautical names. Surely these crow's-nests were not for them. They belonged to the horizontal, not the vertical world. There is also an area of no-man's-land where the time-nerve ticks dangerously. I saw a smashed Victorian letter-box and some forbidden territory where the guard dogs were advertised as by Avant-Garde Limited. Those damned dogs were every-where – though more notices in sight, mercifully, than actual animals. I began to see why the anti-dog movement was gaining momentum. On the river promenade, handsome and spacious, some Georgian cannon were trained on the Isle of Dogs – symbolizing, just possibly, a kind of People's Rebellion.

While Pepys gives his name to a housing estate Evelyn gives

his to a road; but Evelyn's road has lost every trace of his own house, Sayes Court, where he insisted on showing Pepys his mezzotints and also bored his fellow-diarist with long readings from his treatise on gardening. Still less advisedly he lent his house to Peter the Great who came to Deptford to learn about shipbuilding, working at the dockyard as an apprentice and maintaining his differentials by living it up at Sayes Court and showing his gratitude by using poor Evelyn's pictures for target practice. It has been said that the boisterous young czar liked to row on the river and would then drink hugely in the local pubs, his favourite tipple being copious wine followed by hot brandy and pepper. How much of this is myth and how much reality Deptford would now have no way of knowing, even if it asked.

But it was another young man in his twenties who provided Deptford with its darkest mystery story, still unsolved. Every schoolboy knows that Christopher Marlowe was stabbed to death in a tavern brawl, following an argument over the bill. If that is all he knows he runs the risk of being seriously underinformed, if not misinformed. It is not necessary to believe that Marlowe wrote Shakespeare to accept that his life and death were far deeper and more devious than used to be thought, and even the most cautious researchers now agree that the official inquest report – it did not emerge, extraordinarily, until the nineteen-twenties – is a cover-up job. It is now generally thought that Marlowe was a government agent with powerful protection at court; some suspect that he was smuggled abroad to escape grave charges, and that the body of some unfortunate nonentity who would never be missed, lured perhaps from the waterfront, was buried in his name. Certainly the body reputed to be Marlowe's was interred with great haste and in an unmarked grave.

St Nicholas's churchyard was still there, looking suitably enigmatical behind the pair of skulls on the gateposts guarding its entrance. Also still there was the fifteenth-century church tower – it must be immeasurably the oldest thing in Deptford – by the north wall of which the body is supposed to lie. Sir

Frank Benson unveiled a memorial just after the First World War, and Hitler's bombers made their contribution to the conspiracy of silence by destroying it in the second one. I found that a substitute memorial had now gone up, with the somewhat pointed quotation, 'Cut is the branch that might have grown full straight'. The twin skulls, as I left, looked more sardonic than ever. Clearly they would never talk.

11. The Heart of the Enigma

GREENWICH

The end is where we start from — T. S. ELIOT, *Little Gidding*

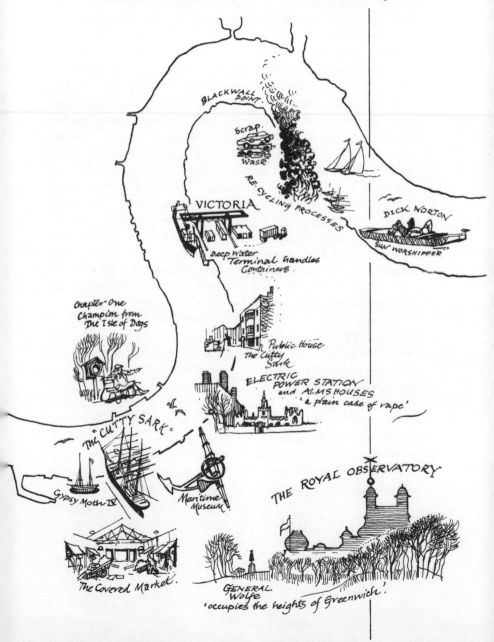

BLACKWALL POINT

Scrap

Waste

RE-CYCLING PROCESSES

VICTORIA

DICK NORTON

SUN WORSHIPPER

Deep Water Terminal handles Containers

Chapter One Champion from The Isle of Dogs

Public House The Cutty Sark

ELECTRIC POWER STATION and ALMS HOUSES 'a plain case of rape'

THE CUTTY SARK

THE ROYAL OBSERVATORY

Gypsy Moth IV

Maritime Museum

The Covered Market.

GENERAL Wolfe 'occupies the heights of Greenwich.'

The Marlowe Affair may be the darkest of the individual Thamesside mysteries, now sunk so deep in time and speculation that the truth may never be finally salvaged; but the whole of the twisting river – not least as it bends towards Greenwich – is an unsolved puzzle. Apart from the enigma of every river's nature – what else in creation is born, matures and dies simultaneously? – there is the enigma of how 'Thames' came to get its name.

Where did the word the Romans adopted and adapted as Tamesis spring from? Was it Celtic, Latinized Saxon, has it a Sanscrit echo? There is still no certainty among the experts. And where was the river born? Two sites have always competed for the honour, and their champions can still, when the mood takes them, get quite testy about it. There are the supporters of Seven Springs near Cheltenham, and there are those who back the better-fancied Thames Head near Cirencester. Without ever having actually been able to prove it, the river authorities favour Thames Head as the presumed source. (Seven Springs, they have decided, though actually farther from the mouth, is really the source of the tributary Churn.) There have been arguments about it in Parliament, where there is a rival constituency interest, to predictable background cries of 'Dry up!' Which, when I went to look for it, was what the source itself had done.

It was one of those burning summers of the mid-seventies when virtually everything dried up everywhere, but I gathered that little water was to be seen at Thames Head at the best and wettest of times. Looking for the source, I was assured, was a job for a water-diviner.

Strictly speaking, of course, I am playing truant from my London beat in shooting off upstream like this. But it is hard for any writer about the Thames, even in its lower reaches, to resist the urge to take a look at where it all began. So I will break off my journey in midstream – stopping the river at Greenwich, so to speak – and tell how I took myself off to Cirencester to look for its supposed source, hidden deep in its Cotswold hill.

A lane goes past the village of Coates, on its way to Kemble and the London trains. Over a stile, a signpost points down a small field path running by a drystone wall. I followed it over three fields, through a herd of surprised bullocks, through a silent wood and along a deep, stony lane between high tangled hedges covered with sloes and brambles. It crossed a little stone bridge over the dry bed of that forgotten pride of eighteenth-century engineering, the canal which once linked the Thames to the Severn; now romantically derelict, full of ferns and rushes, almost hidden by trees and overhanging creepers. On past three more fields and the glimpse of a distant village; and the path, skirting another wood, finally emerged in a clearing and ended at a pile of dry stones.

The place seemed unnaturally quiet, even for the corner of a remote Cotswold wood, and I felt as if I had come to the end of a long journey. A statue of old Father Thames used to guard the place, but they took it away to save it from vandals. In its place I found what looked like a granite tombstone, and at its foot was lying a small bunch of field flowers.

It seemed a strange way of celebrating a birth. The sense of mystery persisted when I returned to the river's middle age at Greenwich; but I have always found Greenwich a mysterious place, charged with an air of rites and ceremonies. Samuel Johnson evidently had the same impression. He was so moved by the presences still haunting the great riverside ex-palace that he knelt (or so he assures us in his one major poem) to 'kiss the consecrated earth', a sight that must have caused considerable ribaldry among the watermen who landed him there. If, that is to say, the celebrated line was meant to be taken literally, which probably it was not. The doctor was a professional too, and poetic licence can be useful.

Still, a due sense of awe is not to be sneered at. If there is any mystery about time and tide Greenwich is the place to contemplate it, and the old Royal Observatory the proper cathedral for such a cult. Time is what Greenwich is about, and it is never likely to let us forget it. The famous red ball on its spindle now goes through its one o'clock time signal routine for the world's tourists rather than the Thames skippers, and the prime meridian – that magical line graven in the courtyard and set in concrete – is more irresistible than ever to the generations of small boys of every size, age and colour who want to stand in two hemispheres at the same time. As for the clock of clocks near by, the basis of the international time zone system, this is the true global head-splitter, a cosmic migraine for most ordinary mortals. I have seen people studying it for so long, and with such bafflement, that they have had in the end to ask the time by an ordinary watch.

Time, superior Greenwich time, is of the essence; it throbs through Tompion's 'great clockes' and animates the gravely beautiful faces of baroque sundials. Those with a mind (and time) for it can apply themselves to the problems of azimuth and almucantarath, trace the shadow of the gnomon across a diversity of elegant grounds, or observe the variations between the ancient Babylonian and the Italian hour. It is evident that time is not always what it seems; and perhaps, when even these most artful of mechanical systems have finally run down, some new generation of super-sophisticated clocks will be set by sundials so that everything can start up again.

All this can be studied – or, for people like myself, goggled at with fascinated incomprehension – at the Royal Observatory which now serves as a museum of astronomy and navigation. Here the riddle of longitude was solved and applied, a greater navigational discovery than any new continent, and the world's tangled shipping snapped into line like beads on tautened threads. Not everyone welcomed this giant step, any more than there was universal joy at the death of pro-fessional sail. In his virtually forgotten *London River*, a book that conveys the lost excitement of being at the watery world's gateway more than any other I know outside Conrad, H. M. Tomlinson shows a marked lack of enthusiasm for what to him were still comparatively new and dubious developments. He laments the days when men 'were seamen and navigators in a way that is lost . . . What is the sea now? Steamers do not make time, or lose it. They keep it. They run to schedule, one behind the other, in processions. They have nothing to overcome . . .'

Such feelings are not extinct. Half a century later, an ex-barge skipper who was unlikely to have heard of Tomlinson was being interviewed on his 101st birthday and echoing his thoughts. His name was Dick Miller; he described how he sailed barges through the First World War and between the wars, and lost his last one at Dunkirk. All his life he refused to work with motor vessels because they would take away his freedom: 'You have to run to time in motors.' His philosophy seemed to have paid off; at least, he had gone on beating time.

Equally undefeated by the common enemy, General Wolfe (well past his double centenary) now occupies the Heights of Greenwich, standing on the hilltop outside the Observatory in a most unmilitary-looking tricorne hat, unperturbed by shell-splinters from later wars than his own. As a local man he is fully entitled to be there, commanding what was in his day and remains now one of the great panoramic views across London. It has changed, but not unrecognizably. Contours are the best conservators; as long as there are hills and river bends we can relate the present to the past, the London or Londons of the Tudors and of Wren, Wolfe, Johnson, Byron, Betjeman. The general's living eye would have swept uninterruptedly across the empty Isle of Dogs to distant Hornsey Rise, the Lea Valley dipping to the right with Epping Forest lifting again farther eastward, and Hainault Forest beyond Greenwich Marshes, now power stations and the surviving impedimenta of dockland. Leftward he would have looked over Deptford Creek straight to St Paul's dome, that 'foolscap crown on a fool's head', as Byron so rudely called it. Now the towers of Deptford's rehousing block the foreground, yet the 'huge, dun cupola' (more buoyant since they cleaned it and younger-looking than in Byron's day or Wolfe's) still rides the commercial clutter. Paul's seems unconquerable, and the general would certainly approve of that.

Nothing but the best is good enough for the distinguished students of the Royal Naval College, dominating the foreground, and Wren has provided them with not one but two foolscap crowns to encourage them in their studies. I must confess that this is a building I admire without beginning to love. Johnson considered it too grand a place for the simple seamen who then went there as resident pensioners. The old sailors seemed to agree; at least, they never settled down there as contentedly as the old soldiers did at Chelsea Hospital, and there was no mutinous reaction when they were displaced in the mid-Victorian period to make way for the grander inmates of the naval college. So the doctor was right again, and the important sailors who study there have lived up to his judgement and not had much to do with the lower orders beyond their ornate railings. They keep themselves to themselves, working out their higher naval problems.

Can these be so abstract as to make the students themselves disappear from view? Universities are normally places of considerable life and bustle, and the RNC is by way of being the naval university. Yet you scarcely ever see a living soul in or around the vast premises, except for the men at the gates and the tourists gazing in awe at the famous Painted Hall. I found the hall deserted as usual, but it was uncanny to see that all the tables were laid. But where were the diners?

It must have been the implacable absence of human life that was beginning to work on the nerves. I started imagining things. The last of the original inmates, those war-battered old pensioners, left more than a century ago. Can they have been *frightened* away? But they had stopped eating in this grand refectory long before their final removal, and probably there were no complaints. It must have been hard to concentrate on your food. Here it was that Nelson's body lay in state, while Pluto chased Persephone across the ceiling in an orgy of English baroque, Minerva and Hercules cleaned up heaven with spear and club, and various symbolic ladies named Peace, Prudence, Temperance, Piety and the like – unperturbed by all this or by the naval action going on around them – calmly received King William and Queen Mary. Sir James Thornhill, the painter, himself appears on the ceiling. So does John Wall, the oldest pensioner, aged ninety-seven. But probably the living Wall was content to consume his biscuits and skilly in some humbler mess.

I decided it must be for the invisible students of today that those tables were laid.

The lower decks of Greenwich have their problems too. Though there are more desolate parts of dockland, areas like Greenwich and Woolwich are at a special disadvantage. It would be hard to see how virtually flattened stretches of riverside such as Wapping could have anything but a radical approach to the future. They have little to build on, except ground. In contrast, the unfashionable end of built-up Greenwich looks as stuck with traditionalism as the fashionable one. There are ranges of old factories it would take a massive demolition and reconstruction campaign or an atomic war to clear away, and the one looks no more imminent than the other. Anyway, many locals would prefer them to stay, if they could go on providing work.

This was always an area where people tended to live and work and amuse themselves without much concern about what went on in other parts of London. They liked it here. Their children and grandchildren liked it too. They specialized in craftsmanly jobs linked to the river, generation following generation into the same wharf or factory. This made for continuity, a strong local identity and social contentment, virtues that understandably embarrass the authorities more than a little as they watch the industrial tide receding – partly through their own steering – from the waterfront that formed and sustained this community.

Everything is topsy-turvy now, thrown into reverse. Instead of bettering themselves like their forebears, men skilled in river-based trades move steadily downwards, worsening themselves. What choice have they? A specialist toolmaker becomes a machineman, then a warehouse hand, then a hospital porter or watchman. And when the factory he watches closes down or moves out, there is nothing left for him to do but what the tourists do – go and watch the hydrofoils or gaze admiringly at the *Cutty Sark*.

Sailing for ever in her concrete sea, *Cutty Sark* is what Greenwich means to most people; and very beautiful she is. But the main appeal of the place lies round corners the tourist never turns. What I like about it most is its obstinate refusal to let the human dimension be crushed out of it by architects, admirals, literary moguls, publicity men or anybody else, though the life is in danger of being shaken out of it by heavy lorries. My Greenwich, which has the added advantage of dodging the lorries, is down alleys of which nobody has heard, across a shabbily handsome market at which nobody looks, informing the world (in an inscription nobody reads) that A FALSE BALANCE IS ABOMINATION TO THE LORD BUT A JUST WEIGHT IS HIS DELIGHT. It follows narrow Georgian and Victorian streets leading to claustrophobic little squares. It is both secret and vertiginous, full of sharp hills and countryfied lanes that suddenly run out into space. A giddy town, still surprisingly well stocked with corner shops and small printing works and all manner of one-man businesses. A fascinating human mess in short – though that could not be said of Croom's Hill, one of the show-places of London.

Croom's Hill, climbing up the west side of Greenwich Park, was probably an old road when the Romans came, joining Blackheath to the original fishing village; now it has an unequalled range of rich Georgian houses. A stone's-throw from this elegance I found a very different scene. For this is a town of sudden surprises, even shocks. I was startled by a window I had never noticed before, full now of staring Victorian dolls wearing flowered hats. An antique shop straight out of Dickens had a shattered window and there was blood on the step; the woman in charge explained calmly enough that there seemed to have been some trouble overnight but of course it was business as usual, if customers didn't mind the draught. I managed to get myself slightly lost – surely a tribute to a place one has lived in for twenty years – and landed up in a narrow, tucked-away street where there were three pubs in a row.

The one I went in was intensely local though not aggressively so; they seemed interested to see a new face. Outside stood an ancient Austin car, a survivor from the Thirties, as lovingly cared for as the *Cutty Sark* and to its owner – he seemed to expect that strangers would want to talk about it– even more beautiful. Caressing its gleaming bodywork, he ran through the short-list of its owners, all of whom had clearly been worthy of their trust, and the routine for keeping the veteran healthy and happy. In Greenwich they like things old and they like them to last. Listening to this man whose devotion to the past was so intense, so Greenwich-like, I doubted whether he or the place he lived in would earn much approval from experts like Dr David Eversley, of the Centre for Environmental Studies. I had just been reading a memorandum the doctor had presented to Parliament in which he gave a stern warning that the conservationist cult and Ye Oldery in general had gone too far.

Undeterred by the Centre for Environmental Studies and its thinkers, donkeys were still busy at the upper end of the park giving rides to children. At the lower end, in the streets leading to the waterfront, shellfish could still be bought from barrows. Kings and cockles seem no unnatural mix to the people of Greenwich, who have never thought that the proximity of the great need cramp their style. (Perhaps the captains and commanders are difficult; children no longer seem to want to play on the old river beach, thronged at one time, below the college steps.) I was glad to be reminded that others live here besides columnists, actors and art studio proprietors.

The town's education in the true East London spirit owes more to Deptford, just across the creek and really part of the family, than to any college or studio. It would not be surprising to find in the Greenwich back streets a survivor or two from the traditional street traders: knife-grinder, boot-black, flower-girl, match-seller, cat's-meat man, crying their wares to the ghostly music of barrel-organs. They say there were dancing bears inside the longest of living Greenwich memories, but such hangovers from the horrors of Bankside or

Paris Gardens could never compete with the horrors of the modern traffic, which seems the one thing capable of bringing the Greenwich story to an end.

One riverside walk not only foils the traffic by pushing it underground, through the Blackwall Tunnel, but also provides a series of visual impacts as strong as anything the industrial river has to offer, and that is a large statement. Most of them are superb; one is so outrageous that it brings every environmentalist I have ever come across to somewhere near apoplexy. Ancient Crane Street, narrow as a gangplank, leads from the naval college's river entrance – surely the most ceremonious back door in Britain – to what must be among the biggest and ugliest of London's power stations. Gripped in its black jaws is one of the smallest and most perfect of Jacobean almshouses, complete with Italianate courtyard and fountain. A plain case of rape, they all say.

The sight is highly provocative, but I have never made up my mind whether to join in the cries of anguish or regard it as an uncommon example of Edwardian forbearance. The marvel was, at a time when we were flexing our industrial muscles and the claims of power in all senses of the word were at their most brutal, that anything as fragile and unproductive as the little Trinity Hospital should have been allowed to survive at all if it got in the monster's way. It did; but the beast retracted a couple of claws, so to speak, to accommodate the almshouse and its tiny garden. Now they have cohabited for the best part of a century. Ironically, the power station's original function, running London's trams, is long over, there being no more trams to run; but the almshouse still carries out its much older commitment to provide a home for twenty-one local men. All those centuries of precarious survival have not, however, contrived to make it worldly. I found a notice on its exquisite front offering ten pounds reward for any information 'leading to the conviction of any person causing damage to this property'. It seemed an inadequate deterrent, like a caution for anyone caught defacing a Rembrandt.

Beyond the power station is a river wall like a fortress and a range of fine old Georgian buildings, including a harbour-master's house and a bow-windowed pub that was once my favourite in all London. You could have a casual drink in the bar, comfortable enough if you didn't mind stumbling over the occasional river-dog or coil of rope, and then wander upstairs to watch the ships go by as you waited – often a long time, but who cared? – for your whitebait supper. It is all grander now, restyled in Brewer's Maritime. But at least nobody has laid hands on the frontage, and the fastidious can always nurse their pint on the river wall.

Outside is best. I never get tired of this scene – of all London river views, though almost totally industrial, perhaps the finest. The very messiness has style, even grandeur.

The dumps and piles of waste look as if they were posing for artists. Chimneys lurch like drunken sailors, and small but famous wharves – Lovell's Wharf, Piper's Wharf – are still in business running freight services or repairing lighters. Barges have names like honest old river-horses, 'Lily' or 'Betty'. But also, as a bonus for pedestrians, one can get a close-up view – rare in London's dockland – of modern processes in action. I was able to walk right through the Victoria Deep Water Terminal which manages to handle container cargo remarkably high upstream – twenty miles up from Tilbury, in fact, and only six river miles from Tower Bridge. Cargo from distant seas swims in by what must seem to the layman the strangest development of transport evolution. Lighters cross the ocean in the holds of mother ships, which spawn them into the Thames at Tilbury to finish their voyage upstream.

And here everything booms and echoes to the clanging, thumping and hissing of rail-mounted gantry cranes and great fork-lift trucks. Technological whales rule this stretch of the river, once famous for shrimps. Not many yards further along is Blackwall Point, where they used to hang pirates and it looks as if they still might; and opposite the River Lea twists into the Thames in the convulsions of Bow Creek, like the last threshings of a dying eel. This was Isaac Walton's river, but he would hardly have relished the things anybody would be liable to fish out of it here.

The main river itself takes one of its most violent bends at this point, performing a U-turn from a northward to virtually a southward flow, and with it comes one of its theatrical changes of character. The upward curve – as far as the point where they hanged the pirates – has a spacious industrial grandeur. The down stretch, past the creek on the one side and the gasworks on the other, grows more introverted and ominous. This is slightly demonic country, as one might imagine one of the less severe suburbs of hell, and not without its perverse attractions. The river path leading towards Woolwich and the new barrier is flanked by mountains of scrap metal and orchestrated with the rumblings and belchings of recycling processes. Small patient fires burn eternally, acrid smoke drifts over rusted rails and pools of black water, dead cars copulate in titanic pile-ups. Behind the riverfront the hellish air is more emphatic and achieves grandeur, especially at night when the gasworks blaze like a city of satanic palaces; and at the entrance to each a little old lady sits in a small fireproof hut, brewing tea.

At Angerstein Wharf I talked to a man in the rain, a murky drizzle that suited the scene and his mood. Some clumsy rivercraft – it still happens, even in these days of thin water traffic – had fouled the river wall and dislodged a few yards of it. This had to be repaired; not much of a job, but it needed to be done, and quickly.

'My last contract,' this engineer said with a kind of resigned bitterness. All his professional life he had been busy on the London river, and now his work had come to this – superintending a couple of men mending a yard or two of broken wall. It was a scene of utter desolation, though active in a scavenging sort of way. A green-funnelled ballast-dredger called *Flamingo* was the only ship to be seen through the clinging mist. On the landward side a fierce crunching of dead metal was going on, as though by monster hyaenas. Waste and recycling: these were the operative words now. His own job would be recycled soon. If it turned out that he had to leave the Thames he would be very unhappy about it. The river was his life, as it had been the life of so many. It might, at that place and time, have reasonably been thought a good thing to leave.

But even then the river was able to operate its gift for transformation scenes. He showed me Bugsby's Hole, a weirdly romantic beach scooped out of this dire stretch of bank, covered with skiffs and little spectral yachts: there was actually one called *Spook*. It was as though Charon had arranged a small private resort where he took favoured customers for a break on the way over. They still speak of such famous local figures as Dick Norton, a barge man whose yard was here; who sunned himself on his working beach when he was not working and when, of course, there was some sun; who quite literally lived and died on the river.

There have been many Nortons over the years and centuries, total rivermen. Like Bugsby, no doubt. Who was this Bugsby? Nobody seems to know, though he had a whole reach of the river named after him, as well as a point, a hole, an island, a tree, a causeway and a flight of steps. He must at one time have been a figure of note, and it seems strange that no clue survives – nothing but hunches. A. P. Herbert, who always liked to look on the bright side, had the cheerful notion that he was a popular longshoreman or general man-about-the-Thames. There was a darker tradition casting him as a captain in charge of prison hulks that used to be moored in the reach. Some thought he was a notorious pirate. Perhaps, as the custom was, he was hung in chains until three tides had washed over him.

We shall never know the source of Bugsby now. Yet somebody must once have known who he was. I often fancy that among the rusting relics on the river bed are the lost keys to many such secrets.

12. Woolwich and Thamesmead

SHADES OF PAST AND FUTURE

Dolorously the shipping clanks
And after me a strange tide turns,
WILFRED OWEN, 'Shadwell Stair'

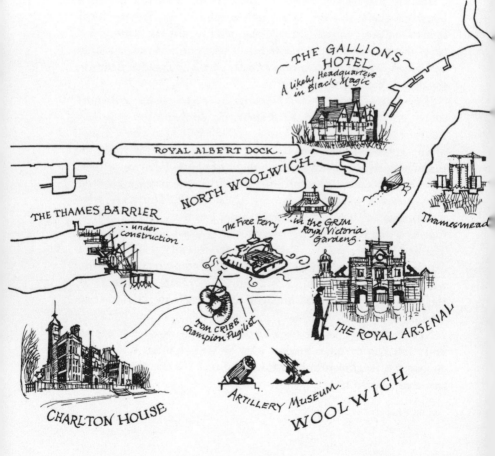

I was looking out of my window across Blackheath, in the silence that only comes to the Dover road early on Sunday mornings, when I saw, or thought I saw, a troop of soldiers on horseback riding slowly through the mist. Nothing ceremonial: just working cavalrymen or artillerymen in khaki, half a century late on parade, wearing (I swear it) puttees.

On their way, I had to tell myself, to some film or pageant rehearsal; but I am not sure I altogether wanted to explain them away. As one whose house overlooks the most potentially haunted stretch of open space in London, gibbering with dead kings, encamped Danes, rebellious peasants, plotters, pilgrims, highwaymen, I think I believe in ghosts and reckon that they have more right around my section of Watling Street than Euro-lorries.

Not so much the obvious guidebook spooks, though we are moving into territory well supplied with those; not only are places like the Jacobean Charlton House and the sham-Gothic Vanburgh Castle reputedly haunted, which is in no way surprising, but even Edward Heath's somewhat denatured constituency of Bexley is credited with its local spectre – the Black Prince, no less. He does his stuff, whatever it may be, away over the other side of Shooters Hill. It must be hard going, haunting the A2.

But those ghosts, if that is what they were, I saw from my window were not Greenwich or Bexley ghosts. They could have been from one place only: Woolwich.

Greenwich and Woolwich are now, officially and inconceivably, one. Local government reorganization recently wedded them, and they have set up house as the London Borough of Greenwich. For the life of me I can't begin to think of them as even cohabiting. To all but official eyes they are still totally separate, each its own place; and whom God or natural development have kept asunder no man or municipality should presume to join. I don't expect anybody at County Hall to believe in ghosts, but I do expect them to believe, as I fervently do, that every human habitation has its own spirit; sometimes this is of the past, sometimes of the future, while lucky communities may find themselves getting along happily with a contemporary one that fits. Where none exists at all the place is simply not alive, and it is the inhabitants who become ghosts.

A place, like a person, must be itself. What else can give it identity, let alone distinction? Greenwich is clearly distinct from Woolwich, whatever the reorganization men may say. A shotgun marriage that must have been, since Woolwich is as plainly Army as Greenwich is Navy, and it's surprising there have not been more brawls already. Yet although Woolwich, municipally speaking, has had to take Greenwich's name it did get one consolation prize out of the losing match.

Since the two used to be separate boroughs, each naturally had its own town hall. Woolwich Town Hall was a jolly number in Edwardian baroque, fat and fussy as a pearly queen. Greenwich, making a surprising leap into the twentieth century around the nineteen-thirties, settled for a new town hall in the then modernistic manner – austere brick, with a tall tower strongly under Continental influence. 'Futuristic' could even have been the word they used for it. Yet which, forty years on, was chosen to rule over the new joint household? Fussy old Woolwich, leaving poor Greenwich the unfashionable one, in the undignified position of having to try and hire herself out to any surviving admirers for balls, meetings and other such public or social occasions.

There are various ways of approaching Woolwich, the most tedious being to drive along the main Woolwich road. The most adventurous is to stumble as far as one can along the river track, past the paper mountains and graveyards of perished machinery, the baleful beaches and old wooden jetties, with the smell of rotting piers and occasionally the sea. Not counting the flood prevention barrier now building, there are liable to be obstacles and even hazards.

I saw a flock of yellow-legged river firemen moving calmly along the bank, and was advised that it might not be a good idea to go much farther as an oil tanker was rather expected to explode at any moment. I watched from a discreet distance but nothing happened. Through the haze of the hot afternoon the water shimmered round the barrier-construction, making it look like Venice lagoon.

Here, perhaps, was the true frontier – between the river of the future, the protected reaches upstream from this point, and the old tidal river beyond the barrier. There lay the old Royal Dockyard, once as famous as Deptford's, dreaming of the past and of such ghosts as the *Great Harry*, built at the considerable cost (at 1515 prices) of £6427.8s.o¾d, not including the timber which was supplied by monasteries and other more or less voluntary bodies. Samuel Pepys was as often here as at Deptford, carrying out his duties as Secretary to the Navy Board, examining the navy stores, unravelling the red tape of the Rope Yard, worrying – though not in any way that interfered with his private life unduly – about the Dutch. He travelled by water, of course.

Since that sensible way is now denied us the best route to Woolwich, while still avoiding the boring, traffic-clogged main road, is through Charlton. This remarkable village has received surprisingly little attention from the guides. Charlton is no mere ghost of a village. There are plenty of those around London, with the configuration providing a skeletal shape on which a mental picture can be built of the way it might once have looked – church, pond, village green, stocks, all the rural props that townsmen love.

Charlton is more than that: it is the village itself, a lucky or clever survivor if ever there was one. Church, green, manor-house are more than just locations, identifiable sites. They are there as much as the famous football ground.

They were really laying on the charm, with village children playing round the fountain, old inhabitants sunning themselves on a bench, a horse and cart standing near by. People were even going about – and I must say I rather thought this was overdoing things – in medieval dress. It turned out that a ceremony was going on at the big house, something connected with the traditional and coarsely named Horn

Fair. This annual frolic, based on an improbable legend involving King John and a local miller's wife, caused such scandal as the centuries rolled by – a 'rabble of mad people', Defoe went so far as to call it – that the fair was eventually banned.

Charlton commands an extensive river view, an essential factor in the legend which also purports to explain another mysterious river name, Cuckold's Point back in Rotherhithe. Caught in the act by the miller, the king is supposed to have bought him off by promising him all the land as far as he could see, looking one way. This turned out to be from Cuckold's Point to Charlton Hill – four miles or less as the crow flies but a good deal more as the seducer flies, and uphill at that. A nice stretch of desirable riverside territory, in short, and the miller settled for it gladly.

The only stipulation was that he had to remind himself how far it was, and also acknowledge his status as a cuckold, by covering the ground in procession with his family every year wearing horns. A jolly old orgy, and any idea of reviving it would undoubtedly chime in with the urge for Merrie Englandry which has sprung up lately in a somewhat self-conscious way, perhaps as a conscientious counterblast to the celtic nationalist movements. Yet even assuming that the respectable suburbanites of Charlton could command much conviction as they strapped on their horns and politely arranged their places in the bawdy procession, any modern version of the abandoned old pageant is bound to be on more decorous lines than the 'rabble' Defoe was writing about.

Charlton House has its own dignity to consider. I would put it second only to Ham House in my short list of London's Jacobean winners. It is often complained, as things are, that what goes on inside hardly lives up to the grandeur of the exterior. The fact is that it is used as a community centre; and to complain that Charlton House is too good for ordinary Charltonians seems a touch superior, like that notion of Dr Johnson's that the naval hospital was too grand a building for simple sailors and would only make them unhappy. I must say that such villagers as I saw strolling about the stately gardens looked contented enough. None appeared unduly overawed, or guilty about being made free of all the magnificence. Better, surely, that the place should be used in this way than kept for high-level occasions, or reserved for important people only, or turned into one of those depressing stately museums. True, there are oddities. The grounds possess what must surely be the only Inigo Jones public lavatory in Britain. It was a summer-house once.

It was also encouraging to see that the common herd were admitted free of charge and without supervision to another local high-quality attraction, the carefully excavated remains of the Augustinian monastery which appears in most of the maps and guides as Lesness, but is properly Lesnes. We have come a long way, and so has Lesnes, since my Victorian guide-book could coldly record that the surviving fragments of the abbey walls were 'of no architectural or picturesque value'. Wrong on both counts. Laid out on their green hillside, against a background of dark woods, the ruins look romantic and precise. The abbey's entire anatomy is now clearly defined: rooms, chapels, walks, arches, steps, even to the kitchen serving hatch. Children were playing about the walls. I somehow doubt whether the monks would chase them off, if they could return. Perhaps they will, for the eighth centenary of this massive foundation is due in 1978, and surely deserves celebrating.

The monks looked from their hillside across the Plumstead marshes, regularly inundated by high tides, and the view can have changed little over the centuries until the sudden rising, in our own day, of a score of tower blocks out of the swamp. This is the start of the new riverside town of Thamesmead, mixed pride and burden of the Greater London Council.

Easy to wince at the gaunt beginnings, the concrete spine and ribs of what will one day – hopefully, to use a vogue word with more than its usual meaning – be a living giant on the south bank, inside ten miles as the crow flies from London

Bridge. Crow? Raven, some would say. There are those who regard the massive enterprise as ill-omened, socially disastrous, on the grounds that a vast new population should never be planted without the advance certainty of adequate work and mobility. Well, certainty is hard to come by, and all intelligent planners bear one thing constantly in mind – how wrong their judgements have often been in the past. The first wave of post-war planners were convinced that it would be impossible to build here at all.

For all the starkness I find it a relief to see the landscape shaped so clearly, using the natural contours, instead of letting everything subside into the mush of instant spaghetti-land so much of outer London has become. Here ancient stone looks across to new, outcrops of the past to signposts for the future. Run-down communities which have retained the shape of their beginnings to a surprising extent, as well as showing their twentieth-century wounds, surround the cradle of one with its whole future to make, and which really belongs to the next millenium.

So although hope is a rare commodity these days it can be found here. The pioneer residents of Thamesmead are an encouragingly mixed lot, some of them refugees from housing conditions so abominable that they could be forgiven for any visionary ideas they may have brought with them about a better future. However, the start of life at Thamesmead has not been wholly idealistic, which is just as well for its chances. Already it has shown itself to be a worldly and combative community, reassuringly and sometimes alarmingly human. It is always getting into public rows about one burning issue or another. But I was soon to find again here what I had frequently found before – the difference between a community as you imagine it from what you read and hear about it, and as it actually looks on the ground.

Taking an actual look at Thamesmead seemed almost unfair, like judging a new play from its first rehearsal or even the preliminary read-through. It could have been registering baffled aspiration, with everybody gone away to think, or a disaster area from which all had fled. Scarcely a soul was to be seen in the streets, whether completed or under construction. Perhaps these were too new to walk in comfortably; perhaps they were all at work or at campaign meetings; perhaps they had already broken through into the post-pedestrian era.

I found a wired-off area that might have been judged central, some kind of official enclave. 'You the dog-catcher, then?' came a voice over my shoulder. So there was life in Thamesmead after all, even if it did ask incomprehensible questions. I took it to be a poker-faced new town joke, and then I saw the notice board. They really were after an official dog-catcher, but far from explaining things I found this more bewildering than ever. Strays, it appeared, had been hunting in packs, which you might expect more in an old town dying than in a new one in process of being born.

THIS AREA IS PATROLLED BY GUARD DOGS, warned another and more familiar notice; presumably nobody would be foolish enough to try and catch *them*. Another mentioned suicide and added YOU HAVE A NUMBER OF CHOICES. It was not as callous as it looked: presumably Thamesmeaders understand this kind of sawn-off language. All the same, none of this had much of an air of the glad hand. Perhaps the pubs would do more in the way of welcoming the stranger to town? I found one called the 'Barge Pole', throbbing with music if not exactly with life. Wide floor-to-ceiling windows looked out on young trees starting to grow round what could become – of all things, should they choose to play it that way – a future old-world village green. Odd if Thamesmead, fifty years hence, were to end up with roses round the door, even if they had to be patrolled by guard dogs. One thing already looked clear: the high-rise planners were already modifying or at any rate mixing their ideas about the levels at which people were being asked or required to live. As well as the glacial peaks under construction there were the lower ranges and the mere hills, and it looked as though even the primitive instincts of the obstinate surface-dwellers were now being catered for too, with a proportion of old-style human-scale houses. From earth to earth in three planning generations? Most people welcomed the signs. When so many East London families were flung into the heavens whether they wanted to go or not, they found no pie in the sky but any amount of neurosis.

Now that planners are increasingly having to accept, often against all their training and instincts, that people can be trusted to know what they really want for themselves, there seems a good chance that the future of a long-term project like Thamesmead will be essentially what its citizens choose to make it. Nobody could ask more than that. It starts with a clean sheet. Nothing was destroyed to build the town, nothing spoiled. There were only the stagnant and malarial Plumstead Marshes, their one memorable feature being the majestic out-fall sewer which the Prince of Wales ceremoniously opened, if that is the right word, in 1865.

Woolwich needs its brash new neighbour; for the old town's best friends (and I count myself one of them) can hardly deny that it has a sadly devitalized air these days, redeemed only by the colour and vigour of its open-air market in the wide, cobbled square opposite the Royal Arsenal. Georgian gilt on weathered brick, the arsenal façade is a sight too, one of those intensely masculine old stars who seem to go on for ever. They get more and more handsome as the years pile up, though I have never been encouraged to ask exactly what they do these days. The arsenal was an economic mainstay once, but only a handful of people work there now, and whatever goes on is sternly withheld from the prying eyes of the public. Police man the gates, and where the fortress walls loom over the town on the western side the Ministry of Defence has thought fit to turn on the whole deterrent works, from Official Secrets Act warnings to the ubiquitous guard dogs. It seems counter-productive. However, I was able to hug the intimidating wall as far as Ship and Half Moon Passage, a weedy lane actually giving access to the river, which is rare enough in Woolwich.

It is hard to believe that anything meaningful goes on there now. Woolwich seems like some antique army pensioner, wounded in the wars and cast upon a not noticeably sympathetic world. It wears its Georgian uniform, shako and empty sleeve, but has lost the habit of looking proud. Things might be different if it could hear the rumble of cannon again, the sound of horses and bugles. Its great ranges of military buildings – the Royal Military Academy, the quarter-mile sweep of the Artillery Barracks – have earned it the name of the English Leningrad; the English St Petersburg would surely be nearer the mark.

The civilian part of the town looks distinctly meaner. Walking round the streets can be dispiriting, with all those big cheap stores and boarded-up little shops. I discovered that a pub called the 'Fortunes of War' had also closed, which seemed symbolical. There used to be a saying that more wealth flowed through Woolwich than any other town in the world. This referred to the geographical oddity that formerly located a detached section of the borough on the north bank of the Thames, and the flow was of course the flow of merchandise along the river itself. It was always a wry sort of joke, and would be even wryer if anybody had the heart to crack it today.

North Woolwich survives only as a name, and on the sailing orders officially displayed on the ferry boat. It is licensed to ply between Woolwich and North Woolwich, a voyage of several hundred yards, and authorized to carry 530 passengers and a crew of eight. I went aboard with a feeling of genuine adventure – an almost forgotten feeling, the authentic lift of the spirits that seldom accompanies jet flights of as many thousands of miles. This Woolwich waterfront has an attractive if absurd deep-sea air, with its surviving cranes and warehouses, bustle of shipping, and seagulls wailing with the special excitement they reserve for ports.

Down the steps in the passenger area, big enough to get lost in, there were enormous smoking and non-smoking saloons, all empty. Was everyone in the dining-saloon, or drinking the captain's start-of-voyage cocktail? I could find nobody at all; she seemed a ghost ship. Her name was the distinctly masculine *Ernest Bevin*, and as I explored deserted companionways I found a handsome plaque commemorating 'the dockers' KC, trade union leader and statesman'. I almost expected to see Ernie himself shambling down from the bridge, dripping with gold braid.

And there was his name on the lifebelts. Lifebelts, to cross a quarter-mile of river? Not so absurd, at that. It was within sight of here, on the appalling evening of 3 September 1878, that over five hundred people died when the outward-bound *Bywell Castle* collided with a pleasure steamer called the *Princess Alice*, returning from a day trip crowded with passengers. After a voyage of a minute or two we were there – the former North Woolwich, once a tiny enclave of Kent in the county of Essex, now the foreign soil of the new metropolitan borough of Newham. It was time to disembark, to gulp the North Thames air, to reacclimatize myself. A few passengers eventually materialized, twice as many cars and lorries, and we made our way down the important ramp.

The whole exercise was ridiculously elaborate and enjoyable, and so much more than value for money. Those who take it for granted that everything has to be paid for, preferably through the customer's nose, must be appalled by the Woolwich Ferry. I am delighted that there should still be such rich exceptions to the huckster principles that rule us. People may pay the earth for a loaf of bread, and the shortest tube or bus journey already costs more than a taxi did yesterday or the day before; yet such luxuries as the National Gallery, the cathedrals, the ruins of Lesnes Abbey, a ceremonious voyage on the Woolwich Ferry, are free. Sheer madness, some would call it.

Is it so mad? Is it even uneconomic, properly considered? In *Crossing London's River* John Pudney describes the part played by the original paddle boats in the social life of the place, and tells how generations of Woolwich mothers took their young families on board 'to picnic and spend the afternoon free-riding between Essex and Kent shores'. And why not? It sounds a better idea than wrecking the lifts of high-rise flats or smashing the windows of empty houses through sheer

boredom and frustration. But these voyages have of course
been routine work-trips to countless thousands who were
infinitely luckier, I think, than most London commuters. One
Greenwich man I know, recently retired after working at the
Royal Docks for many years, often finds himself using the ferry
through sheer nostalgia. I doubt if there are many Londoners
who so enjoyed their journeys to and from work that they continue them after they have retired.

This queer sense of having crossed the sea to another
country, rather than just a river to another county, was
deepened by the disquieting air of North Woolwich: a brooding and somewhat explosive mixture of ages and moods, of old
dockland and new makeshift rehousing. Rows of sedate little
Victorian terrace cottages – pleasant enough, though some
looked as if they could hardly hold a substantial dockworker,
let alone his family – coexisted with prefabs themselves
looking almost old enough to be listed as buildings of historical
interest. There were prefabricated shops and real ones on
adjoining street corners, a prefabricated school, a boarded-up
bank saying OPEN A LIFE SAVINGS ACCOUNT and GIVE
BLOOD. The temporary houses were the most permanent-
looking things in sight, and some of them were suburbanized
with wisteria and garden gnomes in, one would have thought,
distinctly unfriendly country.

There was even a make-believe garden well, which looked
especially provocative. Only a few yards away the Essex River
Board was threatening penalties of £100 against anyone
throwing rubbish into an important stream which, one hardly
needs to add, was clogged with it. At the corner of Milk
Street a pub called the 'California' promised striptease every
Sunday lunchtime, and the old-world-sounding East Ham
Allotment Association displayed warnings against predators.

Even betting shops were ruins in this area, but the unforgettable ruin for me was of something else. A well-preserved
wooden notice still said TO THE GALLIONS HOTEL, pointing
to a lost piece of land opposite No. 12 gate of the Royal
Albert Dock. Inside the dock entrance was the yacht basin of

the London Marina, jaunty with bobbing private craft, a smart
yacht club and sale notices offering four-berth cabin cruisers
for a cool £6000. Outside was the 'Gallions', the ghost of a
hotel, its windows covered with sheets of metal but still
looking solid on its feet – or rather on its piles, for it was on
these that it was originally built.

The 'Gallions' had quite a grand past. It was built in con-
junction with a rail link for the first-class steamer custom,
and there used to be stables and subways connecting it straight
to the docks. It catered for people who were used to substantial comfort with a touch of grandeur in the late Victorian
way – the sirloin and mahogany trade, so to speak – and even its
remains were far more solid than many a living building in
these parts. The massive Tudor-style chimneys were still
upstanding, the weathervane on the turret was working, the
blue-and-white neo-Hellenic frieze round the outer walls
looked very little damaged, and so did the tiles on the
terrace.

But the floors were broken, opening up glimpses of horrific
depths beneath, and though I found my way inside I doubt
whether a braver person than I would have ventured far into
that shadowland, among the stained glass and the broken
panelling. Nobody, it struck me, would ever want to attend a
reunion at the 'Gallions', though it looked a likely headquarters
for black magic.

Another mystery: who, or what, was or were Gallions?
Not 'Gallion': the word is not possessive. Not the more
explicable 'Galleons', though it is sometimes misspelled so.
The name remains as mysterious as Bugsby, or as those mysterious Fiddlers who also have a reach named after them lower
down the estuary.

Having taken a look at the grim Royal Victoria Gardens,
originally conceived as a pleasure garden in the Vauxhall
tradition and still proving that anything green soothes the
spirits where nothing else grows, I returned along the white-
tiled foot-tunnel which is the twin of the Greenwich one,
though a shade longer and straighter. It was over. From

Woolwich to Woolwich, by land and by water, back almost before you started yet a timeless trip to undiscovered country. And all free.

Clearly Woolwich must have been a more vital place fifty years ago, though it can hardly have been a more mysterious one. Few have much to say about it now – and the less the better, judging from such bland write-offs as the one I recently read announcing that below Greenwich the river is nothing but a squalid mess. Those ought to be fighting words. Perhaps Woolwich needs to recover a touch of its old aggressive spirit, symbolized (however inappropriately) by the parish church on the hill overlooking the waterfront. This is a heavyweight Georgian structure trading elegance for strength, and writers have been rude about its uncompromising squareness.

For me it says the last word about Woolwich – or rather the first word, which needs to be heard again. This is to be found in the churchyard: not on the notice-board in the corner announcing, when I saw it last, the Black Bottom Stompers, but in its most elaborate memorial. A lion stands guard over it, massive paw resting on an urn. Here lies buried no poet, statesman, philanthropist, local bigwig, but a man as famous as any in his day – Tom Cribb, champion pugilist. Woolwich was a fighting town once.

13. Turning Tide?

THE WATERMEN FIGHT BACK

One only has to motor round the whole area or fly over the whole area to realise how urgent it is to make a speedy start on creating a new quality environment.

PETER WALKER, sometime Secretary of State for the Environment

SPECIALIST CRAFT MADE FOR DISTANT SEAS

ROAD HAULAGE HAS RENDERED RIVER SITES IRRELEVANT.

THE DOCKERS...

♪ THE CUTTY SARK

...refitted completely after the War, by specialists.....
Would the same services be available to-day?

Watching T.V.

...have been overliberated!

LESS INTERESTED IN LIFTING BALES, THAN..... Cleaning the car, or.

~WHY SHOULD A MAN WORK HARDER IF HE'S NOT GOING TO BE PAID ANY MORE THAN IF HE TOOK IT EASY?

I had reached a natural break in my journey. I was leaving familiar territory, the stretch of the river along which (like many thousands of others) I moved constantly between the places where I lived and worked. And, in my case, walked; for I had formed this eccentric habit of frequently footslogging between Central London and Greenwich, sometimes through Wapping and the Isle of Dogs, sometimes over Tower Bridge and down the 'long street' through Bermondsey and the dead Surrey Docks.

Now, before moving into the wider estuary, it seemed time for a look back, with I hope a little acquired perspective, at the people whose lives were mainly involved in the current upheavals. Whether or not they get Mr Peter Walker's 'new quality environment', whether (to use an equally chilling vogue term) they are 'decanted out' or encouraged to stay where they are, these are the people in the obvious front line of change.

As well as being (to me) very pleasurable, walking across a great city is a humbling occupation. There may be no other virtue in it. A man can be as blind or foolish on his feet as in a car or plane, though at least he has a chance of seeing at close quarters what he is being blind or foolish about. We are conditioned by our vehicles. To survey the environment from a car, which is what most of us (even when we live in it) do most of the time, is to be obsessed by demands of speed and mobility. To survey it from the sky, like some senior statesman or a seagull or an old lady at the top of a tower block, is to be concerned in one aspect or another with problems of lift and the availability of food. At ground level, at four miles an hour, the world looked more human if not necessarily more encouraging.

I am concerned here with people who lived off as well as on the river, who looked to it – and diminishingly still do – for their livelihood. These have always been one of the most cohesive and interdependent communities in London, and are bitter at seeing their work – unnecessarily, as some insist – draining away. They fail to enthuse over brave new schemes for revitalizing the docklands with names like Europa, Thames Park or City New Town; while the planners plan, or – as some would prefer – hesitate to plan, they are there already. They are the natives on the ground, and the natives are understandably restless.

They say that when the *Cutty Sark* went into her dry dock not long after the war, not only did she have to be re-rigged but all manner of highly specialised work had to be done on her; and all the necessary skills were still to be found in London. If she made the return voyage, released from her concrete prison, would the same services be available to send her back to sea? One has to be far gone in romanticism or despair to think we may be driven back to sail. Yet the survival of more contemporary skills is equally in doubt, and there are those who feel that if the commercial tide flows back to the river there will be nobody left to ride it. River crafts are reluctantly leaving the Thames and for some there can be no return trip.

It does no service to the working – the still working – river to exaggerate the decline. It was a quiet Thames I found, but not yet a silent one; its people deeply apprehensive, but not despairing. A bustle of activity was going on in boatyards strung along the waterfront in what to me were often unexpected places, from Eel Pie Island to the tip of Essex. Specialist craft were being turned out for distant seas and rivers, suggesting no falling off in the home skills that produced them.

I found people in the boatbuilding business whose way of meeting the slump – they even used the word in preference to the more modern and euphemistic 'recession' – was a shade old-fashioned though not, on the evidence, ineffectual. Finding the home market at a low ebb they went to look for new business abroad. One quite small firm out on the estuary was busy with high-speed launches destined to be used as patrol and customs boats in Latin America, as well as with motor-sailers for the United States, Finland, France and Italy. Their products were good, and they had no inhibition about saying so.

'You never see our stuff on the second-hand boat market,' they claimed; and it was all achieved in a shed nearly a century old, subject to severe flooding, an ice-house in winter, rattling – sometimes actually shifting – in the south-westerly gales. Some of these original Thames boathouses are more solid and have the appeal of antique barns, showing their ribs like arks; but men spend their time plodding up and down ladders instead of having raised platforms from which to work. Rebuilding may afflict the casual caller with an eye for the picturesque, but it is good for productivity and shows faith in the future.

Along the wharves I found moods as mixed as the cargoes they handled, mostly within the range of black to the lighter shades of grey – the sombreness relaxing, as was to be expected, the farther downstream I moved. One central wharfinger who used to take ships from all over the world, dealing especially in German and French wine, saw no river future at all except, as he gloomily put it, 'for hotels and parks and marinas'. All his surviving business now came to him by road, making his river site an irrelevance. An old man of the river who took a more stalwart view, appropriately enough since the name of his wharf was Dreadnought, refused to be downhearted even though he had already served on two firms that sank under him. Dreadnought used to be the biggest timber wharf in the world, but he now inclined to the view that the future would be safest for small, specialist operators, filling the gaps between the containers which couldn't carry everything. I found others who took this line. The container was not invincible, not the last word. This they had to believe.

'Pig's feet in brine, badminton rackets, cigars, helicopters,' a small man chanted vigorously, like some kind of surreal litany. Variety, it seemed, would be an advantage on a river that could still have work for small ships. At the same time there was a widespread fear of what were seen as the all-powerful and favoured road interests, of bureaucracy and red tape, of contradictory plans for the central river area. The man from Dreadnought thought the planners were in danger of falling between a number of bollards and tangling everybody in a great net of red tape. He had even been to an inquiry where they examined complaints about noise. Noise, on the dockside! It was the lack of it that was the trouble. 'How can you unload a ship without noise? Do they want a working river or don't they?'

As I was making these enquiries another stage in the creeping paralysis of the upper river was reached with talk of the closing to general cargo of the West India and Millwall docks. Straddling the top of the Isle of Dogs, these were the oldest in the London system and could claim to be the most famous. Conrad knew them well as a young seaman in the days when they were still used by the clippers, and he writes about them at length in *The Mirror of the Sea*. There would be a quarter of a mile of these great ships in a row, their gold-and-white figureheads looming over the wharfside. General cargo ports, Conrad wrote, 'belong to the aristocracy of the earth's trading places'; in that aristocracy London held the supreme place, and the West India were London's special pride. At the start of the present decade there were still forty operational berths; at the time of the closure talk these had dwindled to fourteen, and those used less than half their capacity. In the event the docks struggled on.

Small lighterage firms were still managing to make – though some preferred the word scratch – a living; and as I moved down to Gravesend the gloom lifted a little, though the outlook was still highly uncertain. The dockers, or rather the way they had been handled, came in for general criticism. None of the wharfmen wanted, or admitted they wanted, a return to the old casual labour system; but they insisted that the changes had been too sudden. The dockers had been over-liberated. They were less interested in toting barges and lifting bales than in having a nice weekend cleaning the car like the rest of the new working middle class.

'Why should a man work harder if he's not going to be paid any more than if he took it easy?' The question was rhetorical, and typical. The dockers needed a new incentive system.

There was also a new Pool of London, wharfingers plainly thought, threatening to drown them all. It consisted of a surplus labour lake that could no longer be drained off by sackings, and a number of them had already gone under through compulsory overloading.

But the dockers had their history too, and their memories. Whole flocks of lamenting gulls had been coming home to roost. If Conrad's tall ships and their companies were the aristocracy of the maritime scene, the dockers were frankly the serfs. Once they had the simplest and strongest of incentives – food for their families, which was by no means always easy to get. And no sooner had they achieved job security after generations of jungle law in the labour field than the jobs began to go, a bitter irony and a welcome end to the story for some. But not all were content to take their severance pay and disappear from the industrial scene. Some were inclined to wave battle-stained flags like that of the Amalgamated Stevedores Labour Protection League, vibrant with Union Jacks, helmeted maidens and clasped hands of brotherhood, first carried in the historic 'docker's tanner' strike of 1889 in aid of their demand for sixpence an hour and a minimal half-day working stint.

Horror-stories of the days when men massed at the dock gates for casual work have been told and retold, but few realize that the system went on into the nineteen-sixties. There was plenty of grievance in store to fuel the recent strikes, the occasional violence, the angry togetherness and the resentment of such truisms as being reminded that an industry losing out to its European rivals is not best helped by frequent stoppages in its efforts to catch up again. The dockers were convinced that the press and the media were gunning for them, the politicians were unfair to them, the public was being taught to misjudge them by, in particular, unjust productivity comparisons with European ports. They had a deplorable all-round image: they knew it and resented it bitterly.

'Let me tell you,' I heard a docker's wife insisting with great vehemence, 'dockers do *not* beat their wives.' I was not aware that anyone had said they did, but it would have done no good to mention it. This paranoid touch seemed to run right through the docklands, dead and alive. I remember one docker saying outright in a television discussion that dockers were 'hated by the community', which was evidently what he needed to believe. The lightermen also felt bitter about their foundering industry, though they tended to be more restrained. Yet containerization lost them a million tons of work a year after 1963. There are now only a few hundred of them afloat on the Thames, and the shock of so swift a decline in their ancient trade must have been deep.

So all was despair in Deptford and the surviving lanes of Wapping? Hardly that. Dockers and lightermen are also East Londoners. I was going to say Cockneys, but this is dangerous ground. I am well aware that every writer about the East End pledges himself to avoid romantic clichés and then at once commits them – forgiveably, since there is a sense in which the East Ender is himself a cliché. His strong sense of theatre makes him act out what is expected of him, an aggressive self-pity and love of old wounds. At the same time he has a talent for the absurd, for self-parody as well as the self-pity. But before I fall into the trap I warned myself about, let me admit that if there was any fun or social vitality around it was not observed by me. If East End extroversion is still an active impulse that takes to the streets I must have chosen the wrong ones to look at, or the wrong times to look at them. Was the Cockney spirit broken at last, or could it simply be that television and high-rise living have killed the street life?

Traditionally, river people combine the simplicities of the sea with an urban intelligence. The dockers in particular have had a long history of economic precariousness to sharpen their wits. Mayhew tells how men of all classes and callings would be found working or trying to work in the mid-Victorian docks – bankrupts, ex-publicans, refugees, old soldiers, 'broken-down gentlemen'. Now the process is happening in reverse. Many former dockers have gone off with their redundancy pay which their predecessors would have

regarded as riches beyond the dreams of avarice or the Irish
Sweep, while others forced out of the industry have done well
in the most unexpected jobs.

The versatility is still there. It is hard to keep rivermen
down: they bob up again in surprising new roles – clergymen,
hoteliers, managers, lecturers, painters, writers. Some have
turned student in their middle age, learning new trades at
technical college. Most ex-watermen want to stay on the river
if they can manage it, even if it has to be in reduced circumstances: former skippers, mates and tugmasters are glad to
work on ferry-boats. One docker studied in the mornings
before going to work and rose to be one of the top figures in his
chosen industry. Some feel slightly apologetic about their rise
in the world, like the docker of twenty years' standing who
appeared as a witness before the parliamentary sub-committee
on the area's redevelopment. 'I am now, for my sins,' he told
them, 'part of the middle class – I teach.'

It is a pity that none of the displaced watermen are willing
to go back to first principles and man the more primitive
upstream ferries, where one can stand for hours without
managing to get across the river. It is not that they are too
proud to use oars. One of the brightest members of Parliament,
Alan Lee Williams, himself an ex-lightermen, showed in the
1975 Greenwich Festival that he was still capable of wielding
a twenty-foot blade to good effect, helping to win the barge-
driving race for the Transport on Water organization. Their
entry covered four-and-three-quarter miles in an hour and
twenty-two minutes, a bit slower than Concorde but not
comparing too badly with the snarled-up roads and infinitely
better than the postal service. This started something –
restarted, rather. At the memorable Thames Regatta a few
weeks later a dozen of these fifty-ton barges were being
'driven' with all the old cunning. There was a shortage of the
right oars – 'paddles' or 'sweeps', to use more correct terms –
but not, as it turned out, of the men capable of using them. Not
yet.

Indeed, Alan Williams talked with enthusiasm and what

sounded like real hope about Transport on Water, a movement started by a group of surviving Thames lightermen who decided that a spot of self-help would be more useful than a flood of self-pity. They formed themselves into a working group to publicize the benefits and advantages of a trade they provocatively refused to regard as a dying one, and at once encouragement and practical help flowed in from all sides. The movement quickly spready beyond the small crew of Thames watermen who launched it, beyond the Thames itself, seeking to revitalize all the moribund waterways. All manner of industrial and professional people showed not just sympathy but the deepest interest. It was a brainwave that seized their imagination, as though water transport was what the world had been waiting for all these centuries.

The latter-day pioneers must have been feeling a shade sardonic as well as encouraged, but they pressed on. They were supplied with an office where they could feel at home, a mist-wreathed hut in the Royal Albert dock where lightermen used to meet their foremen. They apprenticed themselves to a new trade, learning to deal with the media and to handle that vital freight of our time, publicity material. Unsuspected skills emerged on their own deck. A tug-skipper made them a thirty-minute colour film showing how much better goods were on the water, and how much happier we all were in consequence, than on the clogged and reeking A13 or A2. Employers and unions jostled each other to provide money as well as moral support, and the lightermen still afloat cut in with a voluntary levy. So they, at least, were in business.

Were they rowing gallantly but hopelessly against the tide? One would have thought sanity very much on their side with the growing chaos on the roads, and we had heard often enough of official support for an integrated transport policy which must, if it meant anything at all, include water. But then I was reminded of one of the deadlier oddities of our political life and public attitudes. So often do we seem devoted in principle, and with repeated assurances, to causes we have no intention whatever of allowing to succeed in practice.

And the commercial revival of our canals and rivers is a promise I seem to have lived with all my life. I remember hearing it uttered from the highest quarters in my early days as a journalist, when I was far too naïve to recognize it for what it was – an incantation rather than a declaration of intent. Such was my innocent acceptance of these assurances that I remember wondering if they were not, perhaps, going a little too far in this devotion to our rivers and canals. Had they forgotten that we still had railways and roads? There was no need to worry, of course. Absolutely nothing was done to help water transport, and we were on the brink of the biggest surge of road freight development in history.

I have noticed no change since then, unless it is a lower-tone lip service to the liturgy about a co-ordinated transport system, and a franker acceptance of market compulsions at the crudest and most shortsighted levels. The continuing decline of the working Thames must be particularly galling to watermen who know that the busier they were the better it would be for us all, which is not a boast everyone can make. The more freight on the river, the less burden on the dolorous roads. And why not passengers? Various attempts have been made, though without much sustained effort or certainly much success, to popularize river-bus services. Regular commuting settled down finally to a hard corps of loyalists using a hydro-foil service which gets from Greenwich to the Tower in ten minutes and to Westminster in fifteen, marginally quicker than the trains and much quicker than the roads, as well as safer, more comfortable and infinitely more agreeable.

Yet the planners, when they have looked at the river at all, have done so almost exclusively in terms of visual amenity and a little mild pleasure-boating. Heaven knows that more human access and enjoyment are long enough overdue. What could be disastrous is the assumption that the river's working days are over in these higher reaches, and that the best that can be found for it in the way of serious occupation is some hotel-and-trade-mart activity combined with a little office work and warehousing – all of which greatly increase the transport pressures. Meaning, inevitably, road transport.

Roads for work, water for fun – that is the assumed way of it. So exceptional has it become for industry to start up on the river, and use river transport, that when a telephone cable company recently took a range of premises on the Greenwich waterfront the local authorities were surprised and, naturally, more than pleased. But when the company actually proceeded to move its products direct from the factory by river, they almost fell into the water in their astonishment and delight. It is hard to see why this should be so unusual.

Perhaps it is partly the official assumptions that make it so, since neither passenger tickets nor factory space are likely to be sold very successfully by people who have such small expectation of doing business. In 1975 the Docklands Joint Committee looking into the future of London's inner riverside brought out a series of pamphlets as a basis for public discussion, and the one on transport could not have had a more eloquent title: *The Dockland's Spine – Tube, Bus or Train?* The possibility of river-based transport was not discussed, even though the planners were prepared to be audaciously backward-looking enough to consider bringing back the tram. Why not river-steamers, then? As to that, I noticed that even the dynamic and aggressively contemporary Peter Walker talked about the need to 'go full steam ahead with creating a new East End of London'.

Steam or no steam, not all will accept that the commercial river is dead or dying in these upper reaches. There are those who, whistling bravely into the future, predict that both fares and freight will be back, and in quantity. The state of the roads alone would ensure it, some say. The new lighterage techniques, according to Alan Williams, could not only bring traffic back but return London to the top European league. I challenged him to back his optimism – to peer into the foggy crystal ball and say what he saw at the end of the century. His prediction was that the River Thames could be throbbing with activity, thus hopefully contradicting Dibdin's verse which would otherwise bring a sad end to the chapter:

> Then farewell my trim-built wherry,
> Oars and coat and badge farewell . . . !

14. Fighting Country

THAMES BARRIER TO TILBURY PORT

Lord's Day. After dinner I by water to Woolwich
to see the batterys newly raised
SAMUEL PEPYS, *Diary*, June 1667

I was moving into embattled country. There has never been much peace east of Woolwich; they always seem to have been holding off one invader or another. In Pepys's day – somewhat belatedly, in the correct British style – they were raising batteries against one enemy, and now they are raising a barrier against another. And wherever I went below the flood barrier I found them busy raising The Wall.

Not a Berlin Wall: not to keep people from people, but to keep water from people. All the same, there could conceivably be an unpleasant situation of East versus West London if the riverside territory came to be divided too crudely into Above and Below Barrier. Large stretches of the metropolis, as I have seen, are dangerously threatened by floods. Upstream from Woolwich the barrier will give protection after 1979, or whenever they manage to get it finished. What about downstream? The barrier does nothing for that sector. The ever-sinking land would still, and increasingly, be at the mercy of the ever-rising tides. I doubt if it would be enough for inundated Thamesmead to know that its sister estate at Deptford was high and dry, or for the Dagenham waders and the dyke-watchers of Canvey Island to be able to reassure themselves that the Georgian terrace-dwellers of Hammersmith were safe and that members of Parliament were not going to be swept off their feet in mid-debate.

The lower estuary needs security too – hence the Wall. Everywhere below the barrier-to-be they were lifting the old river defences well above the flood level of 1953, the year of the last major invasion. The estuary-dwellers have always lived dangerously, and their history has been one of improvised defences against enemies that were constantly changing – Danes, Spaniards, French, Dutch – but basically settling into two categories, men and floods; ammunition stores, oil and chemical installations, though presumably on our side, have added more modern hazards. The Dutch have played a particularly intimate part in the river's life, both as attackers and defenders. Sometimes they were busy knocking down the walls, sometimes (as on Canvey) their skill as dyke specialists made us hire them as rebuilders. The Dutch seem to have been better on the whole at keeping out the water than we were at keeping out the Dutch.

For a vivid picture of the scares, shocks and desperate remedies of his day there is no better reading than Samuel Pepys, diarist and secretary to the Navy under Charles II. He was immersed in foggy and dangerous events that must make any modern reader feel at home, and but for those diaries we should know far less than we do about their impact. As a gifted amateur among top professionals, as a producer of enlightening indiscretions, Pepys is in a sense the Richard Crossman of his time. We have no monopoly of crisis. Plague, fire, seamen roving the streets demanding their pay, the Dutch sailing boldly into the lion's jaws which seemed to have dropped open in sheer astonishment – it was one thing after another, or even on top of another. The navy's way of dealing with the Thames invaders carried improvisation to near-demented lengths. One idea was to hold up the enemy by sinking some of our own ships at Barking Creek and elsewhere, a defence strategy that looked all the odder when it was discovered that valuable and much-needed stores had gone down with the ships.

In case there was any danger that these might be regarded as in the nature of panic measures, a steadying example was set at the top. The king – in playful mood even for him – organized a moth hunt with the Duchess of Monmouth, and Pepys himself took a little time off to visit his tailor and kiss a few shop-keepers' wives, which was his way of maintaining the stiff upper lip. All the same, there was a public outcry – more vehement than we tend to get when things go badly wrong nowadays – and the honest Pepys confesses how sad it was 'to see so many good ships there sunk in the River, while we would be thought to be masters of the sea'.

This official bungling – why, after all, should we regard the administrative or military cock-up as a prerogative of our own time? – surprises me less than the public protest. After all, kicking up a fuss about the mismanagement of these high matters was a more dangerous sport in Pepys's day than in ours, or so the historians have always led us to believe. There were stocks and pillories and whipping-posts, with spikes still available on London Bridge for the heads of the more distinguished malcontents. Yet people seem to have grumbled quite openly to this Establishment figure, who could plainly have caused severe trouble for them. Perhaps they sensed that he was sympathetic.

Or can it be that we take too much for granted about the past – and about the present, too? Collecting material for this book I grew more and more astonished, and also ashamed, to discover how little I knew about London. For a Londoner, I had always prided myself on knowing my town rather well. It took no time at all to establish how wrong that idea was.

Take Barking – four miles, perhaps, from where I live. I had never seen the place before. Admittedly it has no obvious appeal. It is not a place people choose to go to on their days off. Indeed, it may have developed a kind of anti-image, since the creek where those ships went down is more famous these days for other sunken matter. This stretch of the river at Barking is one of the world's great sewage depositories: not unloaded into the river in its natural state, as it was in the age of Victoria and cholera, but elaborately treated with the sludge carried out to sea. The parish church has a memorial to the Fishermen of Barking, who can hardly have enjoyed much of a local catch of late years. All the same, this is an exciting spot, with one of the finest churches in London and some prestigious abbey remains. An entire gateway to the abbey survives, the splendid Curfew Tower housing the Chapel of the Holy Rood Loft atte Gate. Miracles were said to grow here like mushrooms.

Perhaps the biggest miracle of all to modern eyes was the power and status of the women who ruled Barking. Equality? The abbesses of Barking would have laughed at the word, if indeed they had ever heard of it. No Barking male would have presumed to cross words with the dominating lady who ruled this distinguished hive, held a seat in the chief councils of state, lived in considerable style, educated the daughters of important people in an abbey annexe that served as the Roedean of the day, and was deferentially addressed by the king as Our Lady of Barking. Her lands stretched to Dagenham, and must have been a considerable worry to her since they were often under water.

Dagenham has another ruler now, and another god. What was it like, before modern times and the A13 led it into the era labelled by Aldous Huxley as that of 'Our Ford'. My Victorian guidebook describes it as a village, 'surrounded on all sides by cornfields and market gardens.' I was even more surprised to find that the village survives. Hidden away behind the flaming temple to the Golden Car – so hideous by day, so riveting by night with its interminable complex of broken shapes and lights – was the authentic old village of Dagenham, small but shapely. They could almost get it on a postcard, and a pretty one it would be, though uncertain of its function. I found a church, some old cottages with a hole punched in the roof as though by a petulant giant, a black-and-white inn scrawled with vague and half-hearted graffiti. There was an air of wetness about the whole place, factory and suburb and village alike, a sense of desolation under vast Judgement-Day skies. No wonder a local legend held that here was the site of the original Deluge.

I tried to picture the awe and terror of the Barking nuns at each new inundation. Or were they splendidly calm, with Roedean standards established already? The river struck often and hard. A famous fourteenth-century flood brought the abbess a royal subsidy to help her reclaim her drowned lands. Another in the early eighteenth century swept away four hundred feet of river wall and left a permanent lake, called Dagenham Breach, which they have never mopped up to this day. As things turned out success in that direction might not have been welcomed, since the lake acquired rural attractions, a good stock of fish and a lakeside villa, 'Breach House'. The official inspection of the wall which began in an atmosphere of natural alarm mellowed, as the years rolled by, into an annual ministerial fish dinner the Premier himself sometimes attended. A good idea, if you must have a deluge, not merely to survive it but turn it to advantage.

Purfleet, a few miles round the bend, ought by rights to be the most neurotic place in Britain. The story of how it got its name ('Oh, my poor fleet!' Elizabeth is supposed to have said after reviewing some of her anti-Armada ships) shares pride of place with the Cuckold's Point legend among my favourite Tall Tales of the Thames. Later farceurs have suggested that what Her Majesty really said, after a heavy ceremonial day on the rough roads of the time, was: 'Oh, my poor feet!' However that may be, any visitor's compassion is surely due to the place itself for having been made to sit for so long on the most awesome kind of manmade volcano. For centuries it was the home of the Government Powder Magazine, and the huge oil installations of our own day can hardly be good for its nerves. It struck me as the strangest place, victim of a split personality. The mixture of ancient Essex village and modern industrial concentrate – oil and mead, meal and gunpowder – is reflected in the building styles, with no attempt at reconciling or disguising the sleepy past and the explosive present. How could they, anyway? Better not to try. If we persist in building a schizoid society it might as well look that way.

On the other side of the river is Greenhithe, which looks on the surface, or just under the surface, as desirable a place to live in, for anyone who likes a quiet life on the waterfront, as could be found in a long day's drive or sail. Yet it is one of the spookiest spots along the whole estuary, white as a sheet or an old-fashioned ghost. It has kept much of the shape and – except in one crucial respect – the atmosphere of an eighteenth-century fishing village which merged into a modest Victorian resort; indeed, my Victorian guide describes Greenhithe as being in modest demand as a summer holiday retreat.

At first I saw no reason why that agreeable label should not still apply. There it stretched, singularly little changed, with its old wharves and lighterages, its jetties and its seaweed, discreet waves washing up the beach like a well-behaved sea, promenade walk kept agreeably simple, spacious views, everything one could wish. Why, then, should the comely High Street look so derelict, the place so unfrequented, 'Ye Village Club' (as it quaintly called itself) so emphatically closed? Why were there no signs of life around those attractive little period houses, with their corbels and rough carvings? I took a deep breath and found the answer. What pricked my nostrils was not ozone but cement dust. I saw why people turn pale when they visit Greenhithe.

In contrast, Tilbury Fort looked marvellously relaxed, and small wonder. This is really the place to come to for a little peace, and always was. Built to protect places like Purfleet and Greenhithe and the dockyards, not to mention London, Tilbury ends up after centuries of inactive service being itself protected by the Ministry of Public Building and Works. Here is that ideal defence work, a fort that never fought.

The structure as we see it now, so handsome and well-preserved, was provided to keep out the Dutch. But since the Dutch had already been, there was really nothing for it to do. And it has gone on doing it ever since. Though only a stroll from the ferry and less than a hoot from the docks, I found it was still being left in peace. The man who gave me my ticket looked a little startled at the intrusion, but showed me the ex-chapel, the old guardhouse with its lock-up, the rows of barracks, the cannon and water-pumps gleaming unnaturally as though worked on each night by spectral defaulters. The solitude did not prevent – perhaps it helped – the strong feeling of being surrounded by presences, of a garrison that was still there and had only just gone off parade.

There were casualties once, they say – two deaths in a brawl following a late-eighteenth-century cricket match. After that the fort was able to revert to its proper business – the peaceful contemplation of the arts of defence, problems (to borrow from its baroque vocabulary) of machicolation, ashlar and culverin, caponier and redan, ravelin, enceinte and terre-plein. And no doubt the garrison swiftly got back to its favourite task of working out co-ordinated lines of fire with Gravesend Fort across the river, a pattern as elaborate and abstract as serial music.

I stayed here for hours, among the cannon-balls and the mysteriously polished pump-handles: why not weeks or years, why not a lifetime? Perhaps every Secretary for Defence ought to go into retreat at Tilbury now and again. If the aim of a defence deterrent is never to be used, here is the classic model. Some, all the same, doubt whether its teeth were ever more than dentures and think it just as well that the fort was never tested in battle, since the builders apparently overlooked an essential part of the scheme, the water bastion. (There is still no water bastion, I suppose it is now safe to tell the Dutch.) But they did remember to make dramatic arrangements for the flooding of acres of flat fields on the landward side by the opening of sluices, to prevent the fort from being surrounded. That, I was assured, can still be done. And Defoe in his day was much impressed, judging from his observations that 'they must be bold Fellows who will venture in the biggest Ships to pass such a Battery, if the Men appointed to serve the Guns do their duty as becomes them.'

Water bastion or no water bastion, those who ventured to approach the fort by river would have a fine view of the Water Gate, one of our most elaborate examples of baroque military architecture. They still do. The river here offers spacious prospects of both banks, with enough distance to make one start instinctively saying 'shores', and there is no better way of enjoying them than from the ferry. Tilbury Ferry has been shuttling across the river for longer than history records. Still more than the one at Woolwich this ferry projects a powerful air of occasion, almost of adventure. I felt I was crossing between continents this time. Pulleys creaked, ramps clanked, old ladies huddled against the rails as though they were saying goodbye to their native land. Some aura from the pre-flying age, when many ferrying their way across to the ocean liners were doing just that, still mingled with the river mist; but the great hotel and pier that so often used to see them off to India were real enough.

This is no free ferry. The charge, with the notice displayed in various languages including Russian, had doubled within months, yet there was an air of crisis on board. The ferry was coming under heavy gunfire, from our own side at that, and there was even talk of closing it. The service was not paying its way, and those who were subsidizing it were evidently being told that they must not devote public funds to such frivolities as encouraging people to travel without cars. Most of the ferry passengers were Tilbury dockworkers, and what was to prevent them from joining the twentieth century and fuming their way with the rest of the motorized procession through the Dartford Tunnel, not so many miles away? In the face of such insanity it seemed to me that Tilbury Fort could do worse than come out of its retirement even at this late stage, and go down fighting for the Tilbury Ferry.

Gravesend was looking marvellous from the river, in spite of the chilly things that have been said and written about it. That is by far the best way to see it, and some say you should never make the mistake of landing. Here is another town sorely needing a restoration of self-confidence. Easy to see what a fascinating place it must have been, full of that individual though introverted Kentish quality still showing in patches through the industrial and suburban spread. Without a little encouragement it may never find the spirit to save what is left of value, which is plenty. This is the best of the estuary towns and should look after itself accordingly. Its losses have already been devastating. By orthodox conservationist standards, in terms of listed buildings and distinguished surviving streets, it may not be much worth bothering about any more. But, taken as a whole, it is well worth bothering about. And never, by the look of things, has the place been more gravely threatened.

The shape and aspect are irreplaceable. It hugs the Thames like a favourite daughter, though in fact it is a grievously neglected one. And nobody can forget that this was the first

English townscape that met the eyes of countless generations
of sailors, home again after months or years at sea. Once
ashore I found the atmosphere far from relaxed. There was
a slight air of siege. I was told of a limitation on building heights
to avoid masking the field of fire from the fort: could they still
be expecting those Dutch?

There were signs of trouble nearer home. BOYS RULE, a
wall message proclaimed. I saw a group of diminutive figures
with cold elderly eyes lighting cigarettes from each other's
ends; and thought how strange it would have been if any of
them happened to be descendants of the ones to whom General
Gordon devoted himself during his six years in Gravesend
supervising the river defences. The general spent his spare
time doing all he could for the poor boys of the town – feeding
them, clothing them, finding them work, entertaining them
at his home.

His influence had clearly faded over the years. OUT OF
ORDER DUE TO VANDALISM, closed public conveniences
were labelled. There could be trouble on the water too. At
the Thames Navigation Centre brisk young officers of the Port
of London Authority were looking for it, scanning the river on
radar screens. These are men of few words; they talk only to
ships. And even with the uncrowded river and the supposedly
sophisticated navigation techniques of today, trouble is always
nearer than you think. Ships still collide, run aground, ram
jetties, sink, even though not deliberately, as in Pepys's day.
They were still talking of the wreck of an ammunition ship,
the *Richard Montgomery*, lying off Sheerness. It seemed the
only way of raising it was verbally, in Parliament; and the
government report was that after the last diving survey it had
been decided that the best and safest course was to leave
the wreck and her cargo undisturbed. Another ship which hit
an oil jetty literally set the Thames on fire, according to the
MP representing South-East Essex, who expressed his fear
to the Commons that as the tankers get heavier their standards
of navigation do not improve.

Sailing people in these parts have a healthy respect for the dangers, both old and new. This is emphatically the professional end of the river, navigational manners are by no means always what they were, and as ships get bigger and faster it is all the more necessary to remember a fact so elementary that it is usually the first to be forgotten – fast ships, like fast cars, can't stop suddenly even if they want to. Old sailing hands warn the novices that the speed of the big ships to be met with in these reaches is highly deceptive. Take their eye off the river for a minute or two, get their sails between themselves and the traffic however briefly, and they may suddenly find a monster bearing down on them. Small wonder that every prudent sailing person has a spouse or a friend to act as personal radar.

They were insisting at the Gravesend Sailing Club how democratic the sport is getting, and the substantial part they have themselves played in breaking down the glacial snobbishness that prevailed not so long ago in yachting circles. Here they claim to have pioneered a new breezy democracy of the river right from the time they launched their club in 1894, and boast a thoroughly mixed membership with working and professional classes all shipmates together. And in case that sounds like the kind of bemused modern society where a man scarcely knows whether he is on the boardroom bridge or the factory deck, I hasten to add that I found the place extremely relaxed and friendly. Also highly conservative, as all sailing communities are. Their agreeably casual clubhouse had changed very little in close on a century. They sat around in their original chairs, and kept their records in the original limp notebooks, neat as a city firm's accounts or a ship's log.

Outside, the flotsam and litter piled itself between the old green-whiskered groynes, with seaweed on the pebbled beach and a tang of distant places on the wind. Indian children – or children of Indian origin, though no doubt Gravesenders now – drifted about the steep streets leading down to the Elephant's Head; and in the churchyard they remembered Pocahontas, an Indian princess. The story of how she came to be buried here is so romantic that I found myself straining every nerve, however unsuccessfully, to believe it true. At grave risk to her life (so the tale goes) she saved an early Virginian settler, the bold Captain John Smith, from her father's braves and – inevitably in such a story – fell in love with him. But she also fell into the hands of the wicked Deputy Governor of Virginia, and married another on being told that the man she loved was dead. Sailing to England with her husband she was received with due honour at King James's court, only to die of a broken heart on discovering that her lover was alive all the time. Poor Pocahontas: the story seems made for a Longfellow epic or a folksy lament to guitar accompaniment. As I watched them unveiling a statue to the sad princess some years ago, her face turned blindly into the rain – which was drenching the wide-brimmed hats of distinguished guests from the American South and bouncing like arrows off Lord Hailsham's bowler – it seemed to me far more likely that she had caught her death at Gravesend.

Leaving the town, dutifully ducking the head to avoid embarrassing the lines of fire from the fort, I went in search of what might be left of the defences further downstream. As late as 1860 there was another scare, and the fear of the French was evidently taken more seriously than the actual presence of the Dutch two centuries earlier. A chance at last for Tilbury? Not seriously. By that time the lower forts had virtually superseded Tilbury and Gravesend as London's front line; it was then that General Gordon, spurred on by the National Defence Committee, began reinforcing them as a matter of high priority. Again, as it turned out, no actual enemy attacked them; yet in marked contrast to Tilbury Fort they look more shattered than if they had been the victims of a destructive war. Coalhouse Fort near East Tilbury is already a kind of instant ruin, a stricken Victorian castle, though the massive walls are still intact.

DANGER – KEEP OUT. The warning is to friends, not enemies.

15. Skylarks Over the Sewers

RIVER WILD LIFE

Type of the wise, who soar, but never roam –
True to the kindred points of Heaven and Home.
WORDSWORTH, 'To the Skylark'

Strange, come to think of it, that Wordsworth's 'ethereal minstrel, pilgrim of the sky' should have chosen, for the Home terminal of his perpendicular commuting, a patch of sour waste land near Beckton. At least, the one I was tuned in to did. With all those thousands of square miles available, a far greater area of choice than most homemakers enjoy, why

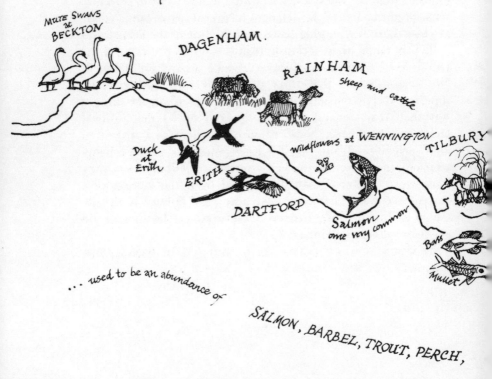

select one of Europe's biggest concentrates of gas and sewage?

The fact is, of course, most plants and creatures are decidedly short on aesthetic taste, but strong on vitality and initiative. What is remarkable is not that certain species seem on their way out, as has been understandably lamented in Parliament and across the country, but that so many should be surviving and even increasing, as air and water grow cleaner and the mysterious processes of adaptation get weaving in what sometimes looks an uncannily speedy way.

People are astonished when they see the unlikely places birds, animals and flowers show up in. For myself, living as I do scarcely more than an owl-hoot from central London, and having fed visiting hedgehogs with saucers of milk and heard foxes bark in the lane at the back of my house, I am less inclined to astonishment at the news that the disused Surrey

Docks turned themselves into a kind of wild Kew Gardens or that Red Admirals, not inappropriately, have been seen drifting around the Wapping waterfront. Birdwatchers have spotted great crested grebes in gravel pits at Richmond and king-fishers at St Katharine's Dock in the shadow of the Tower, wild asparagus lifts its ragged head in the neighbourhood of Gravesend, rabbits burrow and breed in the spoilheaps of the industrial waste land, without causing me any particular surprise.

All the same, one can hardly deny that Nature often sets itself deplorably low environmental standards. Given the slightest opportunity, it seems to enjoy taking over the most dispiriting dumps and derelict sites. I remember at the end – though it seemed it would be endless – of one of the recent long, hot summers seeing a man bent intently over a corner of the least inviting of all the riverside spots near Woolwich. What could he be doing? Defusing explosives? Laying them, maybe? Looking for metal or plastic junk to flog? Nothing of the sort. He was blackberrying.

So why not skylarks over Beckton? There are goldfinches too, they say. 'Leave to the nightingale her shady wood,' Wordsworth chanted on, but even nightingales show up in some strange places these days. Could it be more than just chance and indifference? Could there be a positive attraction for the sleazy life among some birds – a species of *nostalgie de la boue*, or worse than *boue*? Glamour and horror are never far apart along some stretches of the Thames. I remember finding my way down River Road, by the side of Barking Creek; you could be a hundred miles inland for all the sight or sound or sense of the river through those uncompromising cliffs of brick. But it is only necessary to find the right hole in the wall. Go along the path between the main sewage outfall works and the Barking Power Station, past a bank whereon the rosebay willow-herb if not the wild thyme blows, past great drifts of convolvulus – and suddenly, topping a shallow rise, the wind hits you across a major bend in the river. It struck me as one of the great Thames conjuring tricks, with which I was getting familiar. All was not merely revealed but vastly magnified. It was as though the river had become the sea long before its time, and an armada of swans was massing round Beckton Pier at the mouth of the creek. I had never seen so many swans.

Swans are as prominent in the Thames scene as ever they were – more than ever, some would say, and a new carping note tends to be heard when they are mentioned. This could be no more than one of those over-compensatory fashions to which the British are so absurdly prone. They like, from time to time, to knock their darlings. Recently it was dogs. After centuries of dog-worship at a pitch that struck the rest of the world as downright morbid, and bad for all concerned including the dogs, we suddenly and unreasonably turned against them and passed draconian laws to prevent their performing natural functions in public, on the grounds that this was a menace to health as well as decency. Before the poor beast knew what had kicked it, let alone why, the dog was out.

Now it is swans. Not that one can imagine them defecating in public, or even in private for that matter; though their critics insist that they foul precious pasture land. Anyway, it is their turn for disfavour, and anything that can reasonably be held against them – or unreasonably for that matter – will certainly be heard of. They have been pampered birds, specially favoured and protected in the highest quarters, throughout their seven centuries of Thames voyaging. Proud birds too, obviously never able to forget that it was one of our most famous kings, Richard the First, who introduced them to this country.

But now there are signs that they may have to face a colder climate. Perhaps the complexities of the ancient 'swan-upping' routine – marking the birds by cutting their upper mandibles to show which belong to the crown and which to the Dyers and the Vintners, ancient city companies which share the privilege of ownership – have irritated the public at long last, though I can't imagine why the poor birds should be blamed. I should hate to have my mandibles nicked, and possibly this contributes to their well-known surliness. Even so, it is only the swans that belong to the Vintners and Dyers that have their beaks nicked; royal swans are left unmarked. A swan census is also involved in the annual ceremony, and I suppose this fulfils a useful function in keeping track of the numbers.

The markedly less romantic attitude now generally adopted towards these birds may of course have something to do with their unrivalled place in the world of myth and legend, which the current impulse is to deflate. It is not all that much of a testimonial these days to have been Apollo's or Orpheus's bird, or to have an unverified reputation for breaking into song at the point of death. The mood of the time is severely practical, and the citizen is liable to develop a prejudice against creatures he is not allowed to shoot and wouldn't want to eat even if he were. Roast cygnet is long off the national menu, except on highly ritualized occasions in city halls. And the ritual is yet another irritation to our modern debunking urges.

These have gone so far that complaints about the behaviour of the hitherto sacrosanct swans have even been addressed to the Lord Chamberlain, the Royal Swanherd and the Editor of *The Times*. Scientific farmers and other disenchanted correspondents have alleged that they damage river walls, trample pasture, destroy fish spawn and bully all the smaller birds they meet. One expert went so far as to call them 'parasitic pests', at which a thunderbolt on special delivery from Apollo might have been expected to strike the university field station of the Department of Agricultural Science at Oxford, from where this heresy came. What did emerge, under the letterhead of the Athenaeum if not of Olympus, was a dire warning to scientific farmers, swan-knockers and all others it might concern. Due notice was given that there are times of the year when souls of the dead are liable to enter swans, and any attack on them at such seasons can result in dreadful visitations of fire, flood, plague and wine famine at the ancient universities.

Meanwhile the swans, which have never been accustomed to

mix with research agriculturalists any more than they have learned the bourgeois habit of reading *The Times*, sailed on regardless in their customary arrogant and ill-tempered way. They are used to deference and flattery, and to the company of gods, kings and important poets. Though royal birds, they can hardly be expected to have learned the need to adopt democratic attitudes like modern royalty. They are overbearing, useless, beautiful. They are quite indispensable to the river scene.

Perhaps they will have to learn to be more human, all the same, if they are to survive. I have only ever heard of one swan that could be called human. I was visiting a relative, wandering round the rectory garden upstream at Remenham, near Henley, when I came upon a grave and a memorial. It had been placed there by some child, or some child's parent, many mourning years ago and it said:

IN LOVING MEMORY
Died April 26
1956
CLAUDINE
A SWAN

More earthly cries, though only slightly more, are to be heard on the marshlands which start sooner than most Thames explorers think. The inner marshes, like Rainham and Wennington on the north bank, provide a surprising advance taste of the wild in the midst of heavy industrial development – a rehearsal for those great, lonely, wind-buffetted walks farther down the estuary. Rainham village is an unexpected survival, a kind of lucky break; it cowers behind a wilderness of pylons and storage tanks, a near miss from the all-devouring Essex arterial road. It has an identifiable village centre and sheep safely graze off Ferry Lane, which leads past the inevitable sewage works to Frog Island.

There is tradition in this rural-excremental mix. The area used to live by exporting vegetables to central London in barges, which would return laden with coal and manure.

Coming to the river wall here at high tide gave a sense I had not experienced before of the enormous pressure of water, looking ominously higher than the level of the land, and of the ceaseless cat-and-mouse game the river plays. The wall looked massive here, and needed to be. Boys were perched on it, fishing actively, seeming to catch an excitement from the flow of the tide. Marsh looked across to marsh, with Belvedere and Erith over on the Kent side, slightly inimical like a suspicious neighbouring state.

A long walk led south-eastward. The landward side was a sea of mallow, ragwort, purple vetch, with billowing sails of bindweed draping the rusted rigging of industrial wreck, plantain and thistle craning giant heads through broken windows. Cultivated plants like marguerite and hollyhock and golden rod had also seeded themselves in this factory cemetery, while on the other side was implacable life – the sound of the incoming tide and the flotsam, the endless knocking on the wall. Dead workshops, derelict barges, deathless river. FRAGILE ROOF, a notice warned. USE DUCK LADDERS OR CRAWLING BOARDS. Round a bend in the river the marshes suddenly opened out, the mosses and sedges (botanist's and bird-watcher's country) began, a ship or two came to life on the higher level of the water.

Cattle roamed the Wennington Marshes. Spruce old cottages, keeping their heads above water by an elaborate-looking system of dykes and drains, offered fresh eggs and lettuces. There was a hint of deep country, as in a Victorian photograph, but with modern traffic-signs instead of finger-posts beckoning towards places with names like One Tree Hill and Hangman's Wood. Then, again with overwhelming suddenness, I found myself plunged into the territory of detergents and margarine factories and the cement-land of Grays Thurrock. Here the dust flies so free that they say a stranger's hair, when times are really prosperous, can turn white overnight.

But times had not been so prosperous; and it was instructive, gritty with the whitest of white irony, to watch the local reaction to the closing of an important factory which was all the talk of the area. Bad pollution would be eased, but this was not considered a good exchange for lost jobs, at least by the older people. They had learned to live with it, even quietly to glory in it; cement dust had become, if not their oxygen, at least a vital additive to it. Even those who accepted that the pollution was beyond anything human beings ought to endure were not going to admit that this was a good way to stop it.

And there was an epitome of the total Thamesside experience, perhaps of the total experience of modern industrial society. Nobody wants to be made healthier and happier by force or failure. Still, the river and the air have grown cleaner whether we like it or not, and since there seems to be little we can do about it we had better settle for liking it. And even if their standards differ from those of the GLC and the joint planning board, it has to be assumed that the fish like it and the birds like it.

Nobody, or so they claim, likes it more than the river authorities. It is hard not to be impressed by the official boasts about the way the Thames is shedding its pollution, and the way Nature is coming into its own again, though some have suspected a certain exaggeration, or at least over-optimism, about the speed at which this is happening. A few of the New Era fishing stories have stretched credulity to breaking point. One day in 1975 a noise was heard on the central London river, an indescribable sound that might be roughly called a highly amplified bubble-and-shriek, which every true fisherman knew could only be one thing – the bellow of the hump-backed whale. This surely was going too far. It turned out that an expedition launched by Friends of the Earth was making whale noises from a barge to publicize the need for protecting this threatened species, so nobody could complain in the end. Our consciences may have been clearer than in the days when dead whales drifted by the ton into the Greenland Dock, but still not entirely clear since sperm whale oil – or so the campaigners claimed – was still being imported for softening leather. This they wanted stopped.

It must have been a long time since the last whale was sighted or even heard in the Thames; though it is true that watermen, drunk or sober, have reported shoals of porpoises off Canvey and even farther upstream near Gravesend. Some recent salmon stories need to be taken with more than a grain of tidal salt; and my bet would be that the hundred-pound prize offered by a member of Parliament to the first of his colleagues who manages to catch a salmon from the terrace of the Commons will no longer look a particularly handsome prize by the time it is claimed. Yet the Thames used to teem with salmon. Apprentice watermen would complain, or so it is said, of the monotonous regularity with which it appeared at their table, which sounds to us as if kitchen-boys at the Savoy were to grumble about a surfeit of caviare and oysters. By the end of last century there was not – fishermen's stories apart – a salmon left in the river.

Time was when most of London's entire fish consumption came out of the Thames. As well as salmon there was an abundance of barbel, trout, perch, smelt, bream, roach, dace, gudgeon, shrimps and eels, not to mention those famous shoals of whitebait so fancied by Victorian cabinet ministers. As late as 1798, according to evidence produced before a parliamentary commission, four hundred fishermen lived comfortably on their professional catch between Deptford and London Bridge. Thousands of Thames salmon came home to Billingsgate in the season and some boats, crewing a man and a boy, would earn as much as six pounds a week – good money then. By 1828, when this evidence was given, their livelihood was virtually gone. Already the river was polluting steadily, from sewer discharge and the growth of gasworks. Eels and eel-lovers were luckier than most, particularly if they happened to live in the region of the waterside breweries where the waste made excellent eel-food and bait. But it was even getting hard to keep the eels alive.

By that time it must have seemed extraordinary to think that fish were once so plentiful that a man could sit on one of the wide pier-bases of Old London Bridge and pull them out by hand. King James the First is said to have collected cormorants from the coast and trained them to fish in the Chinese fashion, appointing a Master of the Cormorants to organize it all. Henry the Eighth kept a polar bear at the Tower which swam around on fishing forays, held by collar and chain. I hope it was allowed to eat what it caught. There was enough, certainly, for man and beast. For centuries the London Thames must have been like one of those restaurant fish tanks from which the customer chooses his meal. Later, as we have seen, it became more like a refuse bin.

Well, now they are coming back. Lookout-men have been making exciting signals from the most unlikely places about fish and birds ready to resume the joys of hook and net, bullet and snare. They tell of haddock sighted at Barking, sprats and herring near the Dartford Tunnel, coots and moorhens visiting at the most improbable wharves, a mallard seen near Woolwich Reach, a glossy ibis off Swanscombe Point, the re-emergence of birds with shy names like widgeon, pintail, shelduck, pochard, goosander and tufted duck. Sometimes enthusiasm overreaches itself; as when a gannet, posed with a fish in its beak among some reeds and gazing sedately across the water towards a passing container ship, was caught by an official photographer and proudly exhibited as the cover-feature of a Port of London booklet. The bird, it was admitted later, was stuffed.

There were more red faces over the case of the eight-pound salmon – eight pounds four-and-a-half ounces to be exact, according to the newspapers – taken off the screens at the West Thurrock electricity works. This might not be much of a catch compared with the fifty-one-pounder which, according to the *London Chronicle*, was taken out of the river on a May day in 1766. Also the fish was dead, though it was quickly certified as only recently so. Seldom can an inquest have been conducted with such unseemly enthusiasm. One swallow may not make a summer but one salmon could. Salmon men saw it as a massive – or anyway an eight-pound – emblem of hope, the biggest promise for the fishy future they had yet had. The

chief scientific officer of the Thames Water Authority, a Mr
Fish, called it 'a vindication of our policies'. He was already
looking far upstream, to the need for building salmon leaps
to help the homecomers to their spawning grounds.

Unfortunately all this euphoria was somewhat damped when
a man named Yallop, who ran a garage at Tilbury, revealed that
he possessed a fish of exactly that size and description which
he had caught in Ireland. At least, he used to possess it but
had thrown it into the river, not much fancying the look of it
when it came out of the deep freeze. However, there were still
expert rivermen who held to the belief that Mr Yallop's
salmon and the power station salmon were two different
creatures. And the water authority have been backing their
faith by stocking the river with thousands of young fish –
hoping for a happier outcome than the last time this was done,
back in the year 1908, when they were never seen again.

Dead or alive, Irish or homecoming English, it is hard to
get away from salmon as it is from swans. They even swim quite
deeply into politics. I have heard long debates about them
in the House of Lords, where members enjoy a special
relationship with the species, evidently regarding them as the
hereditary peers of the fish world. Their lordships have a better
understanding than most of us of the complex vocabulary of the
salmon, but even they get baffled at times. When is a salmon
not a salmon? Answer – when it is a parr, smolt or kelt; and
even then it is really a salmon all the time. Or is it? I remember
one peer calling a smolt a yearling salmon and being contra-
dicted by another, in the infinitely courteous way their lordships go about these things. With all the deference in the
world, his colleague ventured to suggest that the word his
noble friend was seeking was not smolt but kelt.

'No, it is smolt,' the first peer retorted, rather sharply
by their standards. Doubtless he was right, though no sane
layman would dare to intervene in such a contest, beyond
consulting the dictionary. This clouds the whole issue by
defining a kelt as a 'salmon, sea-trout or herling after spawning', and a smolt as 'a young salmon in the stage intermediate

between the parr and the grilse'. These complexities, which may after all be no worse than those of barons, viscounts, marquesses, hereditary peers and lifers, caused the House little distress. They were delighted that the Thames was being cleaned up and made fit for fishermen to fish in, a campaign that for them assumed a moral aspect at least as strong as that attaching to the cleanliness of the streets, the theatres and the bookshops.

A magnificent achievement, they called the progress that had been made so far, and encouraged Mr Fish to do all he could in the way of providing ladders and any other necessary assistance to help the salmon get up to Oxford. They too looked forward eagerly to the day when they would be able to celebrate the prodigal's return by catching him from the terrace and eating him in the Lord's dining-room. It is a standing world joke that we demonstrate our love of creatures by slaughtering them, and which of us is immune? I must admit that I like fish and duck, as well as fishes and ducks.

But I have always thought that the wild life of Foulness and Maplin, say, called for more concern than solely that wild geese might fly into aircraft if an airport were built there. And without going so far as the late Robert Benchley, who was asked to prepare a study of the Atlantic fisheries and wrote it from the point of view of the fish, I believe that when we plan new towns and other enterprises we should spare at least a thought for the sitting tenants. There does seem a new awareness of these concerns, a growing feeling that accepting ourselves as a part of the natural order is no humiliation. Perhaps a new urban partnership will grow up. The foxes and magpies are coming to town; some regard this as a compliment as well as a challenge and are anxious to repay it. There are people in my suburb who are turning away from polishing their polluting cars and busying themselves with breeding bees and goats, and selling yoghourt, goat cheese, honey and duck eggs. This is the new-style urban farming.

I found two farms. One was old – claiming, surely correctly, to be the last conventional farm in London, and surprising enough to discover not seven miles from the city. It was behind the Albert Dock at North Woolwich; built of whitewashed brick, Manor Way Farm would have looked more at home in the heart of the country than the heart of dockland. Yet until recently it maintained a dairy herd over seventy acres. Now, because of the cost of cattle feed and his neighbours' ignorance of the country code, the farmer had been forced to limit his activities to the smaller livestock.

If that was the last of the old, the farm I discovered still closer in – two miles from Tower Bridge – was the first of the new. Near the abandoned Greenland Dock, where the whalers once sailed in, a landscape gardener named Hilary Peters had established a livestock farm across a waste land of old iron and new brambles that must be the strangest and most appealing landscape she has ever handled. All was on loan, by courtesy of the Port of London Authority, yet the impact

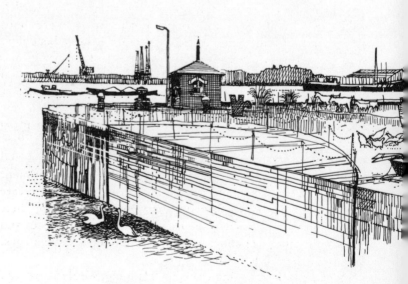

A LIVESTOCK FARM ACROSS A WASTE LAN

was antique, almost classical. A clamour of geese were her burglar or invasion alarm; a herd of goats, fleets of ducks, flocks of hens, flights of bees ranged the brown earth. The natives were mostly friendly. They brought their household waste to help feed her stock, children who had never seen a farm animal or tasted a free-range egg were fascinated by her activities, and some were encouraged to start their own small-holdings. A big dutch barge was moored by the former lock-keeper's house now used as a dairy. When I left Hilary Peters she was talking about getting a horse and cart to help deliver her dairy produce, and also contemplating the breeding of fish in the disused dock basin.

These ventures could provide local jobs. I think they do more. They help people to live with themselves as well as with others, to inhabit their bit of earth with an easier conscience.

Y COURTESY OF THE PORT OF LONDON AUTHORITY.

16. To the End of the World

EAST OF TILBURY

Ours was the marsh country, down by the river, within, as the river wound, twenty miles of the sea . . . I found out that . . . this bleak place overgrown with nettles was the churchyard; . . . and that the dark flat wilderness beyond the churchyard, intersected with dykes and mounds and gates, with scattered cattle feeding on it, was the marshes; and that the low leaden line beyond was the river; and that the distant savage lair from which the wind was rushing, was the sea.

CHARLES DICKENS, *Great Expectations*

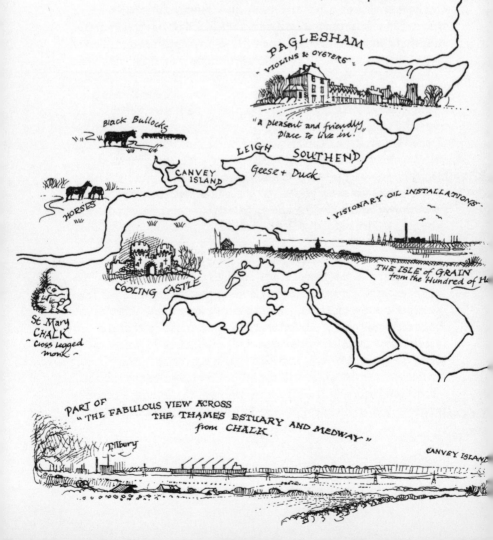

PAGLESHAM
- VIOLINS & OYSTERS -

"a pleasant and friendly, place to live in."

Black Bullocks

LEIGH   SOUTHEND

CANVEY ISLAND   Geese + Duck

HORSES

VISIONARY OIL INSTALLATIONS

COOLING CASTLE

THE ISLE of GRAIN
from the Hundred of H

St Mary
CHALK
- cross legged monk -

PART OF
"THE FABULOUS VIEW ACROSS
THE THAMES ESTUARY AND MEDWAY"
from CHALK.

Tilbury   CANVEY ISLAND

Between the pier at Tilbury and the fort is an old public house called the 'World's End', where the ferry house once stood. It is well named. Though it is really only the beginning of the end, standing at the edge of the marshland, the weather-boarded inn has gathered around itself in its three-and-a-half centuries of existence a sentry-like and protective air, as if it were a wing to shelter wildfowlers, smugglers, escaped felons and other exceptional wayfarers who would be the only people likely to be abroad in those parts.

Those who find flat, bare, desolate countryside afflicting to the spirits had better explore no further, for this territory of marshes, saltings and meandering sea wall is the most desolate I know. A couple of miles of it – let alone Pip's twenty – would plunge many people into a mood of unbear-able melancholy. To others – and I am one – it beckons. It starts at the 'World's End'; it ends in the country of Brent geese and eider ducks out on Foulness Island and Maplin sands beyond, where other than three-toed feet seldom tread.

This estuary walking is an addiction, suitable perhaps for morbid romantics only. But there is nothing else, nowhere else, quite like it: nowhere so forlorn, so lonely, so monot-onous and yet with the power to keep the eye and ear engaged and the nerves at stretch; nor, if even a moderately cold wind happens to be blowing, so physically taxing. Other people's chilly breeze is an icy gale here. The walk is along the wall itself – not the new emergency structure that has been going up in support of the flood barrier but the old dyke, the earthwork built up in a leisurely and pragmatical sort of way over the past seven centuries.

Of all human undertakings, a river flood wall is arguably the least suited to private enterprise, local option and the modest piecemeal approach. Yet it was not before some memorable calamities that a general public interest in this form of defence was recognized. Taxes were imposed to finance it. Various Hollanders, Low Germans and other early flood experts were called in from time to time to reclaim territory that had fallen to the enemy. There was no doubt about who he was, or that he was worse than the French or the Dutch. Call him Thames, Neptune or some unnatural congress of both, there was the invader who somehow had to be dealt with. Naturally the defence strategy was not always consistent or clear-cut. Sometimes the foreign experts we hired demanded by way of fee a substantial stake in the land they reclaimed – a third in some cases, as high as half in others. This led to more than a touch of international friction and also had a measurable effect on immigration patterns. All good early training for the Common Market, no doubt.

If the walls were so vital then they are all the more so now, with the land sinking almost before our eyes. I nearly managed to persuade myself as I walked that I could see it going down. It is easy to frighten yourself in this frightening landscape, particularly at high tide, and the tide was high now. I felt exposed, vulnerable, perilously small. I knew the tide-level was in fact higher than the marshland, but did it have to *look* higher? Was it right for those tankers to appear to be sailing over the fields like huge slow-motion aircraft? Gliders, rather, for the silence was profound, broken only by an occasional commotion of geese or the unnerving creaking sound made by flying swans.

Wild life abounded. The only people I met in a three hours' walk were a pair of bird-watchers, male and female, with a shared pair of Japanese binoculars. I asked what they were after. They were hoping for snipe, they told me reluctantly, as though you didn't really ask that sort of question.

Cattle roamed the marshes, black bullocks against the white swans, and what could be more legendary? To see herds moving free across the landscape is not the commonest sight in modern Britain. These have no doubt been grazing the reclaimed pasture for centuries; yet if there are people who find the sight of them disquieting, and think the beasts should be better disciplined, the reaction is not new. 'Beasts and cattle do frequently come into the fortifications,' it was complained when Tilbury Fort was causing particular alarm because of its suspected inadequacies. They still do, and if it mattered then it plainly matters no longer. With a bit of luck, wild horses have even been known to wander in.

Getting wild itself now, the river swung north along the Lower Hope Reach, and the outer forts scowled at each other across the rapidly widening estuary in a way that made me thankful that Kent and Essex confined their violence to cricket and never came to a shooting war. West Tilbury contributed an unexpectedly rural-orthodox, almost feminine touch, looking like the sort of village the fort at East Tilbury was built to defend. They say that yet another Tilbury, a Roman-British settlement, is under the river but a refuse tip on the bank had obliterated all trace of it. Nor was this out of character with the landscape. A jag of nastiness, a whiff of horror even, was quite in keeping.

I stopped to look at the heavily reinforced stonework at a vulnerable bend where the river swept eastward again. The brownish rushes fringing the wall on the landward side were still as in a Chinese print, but the surge of the river against the stones conveyed an unnerving and more than a little mesmerizing sense of pressure, of sheer power. Unbelievable, certainly, to think London was so close. This was more remote in spirit than Cornwall, than Wales, than farthest Scotland, and not necessarily friendlier. What country, then? A distant water tower could as easily have been some kind of temple, while closer at hand there were stumps sticking out of the water like blackened teeth. It began to look like M. R. James country, unpleasantly haunted. Who could know what might lurk among the wharf and harbour gear of pre-Roman times, or the exhalations of old clay and gravel pits? Buoys marking the deep channel clanged. I quickened my pace, the mist lifted slightly, and round the next bend were the shining cylinders of Thameshaven.

These visionary oil installations that float into view as one moves along the estuary were for me the strangest sights of all. They seemed to have nothing to do with industry; they looked like a product of myth and mirage, cities of the future built out of solid geometry. Perhaps they are more of a warning

than a promise. Yet whatever they do to the oil, and whatever
they and the oil do to us, these were to me the refinements,
the ultimate abstractions, of the industrial landscape between
here and London on both sides of the estuary. This provides
visual experiences which have never, strangely enough, been
much used by artists or photographers while writers, of course,
never notice such things. I remembered extraordinary vistas
opening off the Dartford to Gravesend road. One in particular near Greenhithe, a range of aluminium constructions
with the functional beauty of space rockets, fairly took the
breath away. The spectral whiteness of this chalk, cement and
paper region had a weird structural grandeur. Perhaps our
architects, reviled as null or boring in most sectors, may earn
more credit for their unearthly industrial designing.

But just as civilization, if that is what we have been looking
at, stops at Tilbury on the north bank, it does so with almost
equal abruptness though with a different emphasis at Gravesend on the south. Though linked by their loneliness and their
strangeness, the two wall walks are different in character.
The one on the Kent side is more human, though not in any
reassuring way. Here too I got the feeling that time, if it moves
at all, does so reluctantly. It has to be jogged. They say that
through the entire nineteenth century, when most of Britain
including the upper reaches of Thamesside were being
transformed, certain villages here were so changeless that
the rise or fall in population could be counted on the fingers
of one hand. This was Dickens country, so strongly and
sinisterly described in *Great Expectations*: the territory of
convict hulks, escaped prisoners and gibbets.

If atmosphere goes for anything, there are long stretches
here where these could still be around. I remember reading
a book by the travel journalist H. V. Morton in which he told
how he passed a forgotten gibbet on a hilltop, and the only
thing that surprised the local peasantry was that anyone should
have stopped to notice it. That was long after the days of
Dickens, and provides further proof of the well-known
optical illusion that if you look at a thing long enough and

often enough you cease to see it at all. I got the impression that if there were any surviving gibbets today this would be a suitable area for them, and they would be quite likely to emerge as the signposts of isolated inns.

The south bank has hilltops, but the most remarkable object I found on any of them was nothing more sinister than the church of St Mary at Chalk, commanding fabulous views across the Thames estuary and the Medway. This is a theatrical little church, which naturally made it a great favourite with Dickens. He particularly appreciated the cross-legged effigy of a monk – complete with drinking pot and looking like the central figure of some early publicity campaign put out by the brewers – which fills the niche once presumably occupied by the Virgin Mary. According to his biographer Forster, Dickens would always look into the church porch for a word whenever he was in the neighbourhood. The church, incidentally, has its complete roll-call of seventy vicars across seven centuries, and nobody could ask for more continuity than that. But the old monk provides the last taste of jollity for many a long mile.

I found the wall walk past Shornmead to Higham and Cliffe as dismal as the most Gothic taste could demand, with the tolling buoys and lamenting gulls, black cattle brooding across the picture, agitated swans taking off from pools and drainage ditches for no apparent reason. The gaunt skeleton of a barge – little left but spine and broken ribs – reminded me of Dickens's line about 'the black Hulk lying out a little way from the shore, like a wicked Noah's ark'. NO SEAWALL OR FORESHORE SHOOTING, a half-hidden notice announced. It added that ARMED TRESPASSERS WILL BE PROSECUTED, which would have been more comfort if it had contributed less to the general unease. Why were the swans doing so much flying? They did it so seldom farther upstream. It could be for no light cause, since getting themselves airborne always seems to involve more fuss than a flight of coastal command aircraft would permit themselves. Though actually, as I now noticed for the first time, swans taking off sound like trotting horses.

Geese and duck were also flying about in large numbers, and I was grateful for such signs of life by the time I reached Cooling. The church here has a number of tiny lozenge-shaped graves which look sinister but are in fact merely sad; they are the graves of very small children, from an age and an area where it must have been normal enough for life to be so short. Plague, malaria, cement dust – against such invaders as these no defence was to be found in the massive fortifications of Cooling Castle. Its overbearing gatehouse and much of the rest looks so well preserved, or rather so lovingly ruined in its frowning medieval way, that it would be easy to write the place off as an eighteenth-century folly. But no; it is what it purports to be, built (as an engraved legend puts it) 'in help of the contre' against the French. There seems to have been a persistent fear over many centuries – it was rife in Napoleonic days – that the invaders would come this way. Grim and strange: the double note is maintained by the comparatively modern house someone has built inside the castle gateway, like a cuckoo in an eagle's nest.

Moving into the Hundred of Hoo towards the Isle of Grain, I felt the strangeness intensify and the grimness relax. It is easy to find this territory as odd and secluded as it sounds; to believe that nothing ever happened – not a single measurable event, decade by decade, century after century – in a hamlet like Hoo St Mary; that the outside world made not the slightest impact on it, and that nobody would ever have the least cause or desire to set foot in the region unless driven by some devious business probably connected with ships or smuggling. There was a discouraging jingle that used to run

> He that rideth in the Hundred of Hoo
> Besides pilfering Seamen shall find dirt enoo . . .

As though to prove it, the way to Stoke was riddled with excavations for clay like the desperate digging of some monstrous dog, leaving great holes in the landscape. A fleet of small white-sailed yachts chased each other across ploughed fields – or so it appeared – in a state of panic. The wind was thumping and buffeting, even on a fairly calm day. And in the far distance, across the wide vista of wet meadows and saltings, scored by pylons and plumed chimneys and square stacks of straw, another of those unearthly oil cities was shining in the sun. Vision of hope or of fear, New Jerusalem or necropolis, it was hard to believe in when viewed, as I viewed it, through an orchard of unpicked apples.

How long, I wondered, could this oddly appealing family of villages, St Mary and all the Hoos, hope to survive? Their tenacity of spirit under the hot breath of giants, unless it is simply their capacity not to notice, has so far been remarkable enough. The Isle of Grain beyond, where the peninsula's wet nose pushes into the confluence of Thames and Medway, is more remote still and my Victorian guidebook is dismissive, describing Grain as a grazing district so difficult of access that 'it is very little visited and, indeed, offers scant attraction'. Not all would have agreed with that verdict even in the nineties, when primitive countryside was not much in fashion. Nor is it now, always, among the inhabitants; many of them welcomed such portents as the ceremony in 1975 when the Secretary of State for Energy, Mr Tony Benn, turned a tap to set flowing the first oil from the North Sea fields – into an Isle of Grain refinery. And there have been ominous words from the commanding heights of the Port of London Authority about the 'tremendous potential' for reclaiming new land below Gravesend, with the Maplin airport and seaport project 'only a very small token' of what could be done.

Mercifully, as many others will think, even the 'very small token' proved too big for its time. But it was clear enough then and is even clearer now where our priorities stand. The preservation of some of the loneliest walks in England, the interests of birds and their watchers, the roaming and grazing rights of cattle, the continuity of traditional patterns of country life – such considerations are not going to be allowed to stand in the way of changes that could make this peninsula unrecognizable in a decade. There is plenty of evidence to show that environmental standards, even those of health and safety, would not in themselves be allowed to frustrate what most have been conditioned to regard as progress. Economic slump is another matter; when it comes to amenity, or even preserving the minimal decencies of life, necessity is the mother of abstention. We have been saved or reprieved, environmentalists may well say of the years just past, through unsuccess.

However, although the Maplin airport project has been grounded the authorities have been pressing on for the seaport development to go ahead there. The PLA was insisting in 1973 that 'there must be an estuarial deep-water oil port within the next ten years,' that more refinery capacity is needed in the Thames, and that the environment would in fact suffer less from big ships discharging at Maplin than from a lot of smaller ones sailing up Sea Reach into the river. It looked evident that nobody in St Mary or any of the Hoos was going to be allowed to sleep in peace for another thousand years.

Of all the estuary villages, though, I would choose one on the Essex side to remember as the symbol of changelessness in the hot jaws of change. I say 'remember' because I had never expected to see Paglesham again. It would have been devoured in the Maplin airport development and I had already said goodbye to it, as I am sure most of the villagers themselves, however loud they might whistle to keep their spirits up, had also done. I went there for the first time at the height of the great environmental campaign of the early Seventies, and remember wondering why all the reporters and cameramen had settled for neighbouring Canewdon as the sacrificial picture village. A victim must always be found on these occasions, to be flung as ritual prey before the ravening beast of progress, and the rites are usually conducted with all the sensitivity of the tougher sort of beauty parade. As usual there was tacit agreement about who the winner-victim should be, and the mediamen were busy weeping their professional tears over

Canewdon – for no better reason, as far as I could see, than
that it had just won a prize in a Best Kept Village contest,
which certainly showed spirit in the circumstances.

Canewdon looked an agreeable enough place, but its village-
like qualities hardly looked of the superlative kind that would
justify a last-ditch stand on the part of the Defenders of Essex
or any other of the militant environmental groups busy
campaigning at the time. But neighbouring Paglesham was
different. I could see why anybody might feel impelled to fight
to the last ditch or dyke over Paglesham. Many would doubtless regard a visit to this delightful place as both pointless and
bizarre, like sailing through cornfields on a voyage to nowhere.
All I can say is that the village seemed to me to have more than
charm and continuity. It had life, and demonstrably deserved a
better fate than being trampled to death by the great white
elephant which most people thought had already been un-
leashed and was not to be stopped.

Well, stopped it was, and Paglesham goes on. I cannot
regard it as sentimental or backward-looking to applaud this,
and to hope that however far estuarial 'reclamation' goes it
stops short of here. Supporters of Maplin airport and seaport
quite genuinely presumed that here was a stretch of amphibious territory virtually useless except to Brent geese, army
explosive experts, a handful of introverted farmers and a few
hundred cultural drop-outs from the twentieth century. As far
as Paglesham was concerned, and nowhere could have been
more concerned, I can only report that it looked to me a
pleasant and friendly place to live in, and one that can seldom
have been savourless in all the years since the Romans took to
producing salt there.

And for all its continuity – one family traces eight unbroken
generations of village residence and thinks nothing of it –
Paglesham seems to have the knack of living dangerously as
well as just surviving. Another near miss was a threatened
atomic power station twenty years ago. Just before that there
were the great floods of 1953, breaking the sea wall in three
places, laying six hundred acres under water so that villagers

were rowing about the lanes in boats. They had to do more than mend their dykes as best they could, dry themselves out and carry on. There were others to think of, a habit of mind which is an obstinate tradition in these parts. They had friends and relations on Foulness, the stretch of coast adjoining Maplin sands; and any academic argument there may ever have been as to whether Foulness is truly an island was certainly irrelevant now. Five miles of turbulent flood water surged between those isolated farms and rescue, which took two days and two nights.

Nor will those who lived through them forget the excitements of the Second World War; they had the most unenviable of front-stall seats for the bombing of London in its most helpless period, being able to follow the entire flight path of the rockets, virtually from take-off to target. Paglesham did its own bit by acting as a decoy aerodrome. However, not all its adventures came from war and natural disaster. Paglesham was once as famous for its smuggling as for its oysters. Three hollow elms served as its contraband warehouses, their cavities regularly stuffed with precious stores of silk, spirits or tobacco. One of the leading Paglesham smugglers kept the village shop and served as churchwarden. Another village shopkeeper, William Atkinson, made violins good enough to earn him an international reputation. He set much store by his varnish, and emulated the great men of Cremona by taking the secret with him. According to Rosemary Roberts, who in *Paglesham, Life in an Essex Marshland Village* brings him into one of the most fascinating records of village life I have ever read, Atkinson was trying to pass on the magic formula to his son when he died.

Violins and oysters – a good combination. But there seemed so much good about Paglesham; we are no longer used to coping with such goodness. Even though the shadow of the airport had been removed, it was with some trepidation that I went back to see what had happened to the place. People have to live, and have learned to expect daily comforts and conveniences quite as expensive as oysters or violins if not always as nourishing. Urban reminders to agricultural dwellers about how lucky they were in their way of life, and about the precious nature of good farm land, were currently liable to be received with sourish smiles. Not all Pagleshamians had been against Maplin, any more than they had all been against the earlier power station project. There were even moments – remembering what I had seen, or thought I had seen – when I began to doubt whether the place really existed. Perhaps it was a fantasy village, belonging to some country of the mind like A. E. Housman's land of lost content to which one can never return.

But Paglesham was still there, unchanged as ever. While finding it hard to believe that the sun always shines in Paglesham, I can only report that it has done so on each of the three occasions I have been there. The village still led nowhere, an enviable situation to be in these days; indeed, nowhere twice over, since the place consists of two attractive dead ends connecting with nothing, not even with each other. Lucky Paglesham, twice and many times over. How good it must feel to have been saved from a fate worse than death. But this is also one of those places that make you feel that there are worse things than being alive.

17. Riverside Haunts

ALLHALLOWS, CANVEY, SOUTHEND

There have been many attempts to popularise this part
of Kent, as it is the nearest seaside to London. The ghost
town of Allhallows-on-Sea is a reminder that such ideas
are doomed.

NICHOLSON, *Guide to the Thames*

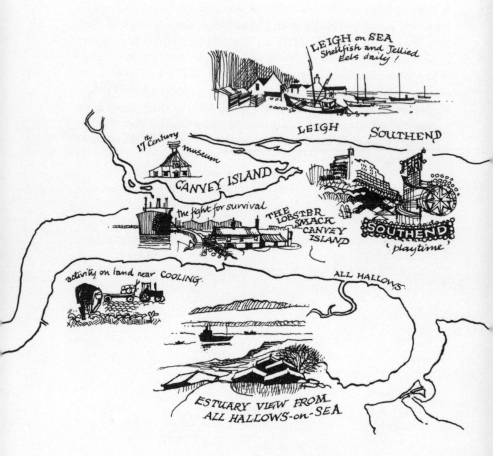

On the other side of Sea Reach, where the dredged channel
runs for the big ships and the width of the estuary begins
to be measured in miles instead of yards, I found a village you
might expect from the map to be a Kentish reflection of
Paglesham. Allhallows-on-Sea also belonged to the marshlands,
and seemed uncannily remote for all its nearness to London. In
every other way Paglesham and Allhallows occupied different
worlds, not just different sides of the river and different
counties. The one looked organic, as if it grew in response to
human needs; the other as though it was built for fun, and
something happened to frighten the revellers away.

The ghosts of pleasure always have a special air of lamentation, and the ghosts of future pleasure – the haunts that never
managed to establish themselves, never took off, but still
kept trying – are the most doleful of all. As against these the
ghosts of past pleasure are unalarming, which is just as well
since they abound on the Thames. The memories and records
they have left behind may even convey a sad charm; but the
more attractive they are the more depressing, since to parade
them is to be reminded of the extent to which the river has
been drained of entertainment as well as work.

Gone, or almost gone, are the water-revels, the routs and
regattas, the music and fireworks, the gaudy processions. The
formal and ceremonial occasions are rare; when such an
occasion does happen in our time it is more likely to be one of
mourning than of rejoicing. I remember a bitter day in January
1965 when Sir Winston Churchill was carried by barge from
Tower Pier to Waterloo, after the funeral service at St Paul's.
It was the river's share of his last journey to his country
churchyard. There was much booming of guns and wailing of
pipes and of bo'suns' whistles, but nothing was more moving
than the apparently spontaneous way the cranes in the working
sectors of the river bowed their heads. Sir Winston, as it
happened, was to return to the river on a very different sort
of occasion, but more of that later.

For the most part it is the ceremonial pleasures, so plentiful
once, that are virtually over. It may be hard at this point of

time to believe in Bermondsey Spa – one of Georgian London's elegant night spots no more than a longish stroll from London Bridge – but nobody doubts that Vauxhall Gardens flourished, or that the fashionable Ranelagh Gardens made an even bigger impression on eighteenth-century London, or that musicians of Handel's stature were happy to write watermusic, or that river festivities of every imaginable kind were frequent. So ungeared is modern London to the spirit of such things that it scarcely believes them even on the rare occasions when they happen. The spectacular Thames Regatta of 1975 – perhaps the outstanding river occasion of our time, coming as it happened exactly two hundred years after the last great Ranelagh Regatta – made curiously little impact measured against the wonders it provided. Even when the great three-masters sailed up the Thames again Londoners watched with unbelieving eyes, as if they were in the middle of a dream.

There are the ghosts of the steam age too, the pleasure cruisers that used to carry boatloads of jolly East Enders to the near coastal resorts (though never, I think, to Allhallows-on-Sea). But the Royal Daffodil is withered, the Queen of the Channel deposed; instead of the jaunty river-steamers loud with Cockneys it is the sludge-carriers that sail silently out to Clacton now, dumping loads of sewage waste into the Barrow Deep; a non-stop service and a necessary one, but hardly convivial. We are the better but not the jollier for it. Some natural law ordains that as we get cleaner we also get drabber and more devitalized, and the tone is caught by the wry commentary of some of the guides on the river launches as they steer the tourists between Westminster and Greenwich.

Something happened to the river, or to London, or to the English nature, that blighted virtually all attempts to use the Thames and its marginal land for enjoyment. Which brings us back to Allhallows, one of the modern attempts at instant resort-making that shrivelled in the bud. It is not a pretty sight. I went there when the main holiday season was over; even so, the weather was still gloriously fine and every other

218

resort would have been thronged. I probed Allhallows for some sign of life, however slight, as if it had been a serious casualty. But soon I was devoutly hoping that nothing would move after all, since the place began to remind me of one of those Parisian cemeteries where the family tombs look like residences and the paths between them like suburban roads, and you wonder what, or who, comes out at nights. There were neat rows of chalets and bungalows, the shells of several large buildings from which anything to do with life had fled, and the bones of an abandoned railway station.

Perhaps there are different things that could be said about Allhallows-on-Sea at other seasons, but I left feeling that nothing in this world would induce me to return there to find out. They say that centuries ago the great house at Allhallows, once occupied by a Speaker of the Commons, disappeared without trace. A happening like that would, I suspect, cause even less surprise at Canvey.

Canvey Island looks an even more improbable location for frolic, as strange as the idea Miss Joan Littlewood once had for a Palace of Fun on the Isle of Dogs. Canvey needs and deserves all the fun it can get, and makes a strong bid – possibly through hearing echoes of Concy Island both in its name and in the brashness of its development – for full amusement status. Let me say at once that I liked the place – admired it too. Nobody could deny that it has spirit. Canvey is something of a mixture of seaside resort, frontier town and unexploded bomb, with the additional chance – being dangerously below high tide level – of being drowned.

A place to escape from at the earliest opportunity, one might think. With fifty-eight Canvey Islanders drowned in the 1953 floods, and a concentration of oil and chemical plants that has led its MP to campaign ceaselessly about the risk, the thirty thousand inhabitants might have been expected to shrink to somewhere nearer the three hundred who occupied the island in its quiet, agricultural Victorian days. Nothing of the sort. Perhaps danger stimulates them, concentrating their minds and their sense of purpose as powerfully as it does

Sir Bernard Braine's. One long summer night in 1974 the member of South-East Essex subjected Parliament to a three-hour speech on why the island could take no more oil refineries, and a few months later he was warning a public inquiry about how this overloading could set the scene for what he called, not mincing his words, 'the largest peacetime catastrophe in our history'.

The islanders are apparently as ready as Sir Bernard to fight for their island, not only its continued existence but its attractions, of which they if few others are aware. The only time they have exploded recently was in the emotional sense, when some bland television voice called Canvey 'a scruffy little island', and the Thames nearly boiled with their rage. Anywhere with such vitality deserves to do better than merely survive; though that, of course, is always a good start if it can be arranged. I found it an extraordinary place, like nowhere else I had ever seen; strong on vigour and protest if short on gracious living, high in spirit but physically sunk so low in its saucer that without climbing the rim the islanders would scarcely be able to get a look at the river. Here too the Wall was rising, and the material for heightening it was to be carried to the island not by water but, circuitously and insanely, by land. There was a row, I was glad to see, going on about that.

It is an island full of anti-smoking warnings which have even more point than usual. Smoke in the wrong place here, and you could blow yourself and your neighbours sky-high. Many of the buildings were mere shacks mushrooming round the founding brick, with a little Essex weatherboarding here and there. A handsome timber-fronted bank with a dashing colonial air looked so out of place that it might have drifted in on some flood. The shopping was energetic and competitive but not all the notices were price-tags.

NO, NO, NO – one of them shouted – NO MORE OIL ON CANVEY. Another added that THIS TIME WE ARE IN FOR THE KILL. Down by the waterfront – if down was the word, since I found I had to climb the barricades to see the water –

the lures were basic, and Americanized in what looked a touchingly old-fashioned way: there were a casino, a fairground, a Platinum Blonde Bar, hot dogs, as well as the inevitable bingo. It all looked far less animated than the town centre. Also there were the sewage treatment works, the cylinders and discs and crowding containers of the methane terminal (NO MATCHES OR LIGHTERS), the demure bungalows with criss-cross curtains and the customary edict forbidding ball games. These might seem frivolous on the very brink of the Big Bang, though it was strange to ban the preaching of sermons on the waterfront as well.

A seventeenth-century cottage, built by the Dutch engineers called in to rescue the island from the river, was still standing and in good shape. They had turned it into a miniature museum. The waves of Canvey development, each one a kind of deluge, were fairly clear. After the Dutch immigrants came the farmers, and after their prosperity had been destroyed by corn imports came the first tide of Londoners looking for a little place by the sea. There was quite a land rush, perhaps helping to explain that curious frontier-town atmosphere. I found an old poster promoting the sale of sites on the 'old Dutch island' with the promise that they would greatly increase in value, and making much of the 'bracing air, good fishing and shooting and boating'. Ten per cent down gave immediate possession; 'free deeds, easy payments' were further inducements. So brisk was the market that an estate office was set up on number four platform at Fenchurch Street Station in London, and plots were sold by auction every Wednesday and Thursday. The heavy industry men settled later.

What stays on this island of change, what survives more than a few tides? An ancient pub called the 'Lobster Smack' clung to a stretch of wall looking out on an oil pier, a ship with golden funnels, ranges of red and silver cylinders like unearthly cheeses with horses and cattle wandering between them, a row of old timber cottages with charming wooden balconies and shattered windows. Warnings against smoking were varied by such ardent cries as UDI FOR CANVEY – this from the top of a crane. In marked contrast to the bustling central streets the silence here on the island's rim was profound. That, I now recognized, was the signal or anti-signal of these macro-industrial sectors of the lower estuary: their deep and implacable silence.

A little farther east lay the answer, so it might be argued, to the notion that Thamesside jollity is over. There is one spot on the unknown estuary everybody knows; and what is Southend-on-Sea – which would be more accurately called Southend-on-Thames – if not jolly? Far from weakening the case I would say that Southend reinforces it. The town's reputation of being a bouncy, boozy East End outlet, London's most obvious escape-hatch from the time when the railway age made day trips possible, has distorted the image and falsified the more sober truth.

It may have been different in the early years of the century, but even at the height of a modern summer season the place seems to have a shadowed air. This may be no more than the social deflation we have all suffered, the difference between the Edwardian Cockney and the contemporary East Londoner. Or it may be something in the nature and development of the town itself, which by higher revelry standards has always been one of the great paddling pools. I have memories of parents rounding up disconsolate flocks, pensive old men in comic hats, women on their way to bingo looking as if their return train is on their minds. Abandonment to revelry? Nothing like that.

But it is out of season that a resort truly reveals itself; it is when the Golden Mile is dimmed, and Madame Rose has put away her crystal ball, and life ticks over in a moribund sort of way, that the spirit of Southend furtively emerges. That was how I saw it now, with the covers on Fun City, Torture Thro' the Ages and the other summertime frolics, and only guard dogs at large in Peter Pan's Playground. One could still go to sea by train, on the little railway rattling up and down the Longest Pier in the World, but pretty well everything else had been put away for the winter. Now the place could be seen in its true, slightly faded colours – a pensive small town with a primly old-fashioned air and more in the way of middle-class aspirations than Cockney bounce. How wrong, it was now obvious, had been those modish gestures towards high-rise building and modern traffic engineering. The town's natural scale is small, domestic, unassuming; and that also goes for its one elegant showpiece which it makes small effort to show, even though the wrought-iron balconies on Royal Terrace would be hard to match in Bath or Cheltenham.

Royal Terrace adds an aristocratic touch. This is really no more in keeping than the plebeian visitations of East Enders. It is in the villadom of Westcliff that the true standards of Southend reveal themselves: a prim, modestly well-off suburbia, lavishly draped in public gardens, falling down to the vast shallow end of the sea – or, more precisely, of the river just as it contemplates striking out to sea. This hillside between the London road and the water sustains three ways of life existing in parallel, but so remote from each other as to be more like three different worlds. The suburbanites up on the road seldom descend from their crest. The view they command is one from which I found it impossible to tear my eyes away until the dark came.

Far below, stretching as it seemed for miles, little coloured boats were caught like flies in the vast expanse of treacly mud. Birds waded over the shining surface, each followed by its delicate reflections. There, close in, was Two Tree Island; brown, silent and deserted now, but when the great flights of geese stop there on their migrations they say that their clamour causes sleepless nights in the villas above.

And there is Leigh-on-Sea, for those who can find it. Hugging the bottom of the shallow cliff, quite out of sight from the upper road, I did discover Leigh and was astonished. It looked the most improbable survivor, a catch many a tourist must miss, a pocket of the eighteenth century trapped between that upper suburbia and the primeval mud. A change of air, of age, of diet – it was all these. Cockle stalls offered shellfish and jellied eels, fresh daily. One had always heard, sceptically, that the cockle fleet still sailed from here. Now I knew it was true. Austere brick terraces were broken by the steep alleys of an authentic fishing port and it looked as though the maritime life really did go on, though one old boathouse had been turned into a shop. Not an ordinary shop, though it would have been ordinary enough three-quarters of a century ago. It was full of those small objects Edwardian children were given as presents, or found in Christmas stockings. Life was less cosy outside. KILL THE WEST ROAD, a poster commanded. A cottager explained that this project had been part of a modernizing move now mercifully shelved. Instead

TALL SHIPS GATHER IN THE UPP

of knocking the cottages down they had settled for injecting a few modern conveniences, and she was not disposed to quarrel with that.

I climbed back to the grossly overloaded A13 and lucky little Leigh-on-Sea, or on Thames, once more disappeared from view. Its inhabitants must be torn between the obvious advantages of being noticed as little as possible and the benefits that could come from a substantial tourist trade. As it is, they and the wild geese and the cockles share a stretch of coast that was the fitting scene for a river occasion as far out of our time as any now living are likely to experience.

OOL TO RACE AROUND THE WORLD.
.V.T

It was here, in that hot late summer of 1975, that the tall ships sailed back out of the past and gathered for the start of the race round the world. This was the climax of the Thames Clipper Regatta, the almost dreamlike exception proving that depressing modern rule about a pleasureless, unceremonial river. The week came and went. There were many Thames-siders, I think, who saw or heard nothing of it.

For myself, I shall never forget joining in the procession that followed the clippers as they sailed down to the wide estuary from the Pool of London, riding the tide with such assurance that they might never have lost the habit. There were certainly ghosts on the river that week. Sixty or seventy ketches, schooners and barques had spread their sails, homed on London and settled on the Upper Pool, six great square-riggers among them. They raked the amazed city sky with their masts, as though we were back in the days when queues of ships would wait a week on end in the congested river to clear their cargoes.

Meanwhile the river was alive again with sights and sounds and skills all presumed dead or near death. Sailing barges opened their great rusty wings like extinct butterflies, dinghies jostled each other in races down the tideway, watermen proved themselves as artful as ever in manipulating wind, tide and oar. There was even a race between oyster smacks. The Thames resounded with gunfire, but this was merely the signalling from the human gods who controlled the events. The week was filled with scenes straight from the paintings of Turner.

But none compared with that last ghostly morning when, at high water, the clippers made off downstream with their escort of mesmerized rivercraft. They loomed above us in the mist, unbelievably, monstrously tall. The ordinary launches most of us followed in were water-beetles to these swans, but more exotic craft had been dreamed up too – a Tudor barge, a Viking longship. Yet neither of these caught the imagination as much as the ferry-boat that had been unable to resist the temptation to desert its post and follow the tall ships.

Children shouted with joy at the sight of the ferry-boat that ran away to sea; their parents sipped their breakfast champagne and peered through the pearly haze to identify the ketch *Arethusa*, the schooner *Sir Winston Churchill*, the towering Russian barque *Tovarisch*, the West German Navy's training ship *Gorch Fock*. The children shouted louder as one of our own training ships loomed past, and suddenly at a word of command the.rigging was alive and swarming with boys. They had seen it, with their own eyes. They were never going to forget it.

The tall ships dissolved eastward into the mist, and we sailed back to Greenwich. That night there was the swishing and yapping of a monumental firework display, shaking the streets and alleys. And after that, silence and again an empty river.

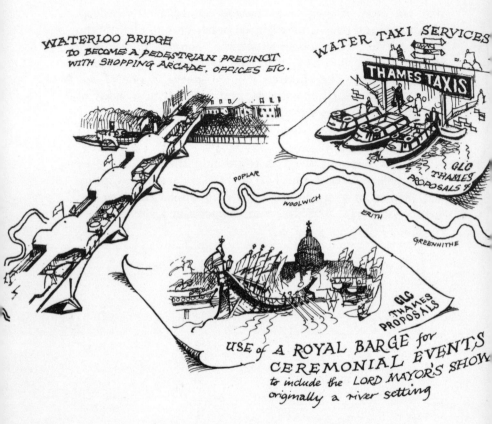

WATERLOO BRIDGE
TO BECOME A PEDESTRIAN PRECINCT
WITH SHOPPING ARCADE, OFFICES ETC.

WATER TAXI SERVICES

THAMES TAXIS

GLC
THAMES
PROPOSALS

POPLAR

WOOLWICH

ERITH

GREENHITHE

GLC
THAMES
PROPOSALS

USE of A ROYAL BARGE for
CEREMONIAL EVENTS
to include the LORD MAYOR'S SHOW
originally a river setting

18. Pipe-dreams to the Future

'Come,' said the Sultan to his hashish-eater in the very
furthest lands that know Bagdad, 'dream to me now of
London.'

LORD DUNSANY, *Tales of Wonder,'* 1916

It (the consultation paper) will attempt to evaluate the
costs and benefits of the options that emerge and to
indicate how and when a preferred option might be
implemented.

Docklands Joint Committee, 1975

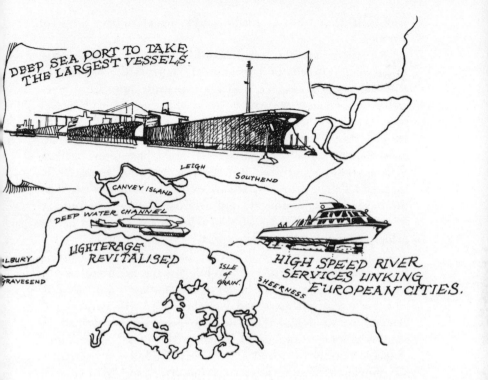

DEEP SEA PORT TO TAKE THE LARGEST VESSELS.

LEIGH
SOUTHEND
CANVEY ISLAND
DEEP WATER CHANNEL
ILBURY
GRAVESEND
LIGHTERAGE REVITALISED
ISLE of GRAIN.
SHEERNESS
HIGH SPEED RIVER SERVICES LINKING EUROPEAN CITIES.

London has had its own pipe-dreams in plenty about its
future and the future of its river. Some of them would strike
us now as mental ravings rather than sober ideas. Yet for the
most part they were not fantasies but plans – technically
worked out, set down on paper with immense care and, in
many cases, duly submitted for consideration to the appropriate
authorities. There were close on a hundred entries for what
was perhaps the key architectural contest of the Victorian age,
the one for rebuilding the Houses of Parliament after the fire
of 1834. Some of them, in particular a magnificent Gothic
frenzy by Thomas Hopper, would have made Barry's winner
look distinctly on the quiet side if they had ever got off the
drawing board. Reticence was a quality for which the period

had little time, but it made a full appeal to the sense of wonder.

'All their camels,' said Lord Dunsany's hashish-eater in his dopey dream of London, 'are pure white.' But they also had water transport, and his trip made him see a river called the Thames on which 'their ships go up with violet sails bringing incense for the braziers that perfume the streets.' The Victorians may not have gone quite as far as that, even though some of their streets could have done with a little perfuming at times. But the river writhed importantly through all their schemes, always excepting the ones that had the idea of straightening it, and even when the great railway frenzy hit the town some kind of wild regard was paid to the principles of co-ordinated transport.

There was water as well as rail. There were roads, sometimes twenty feet in the air. While leaving no doubt about what was regarded as the wonder of the new age – if even a few of those manic planners had had their way, the central rail bridges we so deplore would have been barely noticed in London's total complex of soaring ironwork – the older channels were not ignored. There were mid-century schemes for metropolitan superways over the river, and by 1855 Sir Joseph Paxton, the man who designed the Crystal Palace for the Great Exhibition, had not only dreamed up but worked out his great Victorian Way. Complete with thoroughfare, shops and trains driven by atmospheric pressure, this glass-covered creation would have twisted and (until the Victorian murk got at it) glittered over London's head like a mad boa-constrictor.

There were ideas for ceremonial sewers, for great swan-necked gondolas on the river with cabins pillared like floating town halls, for all manner of piazzas and water frontages with towers, minarets and statuary. Strange bridges were devised, including one that could be placed at whatever point on the river convenience or administrative fancy might dictate, and another that rolled itself up to let shipping through. How did we escape? How did London and the Thames come to be spared or deprived of such inspirations? Neither money nor audacity was lacking, nor was a driving sense of purpose. Probably the sheer pressure of inventiveness was in some degree self-defeating. There were so many ideas that they fell over each other; new techniques were discredited or improved on, new brainwaves outshone by even more brilliant ones, before they could be taken up.

If only because it would be hard to live with them and stay sane, we have to be grateful for being denied most of the Victorian improvements revealed in a Guildhall exhibition called 'London as it might have been', itself one of the brighter thoughts of Architectural Heritage Year. A scheme for ringing the Isle of Dogs with small gunboats and submarines to make it an impregnable fortress gives an awesome sense of the trauma of the times, though it might have come in useful a century later when the island enjoyed its glorious hour of self-declared independence. But projects for carrying people across the river by hydraulic lift or across Greenwich Park by ornamental viaduct no longer offer the least temptation; though an 1862 plan for a street bridge by the Mansion House 'designed for the safety of ladies and children crossing crowded streets' was clearly before its time, and William Moseley's notion of rearing a thirty-foot shopping arcade up in the air between Oxford Circus and Cheapside could have been exciting even if highly destructive of property.

The Victorians were the true revolutionaries. They looked boldly to the future, even if it never happened. Despite all the complaints about brutality our own town planning is timid and visually modest in comparison; we soar blankly into the sky, as if to escape notice, or we nervously echo seventeenth- or eighteenth-century gestures. Personally I am in favour of this cowardice. I would fear the truly bold approach even if we had architects of genius to carry it off. I believe that towns grow imperceptibly, like people, and are subject to much the same satisfactions and tribulations. While realizing all the dangers and disadvantages of gradualism in this field, I would cling to it through sheer nervousness.

We need both the forward-lookers and the backwardlookers. Actually they see eye to eye more often than they admit, or suspect. There is no need to go to the lengths of the nostalgic idea outlined recently for rebuilding Old London Bridge as a lure to the tourists – exactly as it was, complete with shops and houses, but presumably leaving out the traitors' heads on their spikes. Demented as such extreme revivalism may sound, it is perfectly sane and even logical to see London Bridge of the future as part of a traffic-free pedestrian area – so why not flats and shops, at least as fashionable as the ones the bridge carried in the seventeenth century? But the planners would be going back much farther than that. It was King John, close on five centuries earlier, who had the idea of putting houses on the bridge for revenue, and soon rents and tolls were so well organized that the familiar system of paying all ways was in force. You paid if you stayed on the bridge, you paid if you crossed over it, you paid if you sailed under it. Only the heads were admitted free of charge, and they were past caring as they gazed sightlessly down on some of the classiest bookshops, food shops and clothiers in town.

Old London Bridge was in effect a modern flyover, a land street crossing a water street. Also, its bulk was so great that it acted as a partial dam with a significant effect on the tidal levels, probably the nearest thing to a permanent barrage we are now ever likely to get. Even stranger echoes between past and future can be explored. Someone recently asked in Parliament about the possibility of harnessing tidal power, and got a perfectly serious answer as to the chances of a 'feasibility study'. And why not, indeed? Four centuries ago the idea was found feasible enough when a Dutchman set up a tide-operated wheel near London Bridge to pump water supplies to the citizens.

Can we be losing our inventiveness, even our practicality? Certainly nobody who speculates on the river's future can avoid a look back (with whatever appropriate emotion) at Maplin, the abandoned airport and deep-water seaport project. There are those who refuse to accept the word 'abandoned' and insist, at least as far as the seaport is concerned, that it is merely postponed. They maintain that not only does the future of London as a major European port depend on it, but the future well-being of the county of Essex depends on it too – an issue on which there are radically differing views, as I was reminded when the villagers of Paglesham, or most of them, shuddered to hear the drums beginning to roll for the start of a new 'crusade for Maplin' campaign.

Whoever wins in the end, and whoever is right, another contrast between the Victorians and ourselves most glaringly emerges. We nibble nervously, with horrified glances at the price list; they bit off more than they could chew, swallowed it with gusto, and signed the bill without a glance. The confidence of the rich? Perhaps. The Maplin and Tilbury stories make an interesting comparison. Tilbury Docks, built in the 1880s as an aggressive commercial challenge on what many regarded as an already overdocked river, proved a frightening failure at first for all their unequalled deep-water facilities. They were before their time. Three-quarters of a century later the Port of London Authority was frustratedly seeking berths for tankers which had swollen from 70,000 to a quarter-million tons within a very few years, and would be half a million before long. Others would be ready to take them if we could not, and our new partners the Dutch offered as strong a commercial threat as their military threat of three centuries ago when we were enemies. But, for better or worse, the thrusting spirit of the Tilbury days – meaning Tilbury Dock rather than Tilbury Fort – was gone. Tilbury was too early. Maplin might well be too late.

All the same, getting a modern deep-water port some day seems more of a likelihood now than ever getting that major barrage they planned between the wars, the dam that would have converted the upper estuary into a non-tidal, elongated lake. A desolating prospect, some would have considered that. Perhaps more would have welcomed the dam than deplored it. We shall never know, because they were never asked. It was not normal at that time to seek a public attitude on such issues. Things are different now. The deep-water port and

other aspects of the river's development are now accepted as
very much a public concern, needing to be publicly discussed,
and not just in technical terms. On the assumption that what
becomes of the London Thames is of wider concern than just
to those who live on it, even though their interest is primary,
ideas ought surely to have been flooding in about the sort of
future people want to see for the river. At the time of writing
this has not happened. Lacking such pressure of opinion, and
faced with an unnatural stop while the councils and com-
mittees nervously deliberate, it is small wonder that the
smart developers and converters should have slipped in where
they could. A yachting marina here, a trendy row of riverside
apartments there – at least, like the sultan's hashish-eater,
somebody had clear notions of what they thought were the
right things for people to want:

O Friend of God, know then that London is the desiderate
town even of all Earth's cities. Its houses are of ebony and
cedar . . . they have golden balconies in which amethysts
are, where they sit and watch the sunset . . .

Already, so to speak, there are golden balconies where they
sit and watch the sunset at points on the river where the
workaday barges used to bump their way about their own and
the nation's business. And why not? Abandoned wharves have
their morose appeal but it is an unproductive one; better the
rich should get them than they should rot. It would not be
good, all the same, for the natives to be able to complain that
the best river sites were being hogged by wealthy settlers from
Hampstead and the like. And as I moved back through this
disputed territory such complaints were beginning to be
heard.

Clearly the more mundane planners were entitled to the
encouragement, or maybe needed the spur, of knowing what
the locals, and Londoners generally, wanted for particular
riverside localities. And what they wanted might well turn
out to differ widely from one stretch of river to another, as

surely it ought. It could also differ sharply from the sort of professional plans recently floated to test public opinion; and none the worse for that either, many may think. People should have their say, and ought not to be deterred through fear of being thought unenterprising, frivolous or naïve by professional standards. They may be amateurs at planning but they are not amateurs at living. It is their river, if they are bold enough to make the claim, and they should dare to say what they want done with it.

Parliament has given a paltry lead to public discussion. The last full-dress debate on London I heard actually looked as if it might get through from beginning to end without mentioning the Thames once – until Mr Lee Williams, the ex-waterman MP, hove into view. But for his contribution I would have called it a singularly wet debate, though not with river water. They did mention the docklands once or twice, but only to make party points about squabbling local councils. Once they are safe from flooding at the end of the present decade, Westminster politicians have shown little sign – members of the House of Commons Yacht Club presumably excepted – that they will bother their distinguished heads about the river at all; though there are worse things than neglect, and one must hope no official support is ever given to such macabre proposals as one I recently saw outlined. This idea was for double-damming the river at Teddington and Woolwich, draining the stretch between and turning it into a multi-lane inner motorway. They must have been joking, but the sickest jokes are sometimes taken seriously these days. You never know when they may not actually happen.

My own ideas – and now, I believe, is the time for everybody who has ideas about the river to be egotistical enough to project them – are more fluid and less radical. I want the Thames to go on being a multi-purpose river, providing homes and work and recreation along the whole of its metropolitan length; and not distributed too tidily, since the natural flow of the river's life seems to me more desirable than an arbitrary allocation of functions. Even if the old grandeur of being a great port is to be denied the upper reaches – and this looks inevitable whether or not the deep-water port at the mouth ever materializes – there is still, given sensible encouragement, any amount of useful water-work to be done all the way up the London river.

Heavy loads, light loads, goods and passengers, taxi and delivery services of all kinds – the river can surely, to everybody's advantage, take back much of the transport burden from the grossly abused roads. And to the inevitable complaint that people must be allowed to choose for themselves, and what they choose are cars and lorries, the answer must surely be – give them a chance. Give them a genuine choice. The way to do that is by stepping up alternatives, not running them down. The water habit would be hard to form, largely because of the subconscious feeling that it was moving against the current of history; once formed, its attractions could well lift it to flood level. Fast boats and slow boats, work boats and pleasure boats, pollution-free and immune from the ritual slaughter that provides the roads with their own flow of blood unmatched except in major wars – what could be more seductive? Even commuting could be a pleasure. The Thames would be London's High Street again, and it would never need to be closed for surface repairs or because of articulated lorry crashes, or concertina pile-ups of suicide drivers. Piers with short road links would be the easiest things in the world to provide, and it would all make economic sense too. So ingrained is our social masochism, I feel compelled to add, that the chances of such an invasion of sanity must be regarded as slim.

Nobody, surely, would quarrel with the idea that there ought to be more fun and ceremony on the river; and here the tide runs with the argument. The English love of ritual is by no means dead, though it has found itself rather stranded lately. It could be refloated. Take a traditional traffic-stopper like the Lord Mayor's Show; why not put it back on the water, where it began? The mayoral habit of travelling to Westminster by water lasted four hundred years; it was not until the 1850s that

the cavalcade took to the streets, and turned into the annual
ceremony every London driver knows and shuns. A 'Back to
the Lord Mayor's Barge' movement would be universally
popular, the masques and music once a great feature of the
show would provide welcome employment for artists if they
were revived, and the topical tableaux that have formed part
of the procession in recent years, their crews tending to look
stunned by the noise and fumes of the streets, would surely do
better by water.

Royalty, with its strong floating traditions, could also have
a contribution to make to a Thames revival. If they can get out
the state coach for ceremonial occasions, why not the royal
barge? And there is amiable precedent in plenty for the more
relaxed sort of river recreation. The first Elizabeth not only
used the river a great deal – unsurprisingly, since it was the
normal way of getting about Tudor London – but she clearly
enjoyed it too. And a later Charles has something to learn in
this respect from an earlier one. King Charles II had some
attractive traits; not only did he like to amuse himself but he
was on the whole in favour of allowing lesser people to amuse
themselves as well. The river was one of his major pleasures.
Presents were made to him of small but elaborate sailing craft,
and once he took part in a yacht race from Greenwich to
Gravesend and back for £100 stake. (He was behind on the
outward leg but caught up coming home.) He swam in the
river at Chelsea, drank in various riverside inns, and used the
Thames to its full capacity. There was an August day in 1662
when Pepys climbed to the top of the new Banqueting House
in Whitehall and watched the queen being welcomed home
from Hampton Court with a whole fleet of boats and barges.

> Anon come the King and Queen in a barge under a canopy
> with 10,000 barges and boats, I think, for we could see no
> water for them . . .

An exaggeration, no doubt, but it gives an idea of the pageantry
that could attend a perfectly ordinary day. Things seldom went
wrong where royalty was concerned, though there was a

disastrous day in 1641 when the queen's barge overturned at the bridge and a Lady of the Bedchamber was drowned. There was a Chaplinesque evening at Greenwich Pier when George I landed late in a thick fog. The new king, an unknown German, was mistaken for his son, who had arrived on time and been greeted with full royal honours. Since the king knew no English, and his reception committee apparently knew no German, the necessary explanations got a little tangled. He may well have felt like taking himself off again in a Hanoverian huff, but controlled himself and stayed. The fog was still thick, and who could say what humiliations might not accompany a second landing?

As well as a Royal Waterman, a post Prince Philip would be admirably qualified to hold, the river needs a laureate to project and celebrate its revival. It can claim at least two in the past. One thinks a shade dubiously of the famous John Taylor, though the quatercentenary of his birth will be coming up in 1980 and deserves a river celebration. He was one of the best of watermen and a public relations genius centuries before his time, but one of the worst if most energetic of poets. He took up river work after limping out of the navy with a damaged leg, was not afraid to speak up for his fellow watermen before King James himself, and was soon firing angry words at the 'hired hackney hell-carts' which he recognized, if somewhat prematurely, as a menace to their trade. Taylor was never a man to pull his punches, and though there was no Road Transport Federation with which to contend there were plenty of influential quarters where they knew how to deal with low-born audacity. He even dared to attack 'our fur-gowned money mongers', dangerous words in the hearing of a proud and powerful city.

Not only did Taylor get away with his impudence – his moment of greatest danger seems to have been when he was arrested in his own wherry as a suspected pirate – but powerful people took him up and he became a figure in his own right. Perhaps it was his eccentricity they found disarming. In aid of one of his demonstrations he set sail in a boat made of brown paper with a pair of stockfish tied to sticks for oars. His courage was unquestionable. Near the end of his life he kept a pub in Long Acre and renamed it the 'Mourning Crown' when Charles I was beheaded. His artistic gifts were thought good enough for him to direct some important river shows, and he arranged the water pageant celebrating the wedding of James's daughter Elizabeth to the Elector-Palatine. He wrote vast quantities of verse, most of it unreadable now, and went in for eccentric titles like 'A Very Merry Wherry-Ferry Voyage'. But a great river man to remember.

Charles Dibdin, a century later, was equally prolific and a vastly better poet. He was by way of being the Irving Berlin of his day, turning out both words and music of hundreds of songs at astonishing speed. He too specialized in watermen and in unlikely places like Wapping – unlikely now though not, presumably, at a time when the choruses of river songs, some rousing and some sad, would rise from vanished pubs like the 'Ship and Whale', the 'Queen's Landing' and the 'North American Sailor'. Even Wapping Old Stairs, now looking fit only for suicides if they could get at them, were romantic then:

'Your Molly has never been false,' she declares,
'Since last time we parted at Wapping Old Stairs.'

It must be a long time since a pair of lovers last did that. Yet more than anywhere on the riverside Wapping haunts the imagination, just as it haunts all one's Thames reading at any rate up to the time – it seems as remote as Dibdin's now – of that excellent story-writer W. W. Jacobs with his philosophical night-watchmen, laconic skippers and amorous mates.

The past would inevitably play a prominent part in any Festival of the Future, which may be what we need now to help set London's sluggish river-spirit flowing. Taylor, Dibdin, Jacobs and Wapping, as well as Bankside and the great ones of the Globe, would take their bow on equal terms with our own writers and musicians and the new flowering of riverside theatre. Some new watermusic would be more than welcome, a river opera surely a seductive challenge to go with the inevitable revival of *The Beggars' Opera*, in which Gay's Redriff was the earlier name for Rotherhithe. Ideally, such a festival would be launched with a triumphant production of Ben Jonson's lost play *The Isle of Dogs*, providentially rediscovered for the occasion. Not only would this work have obvious river relevance but it would suit the truculent spirit of the times, Jonson's and our own. It so infuriated the establishment of the day that they closed his theatre and sent him and his collaborators to prison for it. What can all the fuss have been about? Probably we shall never know. Lacking *The Isle of Dogs*, we could make do with a lavish summer-evening production of *Bartholomew Fair* on the power-station lawns.

One celebrated villain from the past who would be likely to turn into a kind of hero-figure in a Festival of the Future is Judge Jeffreys, whose unspeakable life and theatrical death look the very stuff that films and pageants are made of – or why not that river opera? After King James's flight the mob were after Jeffreys, who dodged them with fox-like ingenuity; clearly he was fond of life, however unpleasantly he lived it. He managed to hide on a ship moored at Wapping, blacking his face with coal-dust and pretending to be a simple sailor on the Newcastle coastal run. He might have got away with it, but for the misfortune of being seen in an alehouse called the 'Red Cow', near King Edward's Stairs, by a witness he had been bullying in court and who knew the face all too well, disguise or no disguise.

Even then all was not over for him. A train band rescued him from the angry crowd and he was hauled in front of the Lord Mayor, who also knew the face and seems to have been terrified at the sight of it. Still rather splendidly in command of the situation in spite of his own well-justified terror, Jeffreys insisted on being committed to the Tower, clearly the one place where he could depend on being safe from the mob. There he managed to live in something of the style to which he was accustomed, even surviving sick practical jokes like the

one where a man sent him a barrel of oysters with a halter
hidden inside. If this was an invitation to hang himself,
Jeffreys was not the man to oblige. He seems to have remained
in command to the end. He died of drink – not so dramatically
as the unfortunate Duke of Clarence, but simply by drinking
himself to death. Many considered this a better fate than he
deserved; including, no doubt, the man who ran him to earth
in that Wapping pub.

Now Wapping, where once they chased pirates and judges,
is itself lying low, on the run and without any clear idea as to
where it is going to land up. Place of assignations and execu-
tions, suicides and sentimental partings, there is one respect in
which Wapping can disguise itself no more successfully than
Judge Jeffreys could. For all the unnatural quiet, its present
low horizon, it remains unmistakably maritime: a tang of the
deep sea right in the heart of London. Even its policemen are
amphibious creatures, at least half sailors, though they no
longer (as they did once) wear black straw hats and carry
cutlasses. Although at present leading nowhere discernible,
Wapping Old Stairs are still there. Wapping New Stairs too.

As much as Greenwich, this mile of bank is crucial to the
riverside's fate. More so, in one sense. Greenwich stands: its
past and its present are still there, irreplaceable, and must
largely add up to its future. But Wapping is all to do again;
what happens there is a key to the future. A key, not the key.
For we want Wapping *and* Greenwich, just as we want Rotherhithe and Richmond, Wandsworth and Chelsea, Brentford and
Kew: identifiable places, not an extended redevelopment
mush. If we are still going to believe in the identity, the
separateness of people then we also have to believe in the
identity and separateness of the places they live in. The
Thames which originally shaped them still gives them what
unity they need.

An essential character in the Festival of the Future would
have to be Macaulay's New Zealander, the famous tourist who
would one day be perching himself 'on a broken arch of
London Bridge to sketch the ruins of St Paul's'. The curious

thing is that he could do it now, or half of it. In the dead-end churchyard of St Magnus there is a broken arch of Old London Bridge where tourists from New Zealand or anywhere else can sit and sketch to their hearts' content. But London, or a London, would still be there.

Already there have been several London Bridges, several Londons; but only one river, changeless and ever-changing. Eliot, who seems to understand rivers as no other poet does, claims the last word. He called the river a strong brown god; patient, willing to seem tamed, but 'waiting, watching and waiting'. Surely a part of our inner life, whether we recognize it or not; as mysterious as the encompassing sea into which all finally flows.

Bibliography

It would be impossible to make any complete list of the reading I have found useful or stimulating, and which might help others to know and enjoy the river more. However, here are some of the books and documents of central interest. I include no fiction, though Dickens – to name but one novelist – has written better than anybody about the London Thames.

BANKS, F.R., *Penguin Guide to London*, 1958

BESANT, WALTER, *South London*, 1899

BONE, JAMES, *The London Perambulator*, 1925

BOSWELL, JAMES, *London Journal*, 1762-1763

BRIGGS, MARTIN, *Down the Thames*, 1949

BUNGE, J.H.O., *Tideless Thames in Future London*, 1943

CLUNN, HAROLD, *The Face of London*, undated;
   revised edition c1957

CONRAD, JOSEPH, *The Mirror of the Sea*, 1906

COOK, MRS E.T., *Highways and Byways in London*, 1903

CRACKNELL, BASIL E., *Portrait of London River: the Tidal
   Thames from Teddington to the Sea*, 1968

DE MARE, ERIC, *London's Riverside, Past, Present and Future*, 1958

DICKENS, CHARLES, *Dickens's Dictionary of the Thames*, 1893

DOCKLANDS JOINT COMMITTEE, *Working Papers*, 1975

DORE, GUSTAVE AND JERROLD, BLANCHARD, *London, a
   Pilgrimage*, 1970 ed

EBEL, SUSANNE, AND IMPEY, DOREEN, *London's Riverside*,
   1975

FLETCHER, GEOFFREY, *The London Nobody Knows*, 1962

GIBBINGS, R.J., *Sweet Thames Run Softly*, 1940

GIBBINGS, R.J., *Till I End My Song*, 1957

HAMILTON, OLIVE AND NIGEL, *Royal Greenwich*, 1969

HANSARD, Parliamentary Debates 1968-1972

H.M.S.O., *Redevelopment of the London Docklands*, 1975

HERBERT, A.P., *The Thames*, 1966

HOLME, THEA, *Chelsea*, 1972

HOWARD, PHILIP, *London's River*, 1975

Bibliography

JEFFERSON, E.F.E., *The Woolwich Story*, 1970

LINNEY, A.G., *Lure and Lore of London's River*, undated; pre-1939

LONDON DOCKLANDS STUDY TEAM, *Redevelopment Proposals*, 1973

MAYHEW, HENRY, ED. QUENNELL, PETER, *London's Underworld*, 1862

MITCHELL, R.J. AND LEYS, M.D.R., *A History of London Life*, 1958

NAIRN, IAN, *Nairn's London*, 1966

NICHOLSON, ROBERT, *Nicholson's Guide to the Thames*

PEPYS, SAMUEL, *Diary*

PILKINGTON, ROGER, *Small Boat on the Thames*, 1966

PORT OF LONDON, Magazine of the Port of London Authority

The Port, newspaper, fortnightly issues 1975-1977

PUDNEY, JOHN, *Crossing London's River*, 1972

PUDNEY, JOHN, *London's Docks*, 1975

RASMUSSEN, STEEN EILER, *London the Unique City*, 1960 ed

ROBERTS, ROSEMARY, *Paglesham: Life in an Essex Marshland Village*, 1972

RUSKIN, JOHN, *Modern Painters*

SCOTT, W.S., STEVENSON, J. AND SCOTT, S., *Pride of London*, 1947

SHEPHERD, C.W., *A Thousand Years of London Bridge*, 1971

SMITH, ASHLEY, *The East-Enders*, 1961

STOW, JOHN, *Survey of London, 1598:* 1912 ed

TEMPEST, PAUL, *Downstream to Greenwich*, 1975

THAMESSIDE ENVIRONMENTAL ASSESSMENT, G.L.C., 1968

THORNBURY, W. AND WALFORD, E., *Haunted London*, 1880

THORNBURY, W. AND WALFORD, E., *Old and New London*, 1895

THORNE, JAMES, *Handbook to the Environs of London*, 1876

TOMLINSON, H.M., *London River*, 1921

Index

Index

Adelphi 92
Albert Bridge 71
Albert Embankment 72-3
Albury Street, Deptford 135
Allhallows-on-Sea 217, 218-19
Amalgamated Stevedores Labour Protection League 171
'Anchor', Bankside 104
Angerstein Wharf 150
Artillery Barracks, Woolwich 161
Atkinson, William 214

Bankside 99-104
Bankside Power Station 100
Barge bed 106
Barge House Stairs 99
Bargemaster, royal 27
'Barge Pole', Thamesmead 159
Barges 41, 50, 173, 226
Barking 181
Barking Abbey 181-2
Barking Creek 180, 192
Battersea Church Road 67
Battersea Park 71
Battersea Power Station 71
Bear-baiting 102
Bear Gardens Museum, Southwark 43
Beckton Pier 193
Benchley, Robert 201

Bermondsey 127-30, 134
Bermondsey Spa 218
Bermondsey Wall 130
Besant, Sir Walter 96
Billingsgate 49, 104, 107
Birds 115, 192, 199
Blackwall Point 149
Bligh, William 73
Boadicea, Queen 95
Boat-building 168-9
Bondi, Prof. Hermann 79, 82
Boswell, James 90
Braine, Sir Bernard 220
Brentford 53
Broomwater 31-2
Brothels 100-1
Brunel, Isambard Kingdom 134
Brunel, Marc Isambard 131, 134
Brunel Museum 131
Bugsby's Hole 151
Burghers of Calais (Rodin) 87
Bywell Castle 162

Cable Street, Limehouse 124
'California', N. Woolwich 163
Camel Corps Memorial 92
Canals 53, 141, 175
Canewdon 212-13
Canvey Island 179, 219-22
Cardinal's Cap Alley 101
'Cardinal's Hat', Bankside 101

247

Cardinal's Wharf 100, 101
Cargoes, river 50, 169
Carlyle, Thomas 70
Charles II 54, 237
Charlton 155-7
Charlton House 153, 156-7
Chelsea 69-70
Chelsea Flour Mill 68
Cherry Garden Pier 130, 134
Cheyne Mews 70
Cheyne Walk, Chelsea 69, 70
Chinatown 123
Churchill, Sir Winston 217
Classicianus, Julius 118
Cleopatra's Needle 85, 95
Clink prison 102, 103
Clipper Regatta, Thames 226-7
Coalhouse Fort 189
Commuting 175, 236
Conrad, Joseph 170
Containers, 45, 48, 149, 169, 172
Cooling Castle 210
Cormorants 199
Covent Garden Market, Nine Elms 71-2
Crane Street, Greenwich 148
Cribb, Tom 165
Croom's Hill, Greenwich 144
Crossing London's River (Pudney) 162
Cuckold's Point, Rotherhithe 156
Custom House 107
Cutty Sark 20, 146, 168

Dagenham 182

Dagenham Breach 182
Defoe, Daniel 134, 156, 185
Deptford 135
Dibdin, Charles 177, 239
Dickens, Charles 112-13, 128, 209
Dockers 170-3
Dockhead 128
Docklands Joint Committee 176
Docks 117, 123, 131, 163, 170, 174
Doggett, Thomas 41
Doggett's Coat and Badge Race. 41-3, 50
Doré, Gustave 111-12
Dowgate 104, 105
Dreadnought Wharf 169
Drop-outs 88-9
Dunkirk 33, 143

Eel Pie Island 33-4
Eels 31
Eliot, T. S. 104, 242
Elizabeth I 183, 237
Elizabeth II 26, 135
Embankments 86, 94, 114
Evelyn, John 136-7
Eversley, Dr David 147
Execution Dock 121

Farms 203
Ferries 173
Fielding, Henry 127
Fish 30-1, 198-201
Fisher, Dorathea Woodward 45-8, 49, 50, 53, 108

Fisher, Billy 45, 46, 48
Fishmongers' Company 48
'Five Bells and Bladebone', Limehouse 124
Floods 33, 35, 38, 65, 75-83, 85, 179, 182, 213, 219
Fogs 44-5
'Fortunes of War', Woolwich 161
Foulness 214
Fountain Court 97
Freeze-ups 44
Frere, Bartle 93
Fulham Power Station 68

Gallions Hotel, N. Woolwich 164
George I 238
Ghosts 110, 153
Gibbet 208
Golden Hind 135
Gordon, General Charles 187
Government Powder Magazine 183
Gower, John 103
Grain, Isle of 211
Grand Union Canal 53
'Grapes', Wapping 122-3
Gravesend 186-9
Gravesend Sailing Club 188
Grays Thurrock 196
Great Eastern 134
Great Harry 155
Great Stink 113-14
Greenhithe 183-4, 208
Greenland Dock 13, 203
Greenwich 17, 19, 141-9, 241

Greenwich Palace 19
Greenwich Park 19
Greenwich Pier 17
Greenwich Power Station 148
Greenwich Reach 17

Ham House 36-8
Hampton Court 25, 27
'Harp of Erin', Deptford 136
Harris, Harry 43-5
Harrods Furniture Depository 56
Head of the River Race 57-9
Herbert, A. P. 65-7, 83, 151
Hoo, Hundred of 210
Hoo St Mary 210
Hopton, Charles 100
Horn Fair, Charlton 155-6
Houseboats 69
Houses of Parliament 75, 79, 229
Hovercraft 17, 21
Hydrofoils 175

Imports 106, 108, 109
Isle of Dogs 17-23
Isle of Dogs, The (Jonson) 240
Isleworth 36
Ivory House 120

Jacobs, W. W. 239
Jacob Street, Bermondsey 129
James I 199
James, Henry 65
Jeffreys, Judge George 240-1
Jewel Tower, Westminster 87

John, King 156
Johns, Ted 22
Johnson, Dr Samuel 141, 143
Jonson, Ben 240

Kew Gardens 54
King's Bench Walk 97
Kingston 27-8, 35

Lambeth Palace 73
Lea, River 149
Leigh-on-Sea 223-5
Lesnes Abbey 157
Lightermen 40, 41, 109, 170,
    172, 174
Limehouse 123
Little Ship Club 49
'Lobster Smack', Canvey 221
Lockyer, Dr Lionel 103
'London Apprentice', Isleworth
    53-4
London Bridge 44, 104, 232,
    242
*London Labour and the London
    Poor* (Mayhew) 109-10
London Marina 164
London River (Tomlinson) 142
Lord Mayor's Show 236-7
Lots Road Power Station 68

Manor Way Farm, N. Woolwich
    203
Maplin airport 211-12, 232-3
Marlowe, Christopher 137
Marshes 196, 205, 206

'Mayflower Inn', Rotherhithe
    130
Mayhew, Henry 109, 110
Mellish, Robert 133
Metropolitan Water Board 115
Middle Temple 97
Millbank Tower 72
Miller, Dick 143
Mill Street 129
Millwall Dock 170
Millwall Tunnel 18-19
Mirror of the Sea, The (Conrad)
    170
Morton, H. V. 208
Mudlarks, 109

Nine Elms 71
Noel-Buxton, Rufus, 2nd Baron
    76
North Woolwich 161, 162, 163
Norton, Dick 151

'Old California' 96
Old Curiosity Shop, The (Dickens)
    112
Oliver Twist (Dickens) 128
Our Mutual Friend (Dickens) 112-
    13, 122

Paglesham 212-15
Pankhurst, Emmeline 87
Paris Gardens 100
Paxton, Sir Joseph 230
Pepys Estate, Deptford 136
Pepys, Samuel 18, 44, 78, 92,

Pepys, Samuel [*contd.*]
  102, 135, 137, 155, 180, 237
Peters, Hilary 203
Petersham 36
Peter the Great 137
'Pier', Chelsea 70
Pilgrim Fathers 127
Plumstead Marshes 157, 160
Pocahontas, Princess 188-9
Pollution 30, 76, 85, 86, 113,
  197
Princess Alice 162
'Prospect of Whitby', Wapping
  121
Purfleet 183
Putney 59-60

Queenhythe 104, 105-6, 107
Queen's House, Greenwich 19

Raikes, Henry Fawcett 92
Rainham 195
Ranelagh gardens 218
Ratcliff Highway 110, 124
Redevelopment 55, 131-3
Regatta, Thames 218
Richard Montgomery 187
Richmond 59
River-buses 175
Roberts, Rosemary 214
Roman coins 85
Rotherhithe 22, 127, 130-1, 134
Rotherhithe Street 131
Rowing 43, 57
Royal Albert Dock 163, 174
Royal Arsenal, Woolwich 160

Royal Botanical Gardens, Kew
  54
Royal Dockyard, Woolwich 155
Royal Festival Hall 90, 94
Royal Naval College, Green-
  wich 19, 143-5
Royal Observatory, Greenwich
  19-20, 141-2
Royal Society of Arts 92
Royal Victoria Gardens 164
Ruskin, John 64

St George's-in-the-East 124
St Katharine's Dock 119, 192
St Magnus Martyr 105, 242
St Mary Overie's Dock 102-3
St Mary's Church, Battersea 67
St Mary's Church, Chalk 209
St Mary's Church, Lambeth 73
St Nicholas's Church, Deptford
  137
St Paul's Cathedral 94
St Saviour's *see* Southwark
  Cathedral
St Saviour's Dock 128-9
St Thomas's Hospital 73, 87
Salmon 198, 199-201
Sayes Court, Deptford 137
Seven Springs, Glos. 140
Shell building 90, 94
Smith, Capt. John 189
Smuggling 214
Society for Promoting Religion
  and Morality . . . 26
Somerset, Lady Henry 91
Southend-on-Sea 222-3
Southwark 101

Southwark Cathedral (St Saviour's) 103
Spencer, Herbert 82
Spenser, Edmund 14
Statues 35, 87, 92-3, 96, 118, 143, 209
Stow, John 78, 107
Sullivan, Sir Arthur 92
Surrey Commercial Docks 123, 131
Swans 30, 193-5, 209
Swan-upping 194
Swedenborg, Emanuel 124-5
Symphonion 121
Syon House 53, 54

Tata, Sir Ratan 35
Taylor, John 41, 47-8, 238-9
Teddington 29
Temple Gardens 96
Tennyson, Alfred, 1st Baron 85
Thames Barge Sailing Club 49-50
Thames Barrier 81-3, 155, 179
Thameshaven 207
Thames Head, Glos. 140, 141
Thamesmead 157-60
Thames Navigation Centre, Gravesend 187
Thames Regatta 173
Thames River Steamboat Service 17
Thames Tunnel, Greenwich 19
Thames Tunnel, Rotherhithe 131
Thornhill, Sir James 144
Three Men in a Boat (Jerome) 28-9
'Three Pigeons' 35

Tidal range 83
Tilbury 205
Tilbury Docks 233
Tilbury Ferry 185-6
Tilbury Fort 184-5, 206
Tomlinson, H. M. 142
Tower Bridge 107, 117, 118-19
Tower Hotel 107, 117
Tower of London 107, 117
'Trafalgar Tavern', Greenwich 20
Transport on Water 173, 174
Trinity Hospital, Greenwich 148
Tugendhat, Christopher 77
Turner, J. M. W. 64
Two Tree Island 223

Vandalism 59-60
Vauxhall Gardens 71, 218
Victoria Deep Water Terminal 149
Victoria Embankment Gardens 91
Victorian Way 230
Victoria Tower Gardens 86-8
Violins 214
Votive offerings 85

Walker, Peter 167, 176
Wall, John 144
Wall, river 96, 179, 196, 205, 207, 208, 209, 220
Walpole, Horace 56, 64
Walton, Sir Isaac 149
Wandsworth Bridge 67, 68
Wandsworth Road 72

Wapping 120-3, 241
Wapping Lane 121
Wapping Old Stairs 121, 239, 241
Warehouses 104, 119, 130, 131
Water Gate, Tilbury 185
Watermen 26, 40-1, 43, 49, 108
Watermen and Lightermen's Company 48, 49
Waverley, John Anderson, 1st Viscount 78
'Welcome to the Cuckoo', Wapping 121
Wellington, Arthur Wellesley, 1st Duke of 71, 86
Wennington Marshes 196
Westcliff-on-Sea 223
West India Dock 170
Westminster Bridge 89-90
Westminster, Palace of 73, 86

West Tilbury 207
Whales 197-8
Williams, Alan Lee 173-4, 176, 235
Winchester Palace, Southwark 102
Winchester Square 103, 104
'Witness Box', King's Bench Walk 97
Wolfe, General James 143
Woolwich 154, 160-1, 165
Woolwich Free Ferry 161-3
Woolwich Town Hall 154
'World's End', Tilbury 205
Wren, Sir Christopher 100

York House, Twickenham 34-5
York Watergate 91-2